THE BEST INTERNATIONAL WRITING

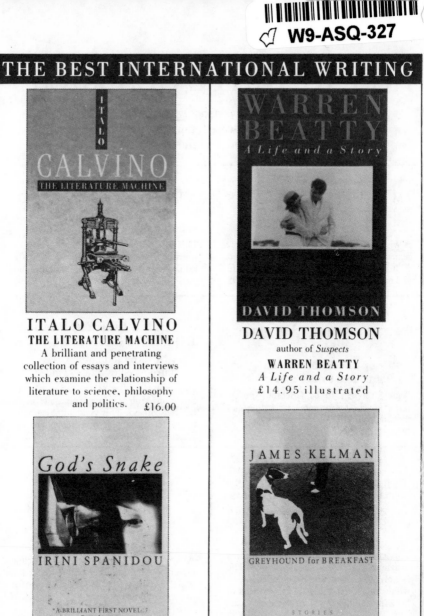

ITALO CALVINO
THE LITERATURE MACHINE
A brilliant and penetrating collection of essays and interviews which examine the relationship of literature to science, philosophy and politics. £16.00

DAVID THOMSON
author of *Suspects*
WARREN BEATTY
A Life and a Story
£14.95 illustrated

IRINI SPANIDOU
GOD'S SNAKE
"A brilliant first novel"
Doris Lessing £10.95

JAMES KELMAN
GREYHOUND FOR BREAKFAST
Stories
"Superbly crafted and a joy to read"
Bernard MacLaverty £10.95

SECKER & WARBURG

CANONGATE CLASSICS

A new, high-quality paperback series which aims to show Scottish
literature as more balanced, universal, and mature
than has often been realised.

GRANTA

THE STORY-TELLER

A PAPERBACK MAGAZINE OF NEW WRITING

21

Editor: Bill Buford
Assistant Editor: Graham Coster
Associate Publisher: Piers Spence
Advertising and Promotion: Monica McStay
Assistant to the Editor: Carole Morin
Subscriptions: Gillian Kemp
Design: Chris Hyde
Editorial Assistants: Vicky Ross, Alicja Kobiernicka, Christina Baker, Helen Casey
Contributing Editor: Todd McEwen
Executive Editor: Pete de Bolla
US Editor: Jonathan Levi, Granta, 250 West 57th Street, Suite 1203, New York, NY 10107, USA.

Editorial and Subscription Correspondence: Granta, 44a Hobson Street, Cambridge CB1 1NL. (0223) 315290.
All manuscripts are welcome but must be accompanied by a stamped, self-addressed envelope or they cannot be returned.

Subscriptions: £15.00 for four issues. Overseas add £3 postage.

Granta is photoset by Hobson Street Studio Ltd and Goodfellow & Egan, Cambridge, and is printed by Hazell Watson and Viney Ltd, Aylesbury, Bucks.

Granta is published by Granta Publications Ltd and distributed by Penguin Books Ltd, Harmondsworth, Middlesex, England; Viking Penguin Inc., 40 West 23rd St, New York, New York, USA; Penguin Books Australia Ltd, Ringwood, Victoria, Australia; Penguin Books Canada Ltd, 2801 John Street, Markham, Ontario, Canada L3R 1B4; Penguin Books (NZ) Ltd, 182–90 Wairau Road, Auckland 10, New Zealand. This selection copyright © 1987 by Granta Publications Ltd.

Cover photograph by Bruno Barbey/Magnum   SUPPORTED BY THE EASTERN Arts ASSOCIATION

Granta 21, Spring 1987

ISBN 014-00-8601-3

FABER PAPERBACK FICTION

DENNIS POTTER
Ticket to Ride
A brilliant psychological thriller from the award-winning author of
The Singing Detective.
'Magnetically unputdownable.' *Observer*
Faber Paperback £2.95

KAZUO ISHIGURO
An Artist of the Floating World
Whitbread Book of the Year 1986
Shortlisted for the 1986 Booker Prize
'Kazuo Ishiguro writes with humour and delicacy . . . We are seeing here the
emergence of one of the masters of contemporary English writing.' *Financial Times*
Faber Paperback £3.95

GARRISON KEILLOR
Lake Wobegon Days
'Keillor writes so beautifully . . . He is, I feel confident in asserting, the best
humorous writer to come out of America since James Thurber . . . Garrison
Keillor's book is certain to become a comic classic.' Paul Bailey, *Observer*
Faber Paperback £3.50

EMMA TENNANT
The Adventures of Robina
A brilliant *tour de force* that provides hilarious and frequently outrageous proof that
among Britain's 'highest in the land' neither manners nor morals are much changed
since the early eighteenth century.
Faber Paperback £2.95

CARYL PHILLIPS
A State of Independence
'Confirms his gifts as a novelist . . . wry and sensitive . . . Phillips skilfully
conveys the clash of three different cultures in the West Indies.' *The Listener*
Faber Paperback £3.95

MAGGIE GEE
Light Years
'Sublimely funny and infinitely subtle, Maggie Gee understands the complexities of
the human condition better than most. Her latest novel, *Light Years*, is pure delight.'
Sunday Telegraph
Faber Paperback £3.95

faber and faber

FIRST EDITIONS

BLOOMSBURY

PAUL BRYERS
Coming First
Introducing Preston Moody, 1987's *Lucky Jim*
£10.95 May

MONA SIMPSON
Anywhere But Here
'A wonderful debut'
Jay McInerney
£10.95 June

DAVID HERBERT DONALD
Look Homeward
A LIFE OF THOMAS WOLFE
'This is easily the best biography of an American novelist.' Gore Vidal
£16.95 April

MARY FLANAGAN
Trust
Her stunning first novel
£10.95 April

JOSEPH OLSHAN
A Warmer Season
The award-winning author of *Clara's Heart*
£10.95 April

CONTENTS

1987

1947

Collins

As part of the celebration of Collins Harvill's 40th birthday, there will be readings in the following cities:

Cambridge (in association with Heffers)		June 4
Edinburgh (in association with Waterstone's)		June 10
Glasgow (in association with John Smith)		June 11
Bath (in association with Waterstone's)		June 15
Manchester (in association with Willshaw's)		June 17
London (in association with the Poetry Society)		June 18
Paris (in association with the Village Voice)		June 26

Further venues and all details to be confirmed. For more information, contact Steven Williams on 01-251 0993.

Collins Harvill publishers in 1987 of Robert Hughes's The Fatal Shore, Georges Perec, Salvatore Satta, Philip Glazebrook, Marta Morazzoni, Josephine Humphreys, John Bayley, Peter Levi, Yashar Kemal, Harry Mulisch, Leonid Borodin, J K Mayo, George MacDonald Fraser, Gerald Seymour, Adam Zagajewski, Patrick O'Brian, Nicholas Gage and Vercors.

Harvill

Raymond Carver
To mark the publication of his poems
In a Marine Light

Richard Ford
To mark the publication of his novel
A Piece of My Heart

Jonathan Raban
Author of:
Coasting
Foreign Land
Arabia Through the Looking Glass
Old Glory

1987

1947

A Letter to our Subscribers

Dear Subscriber

Over the past year the size of <u>Granta</u>'s readership has grown at a phenomenal rate, and our subscriptions are now maintained on a computer. To ensure a fast, efficient service, there are a number of things to bear in mind:

■ If you have problems with your subscription please let us know as soon as possible.

■ We can deal with your queries much more quickly if you quote your subscriber number when writing. You will find this on the top line of your mailing label.

■ Should you change your address, please inform us in good time. Hundreds of copies of the magazine are returned after each dispatch because subscribers have moved without telling us.

■ Please use your postcode in all communications with us. This will ensure that your copy of <u>Granta</u> reaches you without unnecessary delays.

■ We occasionally exchange our mailing list with other publications whose aims are broadly similar to our own. If you would rather not receive mailings from these publications, simply write and tell us, and your name will not be included.

Yours sincerely,

Gillian M. Kemp

Gillian M. Kemp
Subscriptions Manager

P.S. *If you're not already a subscriber, isn't it about time you became one?*

JOHN BERGER
A STORY FOR AESOP

The image impressed me when I set eyes upon it for the first time. It was as if it was already familiar, as if, as a child, I had already seen the same man framed in a doorway. The painting is about half life-size. It was painted by Velázquez in about 1640. It is an imaginary portrait of Aesop.

He stands there, convoked. By whom? A bench of judges? A gang of bandits? A dying woman? Travellers asking for another story?

Where are we? Some say that the wooden bucket and the chammy leather indicate a tannery, and these same commentators remember Aesop's fable about the man who learned gradually to ignore the stench of tanning hides. I'm not entirely convinced. Perhaps we are at an inn, among travellers on the road. His boots are as worn as a tired horse with a sway back. Yet at this moment he is surprisingly dust-free and clean. He has washed and douched his hair, which is still a little damp.

His itinerant pilgrim's robe has long since taken on the shape of his body, and his dress has exactly the same expression as his face. It has reacted as cloth to life, in the same way as his face has reacted as skin and bone. Robe and face appear to share the same experience.

His gaze now makes me hesitate. He is intimidating, he has a kind of arrogance. A pause for thought. No, he is not arrogant. But he does not suffer fools gladly.

Who was the painter's model for this historical portrait of a man who lived two thousand years earlier? In my opinion it would be rash to assume that the model was a writer, or even a regular friend of Velázquez. Aesop is said to have been a freed slave, born perhaps in Sardinia. One might believe the same of the man standing before us. The power of his presence is of the kind which belongs exclusively to those without power. Somehow I think of the convict in a Sicilian prison who once said to Danilo Dolci:

> With all this experience reading the stars all over Italy,
> I've plumbed the depths of the universe. All of humanity
> under Christendom, the poor, the rich, princes, barons,

counts, have revealed to me their hidden desires and
secret practices.*

Legend has it that, at the end of his life, Aesop too was condemned
for theft. Perhaps the model was an ex-convict, a one-time galley
slave, whom Velázquez, like Don Quixote, met on the road. In any
case he knows 'their hidden desires and secret practices.'

Like the court dwarfs painted by Velázquez, he watches the
spectacle of worldly power. As in the eyes of the dwarfs, there is an
irony in his regard, an irony that pierces any conventional rhetoric.
There, however, the resemblance ends, for the dwarfs were
handicapped at birth. Each dwarf has his own expression, yet all of
them register a form of resignation which declares: this time round,
normal life was bound to exclude me. Aesop has no such
exemption. He is normal.

The robe clothes him and at the same time reminds us of the
naked body underneath. This effect is heightened by his left hand,
inside the robe against his stomach. And his face demonstrates
something similar concerning his mind. He observes, watches,
recognizes, listens to what surrounds him and is exterior to him, and
at the same time he ponders within, ceaselessly arranging what he
has perceived, trying to find a sense which goes beyond the five
senses with which he was born. The sense found in what he sees,
however precarious and ambiguous it may be, is his only possession.
For food or shelter he is obliged to tell one of his stories.

How old is he? Between fifty and sixty-five? Younger than
Rembrandt's Homer, older than Ribera's Aesop. Some say the
original story-teller lived to the age of seventy-five. Velázquez died
at sixty-one. The bodies of the young are gifts—both to themselves
and others. The goddesses of ancient Greece were carriers of this
gift. The bodies of the powerful, when old, become unfeeling and
mute, already resembling the statues which they believe will be their
due after their death.

He is no statue. His physique embodies his experience. His
presence refers to nothing except what he has felt and seen: to no
possessions, to no institution, to no authority or protection. If you

---

* Cited in Danilo Dolci's *Sicilian Lives* (1981), p. 171.

weep on his shoulder you'll weep on the shoulder of his life. If you caress his body, it will still recall the tenderness it knew in childhood.

Ortega y Gasset described the kind of experience I feel standing before this man:

> At another time we shall see that, while astronomy for example is not a part of the stellar bodies it researches and discovers, the peculiar vital wisdom we call 'life experience' is an essential part of life itself, constituting one of its principal components or factors. It is this wisdom that makes a second love necessarily different from a first one, because the first love is already there and one carries it rolled up within. So if we resort to the image, universal and ancient as you will see, that portrays life as a road to be travelled and travelled again—hence the expressions 'the course of life, *curriculum vitae*, decide on a career'—we could say that in walking along the road of life we keep it with us, know it; that is, the road already travelled curls up behind us, rolls up like a film. So that when he comes to the end, man discovers that he carries, stuck there on his back, the entire roll of the life he led. *

His virility has little to do with mastery or heroism, but a lot to do with ingenuity, cunning, a certain mockery and a refusal to compromise. This refusal is not a question of obstinacy but of having seen enough to know that in not compromising one has nothing to lose. Women often fall in love with energy and disillusion, and in this they are wise for they are doubly protected. This man, elderly, ragged, carrying nothing but his tattered life's work, has been, I believe, memorable to many women.

I know old peasant women with faces like his. He has now lost his male vanity. In the stories he tells he is not the hero. He is the

---

* *Historical Reason,* (New York, 1984), p. 184.

witness become historian, and in the countryside this is the role which old women fill far better than men. Their reputations are behind them and count for nothing. They become almost as large as nature. (There is an art-historical theory that Velázquez, when painting this portrait, was influenced by an engraving by Giovanni Battista Porta which made a physiognomical comparison between the traits of a man and an ox. Who knows? I prefer my recollection of old peasant women.)

His eyes are odd, for they are painted less emphatically than anything else in the picture. You almost have the impression that everything else has been painted *except* his eyes, that they are all that remains of the ground of the canvas.

Yet everything in the picture, apart from the folio and his hand holding it, points to them. Their expression is given by the way the head is held and by the other features: mouth, nose, brow. The eyes perform—that is to say they look, they observe and little escapes them, yet they do not react with a judgement. This man is neither protagonist nor judge nor satirist. Compare Aesop with Velázquez's companion painting (same size and formula) of Menippus. Menippus, one of the early cynics and a satirist, looks out at the world as at something he has left behind. His leaving has afforded him a certain amusement. In his stance and expression, there is not a trace of Aesop's compassion.

Indirectly Aesop's eyes tell a lot about story-telling. Their expression is reflective. Everything he has seen contributes to his sense of the enigma of life: for this enigma he finds partial answers— each story he tells is one—yet each story, each answer, uncovers another question, and so he is continually failing and this failure maintains his curiosity. Without mystery, without curiosity, and without the form imposed by a partial answer, there can be no stories—only confessions, communiqués, memories and fragments of autobiographical fantasy which for the moment pass as novels.

I once referred to story-tellers as Death's Secretaries. This was because all stories, before they are narrated, begin with the end. Walter Benjamin said: 'Death is the sanction of everything that the story-teller can tell. He has borrowed his authority from death.' Yet my phrase was too romantic, not contradictory enough. No man has less to do with death than this one. He watches life as life might watch itself.

Astory for Aesop. It was the sixth of January, Twelfth Night. I was invited into the kitchen of a house I'd never been into before. Inside were some children and a large, bobtail sheep-dog with a coarse, grey coat and matted hair over her eyes. My arrival frightened the dog, and she started to bark. Not savagely but persistently. I tried talking to her. Then I squatted on the floor so as to be the same size as she. Nothing availed. Ill at ease, she went on barking. We sat round the table, eight or nine of us, drank coffee and ate biscuits. I offered her a biscuit at arm's length. Finally she took it. When I offered her another, close to my knee, she refused. She never bites, said the owner. And this remark prompted me to tell a story.

Twenty-five years ago I lived in a suburb on the edge of a European city. Near the flat were fields and woods where I walked every morning before breakfast. At a certain point, by a makeshift shed where some Spaniards were living, I always passed the same dog. Old, grey, blind in one eye, the size of a boxer, and a mongrel if ever there was one. Each morning, rain or shunny, I would stop, speak to her, pat her head and then continue on my way. We shared this ritual. Then one winter's day, she was no longer there. To be honest I didn't give it a second thought. On the third day, however, when I approached the shed, I heard a dog's bark and then a whine. I stopped, looked around. Not a trace. Perhaps I had imagined it. Yet no sooner had I taken a few steps than the whining started again, turning into a howl. There was snow on the ground. I couldn't even see the tracks of a dog. I stopped and walked towards the shed. And there, at my feet, was a narrow trench for drain-pipes, dug, presumably, before the ground was frozen. Five feet deep with sheer sides. The dog had fallen into the trench and couldn't get out. I hesitated. Should I try to find its owner? Should I jump down and lift it out? As I walked away my demon's voice hissed: 'Coward!'

'Listen,' I replied, 'she's blind. She's been there for a day or two.'

'You don't know,' hissed the demon.

'At least all night,' I said. 'She doesn't know me and I don't even know her name!'

'Coward!'

So I jumped down into the trench. I calmed her. I sat with her till the moment came to lift her up to the level of my shoulders and put her on the ground. She must have weighed a good thirty kilos. As soon as I lifted—as was to be expected—she bit me. Deep into the pad of my thumb and my wrist. I scrambled out and hurried off to the doctor. Later I found the dog's owner, an Italian, and he gave me his card and wrote on the back of it the name and address of his insurance company. When I recounted to the insurance agent what had happened, he raised his eyebrows.

'The most improbable story I've ever heard,' he said.

I pointed at my bandaged right arm in its sling.

'Then you're mad!' he said.

'The owner of the dog asked me to report to you.'

'Of course! You're in it together. How much do you earn?'

At that moment I was inspired. 'Ten thousand a month,' I lied.

'Please take a seat, sir.'

The people listening around the table laughed. Somebody else told a story and then we got to our feet, for it was time to go. I walked over to the door, buttoning up my coat. The dog came across the room in a straight line towards me. She took my hand in her mouth, gently, and backed away, tugging.

She wants to show you the stable where she sleeps, said one of the children.

But no, it was not to the stable door the dog was taking me; it was to the chair where I had been sitting. I sat down again and the dog lay down by my feet, undisturbed by the laughter of everyone else in the room and watchful for the smallest sign that I intended to leave.

A small story for Aesop. You can make what you like of it. How much can dogs understand? The story becomes a story because we are not quite sure how much life's experience of itself (and what else are stories if not that?) is always sceptical.

Legend has it that Pyrrhon, the founder of scepticism, was at first a painter. Later he accompanied Alexander the Great on his voyage through Asia, gave up painting and became a philosopher, declaring that appearances and all perceptions were illusory. (One day somebody should write a play about his journey.) Since the fourth century BC, and more precisely during the last two centuries, the sense of the term *scepticism* has radically changed. The original sceptics rejected any total explanation (or solution) concerning life because they saw experience as being primary yet enigmatic. They thought of their philosophical opponents as privileged, protected academicians. They spoke for common experience against élitism. They believed that if God existed, he was invisible, unanswerable and certainly didn't belong to those with the longest noses.

Today scepticism has come to imply aloofness, a refusal to be engaged, and very often—as in the case of logical positivism—privileged pedantry. There was a certain historical continuity from the early sceptics through the heretics of the Middle Ages to modern revolutionaries. By contrast, modern scepticism challenges nobody and dismantles only theories of change. This said, the man before us is a sceptic in the original sense.

Looking at him, I am reminded that I am not the first to pose unanswerable questions to myself, and I begin to share something of his composure: a curious composure for it co-exists with hurt, with pain and with compassion. The last, essential for story-telling, is the complement of the original scepticism: a tenderness for experience because it is human. Moralists, politicians, merchants ignore experience, being exclusively concerned with actions and products. Most literature has been made by the disinherited or the exiled. Both states fix the attention upon experience and thus on the need to redeem it from oblivion, to hold it tight in the dark.

He is no longer a stranger. I begin, immodestly, to identify with him. Is he what I have wanted to be? Was the doorway he appeared in during my childhood simply my wished-for future?

This confusion of selves offers me now a sudden insight. It is at himself that Aesop is looking. Sardonically, for his imagination is already elsewhere. In a moment he will turn away and join his public. The mirror will reflect an empty room, through whose wall the sound of occasional laughter will be audible.

MICHAEL IGNATIEFF
AN INTERVIEW WITH
BRUCE CHATWIN

He is forty-seven years of age, tall and lean, with fierce blue eyes. Thinner than he ought to be: the skin is tightly stretched on his face and his colour is too high—the effects of a recent brush with illness. The shooting jumpers, corduroys and walking shoes mark him down as English country middle class, an identity he has spent a lifetime escaping. He is English in his use of self-deprecation as a strategy of disguise. An indefatigable fabulist and story-teller, he laughs with a high merry cackle. A lapidary talker, an enviably economical writer.

He came to writing after a career at Sotheby's. Each of his books escapes the last one: *In Patagonia,* a travel narrative and voyage of self-discovery; *The Viceroy of Ouidah,* a lushly coloured miniature about a Brazilian slaver in Dahomey; *On the Black Hill,* his only novel set in Britain, about the lives of two Welsh hill-farmer brothers; and now *The Songlines,* a novel of a journey in search of the Australian Aborigines' songlines, and an inquiry into the origins of nomadism, story-telling and the roots of human restlessness.

He has been married to Elizabeth for more than 20 years. There are no children. They live in a raspberry-red clapboard farmhouse, which belongs on a Vermont hillside but is actually on the edge of sloping pastures in the Chilterns near Oxford. His sojourns here are a prelude or epilogue to travel. He is off next week to Ghana: Werner Herzog is shooting *Cobra Verde,* based on *The Viceroy of Ouidah.*

After lunch in the white study, with the wooden slat blinds drawn against the fierce bright sun reflecting off the snowy fields, he sits down in a canvas chair in front of the fire, hands together, fingers touching his lips, waiting: wary, amused, elusive.

Michael Ignatieff: *Songlines* is a bit of everything: autobiography, fiction, anthropology and archaeology. How would *you* describe it?

Bruce Chatwin: It has to be called a novel because I've invented huge chunks of it in order to tell the story that I wanted to tell. But I suppose as a category it's indefinable.

Ignatieff: I'm puzzled that you chose a fiction form to tell us a lot of interesting theories about nomadic origins, about story-telling, restlessness and so on . . .

Chatwin: To write it as a fiction gives you a greater flexibility; otherwise, if you were laying down the law on these subjects, and indeed I had a go at laying down the law, I can't tell you how pretentious you sound. Or else you have to hedge the whole thing around with so many qualifications that it collapses.

Ignatieff: Were there any books that served as models?

Chatwin: I'm interested in an eighteenth-century form, the dialogue novel, I mean particularly Diderot's *Jacques Le Fataliste*. The *philosophes* of the eighteenth century had a way of expressing serious concepts very lightly indeed. That was one of the things I was trying.

Ignatieff: Where in your work is the division between fiction and non-fiction?

Chatwin: I don't think there *is* one. There definitely should be, but I don't know where it is. I've always written very close to the line. I've tried applying fiction techniques to actual bits of travel. I once made the experiment of counting up the lies in the book I wrote about Patagonia. It wasn't, in fact, too bad: there weren't too many. But with *Songlines,* if I had to tot up the inventions, there would be no question in my mind that the whole thing added up to a fictional work.

Ignatieff: There's one character in *Songlines* who isn't fictional, and that's Bruce, the narrator. You.

Chatwin: Ah well, I don't think you can invent yourself—though you have, of course, to keep a firm reign on yourself. All one hopes to be is the first-person narrator who is like a camera shutter, taking flashes on the story as it develops in front of his eyes.

Ignatieff: *Songlines* originated, didn't it, in a book you were planning to write about nomads?

Chatwin: I went to the Sahara at the time when I was working in the art world, and completely by chance spent time with a very extreme nomad people called the Beja. They alerted me to certain things which were obviously close to me but which I hadn't realized before. They started my quest to know the secret of their irreverent and timeless vitality: why was it that nomad peoples have this amazing capacity to continue under the most adverse circumstances, while the empires come crashing down? It seemed to me to be an immensely interesting subject to tackle. But the literature of nomad peoples is very difficult to handle, and the more I delved into it, the less wise I became. So this is why I did a lot of travelling and why I left a conventional job at the age of twenty-six.

Ignatieff: In the nomads you saw a clue to your own restlessness?

Chatwin: I was working at a job which was making me tremendously unhappy—

Ignatieff: —so unhappy that at Sotheby's you seem to have gone blind.

Chatwin: Yes, one day I came back from America on a pretty nasty flight to stay with a friend in Ireland. I drove from Dublin to Donegal and the next morning I woke up blind. The sight came back in one eye during the day, but when I got to England the eye specialist who looked at me said, 'You've been looking too closely at pictures. Why don't you swap them for some long horizons?' So I said, 'Why not?' He said, 'Where would you like to go?' I said, 'Africa.' And so instead of writing a prescription for new spectacles, he wrote a prescription saying that he recommended travel to Africa. The chairman of Sotheby's said, 'I'm sure Bruce has got something the matter with his eyes, but I can't think why he has to go to Africa.' (*Laughter.*)

Ignatieff: Let's come back to restlessness. Why is it the question of questions for you?

Chatwin: Well, obviously we are the most restless species on the planet. And it seems very important to control that restlessness to prevent it getting out of hand in destructive ways. These were ideas which grew on me as I started reading the literature of nomad peoples, but they became an obsession, particularly after I left the art world. It was at the time of the Vietnam War, and I was having to think for the first time. My career was the reverse of most people's in that I started as a rather unpleasant little capitalist in a big business in which I was extremely successful and smarmy, and suddenly I realized at the age of twenty-five or so that I was hating every minute of it. I had to change. I became quite radical and I intended to write a big radical book, which came to nothing because it was unprintable.

Ignatieff: But in *Songlines* you've kept faith with that earlier project.

Chatwin: Let's just say I felt that the time had come when if I didn't write it now, the whole thing would go sour on me.

Ignatieff: In *Songlines* you've put together a narrative of your voyage in search of aboriginal wisdom in the Australian Outback, and interspersed it with some extraordinary passages of theorizing and quotation culled from twenty years of your notebooks. These give the impression of being put down just as you thought of them, but in fact they struck me as the most heavily worked, the most fictional parts of the book.

Chatwin: The juxtapositions are artful—I hope not arty—a collage of disparate things, whether it's a description of a bus journey in downtown Miami or a quotation from the ancient Greek.
   I was impressed by that essay of Walter Benjamin in which he says the ideal book would be a book of quotations, and then there's a wonderful commonplace book by Hofmannsthal, which is a sort of dialogue of quotations and his own thoughts as well,

all jammed in. I also had the remains of an essay about nomads, about the metaphysics of walking, and it struck me that the only way to use it was to graft it on to a narrative of a journey to Australia.

Ignatieff: At one level *Songlines* is a travel book. What does travel mean to you?

Chatwin: The word travel is the same as the French *travail*. It means hard work, penance and finally a journey. There was an idea, particularly in the Middle Ages, that by going on pilgrimage, as Muslim pilgrims do, you were reinstating the original condition of man. The act of walking through a wilderness was thought to bring you back to God. That is something you find in all the religions.

Ignatieff: Do you think of your travelling in terms of pilgrimage?

Chatwin: Pilgrimage is too strong, really. It's just that I'm a footloose sort of character and can't do anything else.

Ignatieff: Do you think of yourself as a travel writer?

Chatwin: It always irritated me to be called a travel writer. So I decided to write something about people who never went out. That's how *On the Black Hill* came into being.

Ignatieff: But it is true that you yourself can't write unless you travel.

Chatwin: That's very true.

Ignatieff: Then the question is why?

Chatwin: I wish I knew. I do find it quite interesting that in one form or another all the great early epics—whether it's the *Odyssey* or *Beowulf*—are traveller's tales. Why should it be that the metaphor of the voyage is at the heart of all story-telling? It's not simply that most stories are traveller's tales, it's actually the way these epics are patterned into a voyage structure. Lord Raglan, a British folklorist, took the great myths and showed that they have a common paradigm. The story begins with a young man, who is often a foundling, who goes on a journey and finds a population menaced by some kind of monster or wild beast. He saves the population, rescues the damsel in distress and receives a reward, usually of the damsel in marriage, the kingdom and treasure. In his maturity he rules people who are strangers to him, and then in old age the forces of destruction close in, restlessness strikes again, and he departs to do battle with another monster, and then vanishes. I once mapped Che Guevara's life against this paradigm and it fitted pretty well. (*Laughter.*) The point is that the classical hero cycle is an idealized programme for the human life cycle. Each stage corresponds to a biological event in human life.

Ignatieff: So let's get clear about this. You think that most fictions replay archetypal, universal stories.

Chatwin: We're on tricky ground here.

Ignatieff: That's the ground that's interesting.

Chatwin: I do in a way, yes.

Ignatieff: But doesn't that go against the idea of the modern writer as the inventor, the originator of his stories, the creator of something new?

Chatwin: I'm unimpressed by the idea of the new. Most advances in literature usually strike me as being advances into a cul-de-sac.

Ignatieff: And so a good writer ought to be in touch with the recurring character of certain story forms?

Chatwin: He may be in touch with them although he doesn't realize it. There's a strong instinctive bias in human behaviour, a template into which we slot. I don't believe *all* behaviour is learned. We're not a blank slate.

Ignatieff: Instincts pose limits to what you can do with human beings, and that's a good thing?

Chatwin: Absolutely. The Greeks had the idea that there were limits to the range of human behaviour and, if anyone had the *hubris* to go beyond those limits, he was struck down by fate. Well, one would agree. In other words an instinctive paradigm does impose limits as to how people can or should behave.

Ignatieff: And you think some story-telling is instinctual?

Chatwin: Again, we're on tricky ground, but Konrad Lorenz has worked out that an animal experiences certain stages or 'calls' in its career. The animal may or may not take up the call, because if the natural target or partner of a particular paradigm of behaviour is not available, then it will get deflected onto a substitute. It struck me that these 'behavioural chains' which Lorenz talks about are similar to the structure of myths. If myths have a sort of spontaneous activity in the human psyche, then a section of that myth corresponds to a certain section of the human life cycle. I would say tentatively that there is a connection between instinct and the structure of story-telling.

Ignatieff: Let me see if I understand this. Human beings originate on the desert plains of Africa three million years ago . . .

Chatwin: Yes . . .

Ignatieff: . . . and they gradually acquire a set of instinctual behaviours that enable them to survive on the grasslands and vanquish their predators . . .

Chatwin: Yes . . .

Ignatieff: . . . and as they acquire a set of instinctual nomadic patterns of behaviour they also acquire a meaning system, a set of myths which are imprinted on the brain over millions of years . . .

Chatwin: Yes . . .

Ignatieff: . . . and these are the story patterns that keep recurring even in the modern day.

Chatwin: Absolutely.

Ignatieff: An example of this kind of eternal story would be the young man who leaves home, goes off into the wilderness to find himself. Bruce Chatwin, archetypal hero, goes out into the desert in search of . . .

Chatwin: You make me sound very pretentious . . .

Ignatieff: Not at all. I'm just taking seriously the idea that *Songlines* itself works through a certain mythic story form.

Chatwin: I would hope so.

Ignatieff: In your version of the myth, the callow young man travels into the Australian desert in search of enlightenment and finds Aboriginal peoples engaged in precisely the same quest . . .

Chatwin: Exactly.

Ignatieff: . . . finding the knowledge of their ancestors, following a songline in search of their destiny. What *are* the songlines?

Chatwin: The songlines are a labyrinth of invisible pathways which stretch to every corner of Australia. Aboriginal creation myths tell of the legendary totemic ancestors—part animal, part man—who create themselves and then set out on immense journeys across the continent, singing the name of everything that crosses their path and so singing the world into existence. In fact, there's hardly a rock or a creek or a stand of eucalyptus that isn't an 'event' on one or other of the songlines. In other words, the whole of Australia can be read as a musical score . . .

The ancestors, while walking through the land, are thought to have scattered a kind of 'scent-trail' of words and musical notes. Each new-born baby inherits a section of the song as his birthright. His stanzas are his inalienable private property and define his territory. But he is entitled to 'lend' these stanzas up and down a songline and so acquire rights of passage from his neighbours—so that, in case of catastrophe, he can always expect help and hospitality providing he sticks to the line. At the end of the last century, an English ethnologist, W. E. Roth, was the first to indicate that the so-called Aboriginal 'walkabout' was, in fact, part of a gigantic diplomatic and trading system which kept the most far-flung tribes in peaceful contact with each other. What has since emerged is that the trade-routes were also songs, and that the principal medium of exchange was song. A songline changes language from one people to the next, but the melody remains constant over colossal distances: so that, in theory at least, a man can sing his way across a landscape without ever having been there.

I felt the songlines were the most fascinating concept I'd ever had to deal with. I still don't quite know what implications to draw from them. But I do know they make nonsense of the various theories touted around in the name of science: that man is a territorial predator whose impulse is to raid or destroy his neighbour.

Ignatieff: *Songlines* could be read as a pretty grandiose metaphysics of your own restlessness. It grounds your wanderlust in a big scheme that involves Darwinism, nomads, instincts—but a sceptic would say, 'Come off it, Bruce, the *real* story is that you're an Englishman who wanted to get out of Sotheby's, who wanted to get out of this bloody little country and see the world.'

Chatwin: That may also be true. Being an Englishman makes me uneasy. I find I can be English and behave like an Englishman only if I'm not here.

Ignatieff: Why is that?

Chatwin: I think the English survive rather well under conditions of exile. And the fact that they tend to disintegrate while they're at home is not true of all peoples.

Ignatieff: Why do you think that is? The imperial past?

Chatwin: I don't like the imperial past. When I was at my prep school it was somehow assumed that when you left you would take the Colonial Service exam and suddenly find yourself on a South Sea island pulling down the Union Jack at sunset. That was the image not only I but a lot of people had of themselves.

Ignatieff: But in fact you were on the tail-end of that, when all that old rubbish was over. You're actually a Vietnam era traveller—and therefore part not so much of something English, but of something international. Everybody hit the road in the Sixties.

Chatwin: That's what I feel part of.

Ignatieff: But there's still an English story to your wandering, a story of escaping the suffocation of 'our island home'.

Chatwin: If you travel, you escape being labelled with class stereotypes. I come from a very middle-class family of lawyers and architects. Travel was an immense relief—it got rid of the pressure from above and from below. If you're out on the road, people have to take you at face value. You're the 'travelling Englishman'. I find that very relaxing. The English class struggle, with all its nit-picking, is alien to me. Perhaps this has to do with the fact that during the war, while my father was away in the Navy, I lived in NAAFI canteens and was passed around like a tea urn.

Later, when I went to prep school, I was shocked by the class hatred. I didn't understand what it was. For example, during the 1949 election, I think it was, on Guy Fawkes Day, we boys were required to make images of Mr and Mrs Attlee and burn them on a bonfire. We were told that Aneurin Bevin was an appalling ogre. It made me really outraged.

Ignatieff: Let's talk about another kind of politics: the struggle for Aboriginal land rights in Australia. What's your attitude to that?

Chatwin: Australia is the only great colonial land mass in which the native population did not fight back. They just folded their arms and looked with a reproachful smile at their murderers, and that made the murderers jittery beyond belief.

There is an idea in Australia that the Aboriginals have got the country by the throat. I remember in Sydney talking to somebody who said, 'I can't think why you want to go and see the Aboriginals. Here in Sydney we never meet Aboriginals; we don't see them at parties. I am not conscious of ever having shaken an Aboriginal by the hand. They don't mean anything to us.' One watched his knuckles whitening out of sheer rage at something he didn't know anything about. It was an interesting insight into the immense power these old Aboriginal men have over the country. To be confronted by them is like going to pay a visit to one of the pre-Socratic philosophers. They seem immensely wise, even though they simply rattle out a few sharp words at you. They sit there, legs folded, rather in the position of the Buddha, and you feel this immense intelligence coming out at you in waves.

Ignatieff: But what about the rights and wrongs of their land case?

Chatwin: Obviously, the whole of Australia is Aboriginal land. There's no end to the claim. You see, a tribal group who might be sitting in western New South Wales would actually know what part of downtown Sydney belonged to their moiety. And white Australians do feel with some justification that once you've opened this particular can of worms there's absolutely no end to it.

Ignatieff: I was struck by the edginess, the bitterness of your relationship with these Aboriginal pre-Socratics.

Chatwin: Yes. There was that rather curious exchange I had with a man who was a defrocked priest, an Aboriginal, who had been to Rome, been blessed by the Pope, and had then returned to his people. I tried to interest him in the themes I was pursuing. Hopeless! Not a glimmer! Then I thought I'd try a different tack. I'd try and interest him in the gypsies, because there are certain ways in which gypsies use the international telephone system in the same way that Aborigines use the songlines. Again, he said, 'I can't see what gypsies have to do with it.' And I said, 'The gypsies also see the white man as a resource, as "sitting game", to be preyed upon. In fact the gypsy word for white settlers is "meat".' The Aboriginal suddenly turned on me and said, 'Do you know what we call white men?' And I said, 'Meat.' And he said, 'Do you know what we call the welfare cheque?' 'Also meat.'

Ignatieff: How much closer could you have gotten to them?

Chatwin: I would have chosen to go and live on an Aboriginal settlement. Then I would have had to undergo some kind of ritual initiation. But my stance was to remain an observer, to get as close as I possibly could without going through all that. I just didn't want to.

Ignatieff: An accusatory voice would say, you've managed just enough entanglement with the Third World to get some fiction out of it, but you've never actually got *involved*.

Chatwin: *Now* you've caught me on tricky ground. (*Pause.*) If I had become involved, I wouldn't write the books I do.

Ignatieff: But isn't there a recurring contrast in *Songlines* between Bruce, the narrator, and characters like Arkady, Marion and Wendy, who make a commitment to Aboriginal reality incomparably deeper than your own?

Chatwin: *Incomparably* deeper than mine! The point of inventing a character like Arkady is that I was able to take a load off my back as an observer by turning it into dialogue with Arkady. And he is admirably involved. But if I had been involved then I couldn't have described him and his involvement.

Ignatieff: Now we come to the fine line between the traveller and the tourist.

Chatwin: There's nothing necessarily wrong with being a tourist. A tourist is somebody who happens to be more interested in the rest of the world than he is in his own little puddle.

Ignatieff: And what redeems this particular tourist—Bruce Chatwin—is the writing he brought back?

Chatwin: Well, it either works or it doesn't.

Ignatieff: *Songlines* ends with an unforgettable image of three Aboriginal ancients who have followed their songlines to a sacred place where the songline starts. And they're dying, but in a state of beatific happiness. It struck me that the book ends with an image of a happy death, and that when you wrote that you yourself happened to be near death.

Chatwin: Ah yes. Well, a young German Lutheran missionary took me to see these three old men dying under a tree. And it was obviously the way to end the book; there were no two ways about it. But somehow fiction and real life all came together: the year before I had been to China and picked up a completely unknown disease of the bone marrow; I handed in this book—which is, above all, about walking—and the day after I couldn't walk across the hotel bedroom. I wrote that last chapter about three old men dying under a gum tree, when I was just about to conk myself. It was done with great speed. Often I have to *labour* over sentences, but this time I just wrote it straight down on a yellow pad, and that was the end of the book. It did bring home how writing a fiction impinges on your life.

Ignatieff: Bruce, we're talking in a sunlit room of a farmhouse that looks over a banked meadow in which black sheep are grazing. There's a crackling fire in the grate, and we've just finished a delicious roast of lamb which Elizabeth prepared for us. The whole scene is a picture of home. For a wanderer, are you surprised at where you sit now? Is this home?

Chatwin: (*Long pause.*) Terrible to say so, but it isn't. I don't know why, but it can never be. I couldn't explain why. It drives Elizabeth insane, but . . . we have everything here, but I always wish I was somewhere else. It's a condition that makes one very difficut to live with.

Ignatieff: (*Pause.*) So *Songlines* is finished, but in some sense the voyage is not over. You'll be back on the road again.

Chatwin: Yes, all my plans are geared to the idea of the road. I have an idea that I should try and write a 'Russian novel', as seen from the viewpoint of an outsider. So I shall be off again.

Ignatieff: During your convalescence you began a novel about Prague, didn't you?

Chatwin: It's a memoir of things that happened to me in Prague in 1967. I met a character who was a great collector of Meissen porcelain. He had shrunk his horizons down to those of his best friends, who were all porcelain figures seven inches high. He lived like a monk. It is, of course, a fantasy of people like myself to want to sit in a cell and never move again. That's what this man did.

Ignatieff: Final question. Who are your heroes?

Chatwin: The writers I adore are nearly always the Russians. Mandelstam especially; his *Journey to Armenia* went with me on my journey to Patagonia. As a Jew, he understands restlessness—at one point he speaks about 'our fantastic homelessness.' His life was a series of the most extraordinary dislocations, which ended up in Siberia. He seems to have postulated, very early in his writing, the fate that would eventually overcome him.

Ignatieff: There's a quotation from Mandelstam in *Songlines*.

Chatwin: And how! It's from his *Conversations about Dante*. It goes something like:

> The question occurs to me—and quite seriously— how many shoe soles . . . how many sandals Aligheri wore out in the course of his poetic work, wandering about on the goat paths of Italy.
>
> The *Inferno*, and especially the *Purgatorio*, glorify the human gait, the measure and rhythm of walking, the foot and its shape . . .

I love it. It's a key text.

Ignatieff: And talismanic for a book like yours about the relationship between walking and writing.

Chatwin: Absolutely. Mandelstam himself could *only* compose on the hoof. He had to be walking, when actually writing a poem. He had an idea that the production of words in the larynx was dependent on the action of the feet.

Ignatieff: You believe this . . . ?

Chatwin: Oh yes. Like dogma!

BRUCE CHATWIN
DREAMTIME

Arkady

In Alice Springs—a grid of scorching streets where men in long white socks were forever getting in and out of Land Cruisers—I met a Russian who was mapping the sacred sites of the Aboriginals.

His name was Arkady Volchok. He was an Australian citizen. He was thirty-three years old.

His father, Ivan Volchok, a Cossack from a village near Rostov-on-Don, was arrested in 1942, and sent with a trainload of other *Ostarbeiter* to work in a German factory. One night, somewhere in the Ukraine, he jumped from the cattle car into a field of sunflowers. Soldiers in grey uniforms hunted him up and down the long lines of sunflowers, but he gave them the slip. Somewhere else, lost between murdering armies, he met a girl from Kiev and married her. Together they drifted to a forgetful Adelaide suburb where he rigged up a vodka still and fathered three sturdy sons.

The youngest of these was Arkady.

Arkady had married and had a daughter of six. Yet, preferring solitude to domestic chaos, he no longer lived with his wife. He had few possessions apart from a harpsichord and a shelf of books.

He was a tireless bush-walker. He thought nothing of setting out, with a water flask and a few bites of food, for a hundred-mile walk along the Ranges. Then he would come home, out of the heat and light, and draw the curtains, and play the music of Buxtehude and Bach on the harpsichord. Their orderly progressions, he said, conformed to the contours of the central Australian landscape.

Arkady's parents had never read a book in English. He delighted them by winning a first-class honours degree in history and philosophy at Adelaide University. He made them sad when he went to work as a schoolteacher on an Aboriginal settlement in Walbiri country to the north of Alice Springs.

He liked the Aboriginals. He liked their grit and tenacity, and their artful ways of dealing with the white man. He had learned, or half-learned, a couple of their languages and had come away astonished by their intellectual vigour, their feats of memory, and their capacity and will to survive. They were not, he insisted, a dying

Photo: Penny Tweedie/Colorific

41

race—although they did need help, now and then, to get the government and mining companies off their backs.

It was during his time as a schoolteacher that Arkady learned of the labyrinth of invisible pathways that meander all over Australia and are known to Europeans as 'Dreaming-tracks' or 'Songlines', to the Aboriginals as the 'Footprints of the Ancestors' or the 'Way of the Law.'

Aboriginal Creation myths tell of legendary totemic beings who wandered over the continent in the Dreamtime, singing out the name of everything that crossed their path—birds, animals, plants, rocks, water-holes—and so singing the world into existence.

Arkady was so struck by the beauty of this concept that he began to take notes of everything he saw or heard. At first, the Walbiri elders mistrusted him, and their answers to his questions were evasive. With time, once he had won their confidence, they invited him to witness their most secret ceremonies and encouraged him to learn their songs.

The Land Rights Act of 1976 had given Aboriginal 'owners' the title to their country, providing it lay untenanted; and the job Arkady invented for himself was to interpret or translate 'tribal law' into the language of the law of the Crown.

No one knew better that the 'idyllic' days of hunting and gathering were over—if, indeed, they were ever that idyllic. What could be done for Aboriginals was to preserve their most essential liberty: the liberty to remain poor, or, as Arkady phrased it more tactfully, the space in which to be poor if they wished to be poor.

Now that he lived alone he liked to spend most of his time 'out bush'. When he did come to town, he worked from the shop-floor at a disused newspaper, where rolls of old newsprint still clogged the presses and his sequences of aerial photos had spread, like a game of dominoes, over the shabby white walls.

One sequence showed a 300-mile strip of country running roughly due north. This was the suggested route of a new Alice-to-Darwin railway. The line, Arkady told me, was going to be the last long stretch of track to be laid in Australia, and its chief engineer, a railwayman of the old school, had announced that it must be one of the best. The engineer was close to retiring, and concerned for his posthumous reputation. He was especially concerned to avoid the kind of rumpus that broke out whenever a mining company moved its machinery into Aboriginal land. So, promising not to destroy a single one of their sacred sites, he had asked their representatives to supply him with a survey.

Arkady's job was to identify the 'traditional landowners'; to drive them over their old hunting-grounds, even if these now belonged to a cattle company; and to get them to reveal which rock or soak or ghost-gum was the work of a Dreamtime hero. He had already mapped the 150-mile stretch from Alice to Middle Bore Station. He had 150 to go.

'I warned the engineer he was being a bit rash,' he said. 'But that's the way he wanted it.'

'Why rash?'

'Well, if you look at it *their* way,' he grinned, 'the whole of bloody Australia's a sacred site.'

'Explain.'

He was on the point of explaining when an Aboriginal girl came in with a stack of papers. She was a secretary, a pliant brown girl in a brown knitted dress. She smiled and said, 'Hi, Ark!' but her smile fell away at the sight of a stranger. Arkady lowered his voice. He had warned me earlier how Aboriginals hate to hear white men discussing their 'business'.

'This is a Pom,' he said to the secretary. 'A Pom by the name of Bruce.'

The girl giggled diffidently, dumped the papers on the desk and dashed for the door.

'Let's go and get a coffee,' he said.

So we went to a coffee shop on Todd Street.

Arkady ordered a couple of *cappuccinos* in the coffee shop. We took them to a table by the window and he began to talk.

I was dazzled by the speed of his mind, although at times I felt he sounded like a man on a public platform, and that much of what he said had been said before.

The Aboriginals, he said, had an earth-bound philosophy. The earth gave life to a man; gave him his food, language and intelligence; and the earth took him back when he died. A man's 'own country', even an empty stretch of spinifex, was itself a sacred icon that must remain unscarred.

'Unscarred, you mean, by roads or mines or railways?'

'To wound the earth,' he answered earnestly, 'is to wound yourself, and, if others wound the earth, they are wounding you. The land should be left untouched: as it was in the Dreamtime when the Ancestors sang the world into existence.'

'Rilke,' I said, 'had a similar intuition. He also said Song was Existence.'

'I know,' said Arkady. 'Third Sonnet to Orpheus.'

The Aboriginals, he went on, were a people who trod lightly over the earth; and the less they took from it, the less they had to give in return. They had never understood why the missionaries forbade their innocent sacrifices. They slaughtered no victims, animal or human. Instead, when they wished to thank the earth for its gifts, they would simply slit a vein in their forearms and let their own blood spatter the ground.

'Not a heavy price to pay,' he said. 'The wars of the twentieth century are the price for having taken too much.'

To get to grips with the Dreamtime, you had to understand it as an Aboriginal equivalent of the first two chapters of *Genesis*—with one significant difference. In *Genesis*, God first created the 'living things' and then fashioned father Adam from clay. Here in Australia, the Ancestors created themselves from clay, hundreds and thousands of them, one for each totemic species.

'So when an Aboriginal tells you, "I have a wallaby Dreaming," he means, "My totem is wallaby; I am a member of the Wallaby Clan."'

'So a Dreaming is a clan emblem? A badge to distinguish "us" from "them"? "Our country" from "their country"?'

'Much more than that,' Arkady said.

Every Wallaby Man believed he was descended from a universal Wallaby Father, who was the ancestor of all other Wallaby Men and of all living wallabies. Wallabies, therefore, were his brothers. To kill one for food was both fratricide and cannibalism.

'Yet,' I persisted, 'the man was no more wallaby than the British are lions, the Russians bears or the Americans bald eagles.'

'Any species,' he said, 'can be a Dreaming. A virus can be a

Dreaming. You can have a chicken-pox Dreaming, a rain Dreaming, a desert-orange Dreaming, a lice Dreaming. In the Kimberleys they've now got a money Dreaming.'

'And the Welsh have leeks, the Scots thistles, and Daphne was changed into a laurel.'

'Same old story,' he said.

He went on to explain how each Ancestor, while travelling through the country, was thought to have scattered a trail of words and musical notes along the line of his footprints, and how these Dreaming-tracks lay over the land as 'ways' of communication between the most far-flung tribes. 'A song,' he said, 'was both map and direction-finder. Providing you knew the song, you could always find your way across country.'

'And would a man on "walkabout" always be travelling down one of the songlines?'

'In the old days, yes,' he agreed. 'Nowadays, they go by train or car.'

'Suppose the man strayed from his songline?'

'He was trespassing. He might get speared for it.'

'But as long as he stuck to the track, he'd always find people who shared his Dreaming? Who were, in fact, his brothers?'

'Yes.'

'From whom he could expect hospitality?'

'And vice versa.'

'So song is a kind of passport and meal-ticket?'

'Again, it's more complicated.' In theory, at least, the whole of Australia could be read as a musical score. There was hardly a rock or creek in the country that could not or had not been sung. One should perhaps visualize the songlines as a spaghetti of Iliads and Odysseys, writhing this way and that, in which every 'episode' was readable in terms of geology.

'By episode,' I asked, 'you mean "sacred site"?'

'I do.'

'The kind of site you're surveying for the railway?'

'Put it this way,' he said, 'anywhere in the bush you can point to some feature of the landscape and ask the Aboriginal with you, "What's the story there?" or "Who's that?" The chances are he'll answer "Kangaroo" or "Budgerigar" or "Jew Lizard", depending on which Ancestor walked that way.'

'And the distance between two such sites can be measured as a stretch of song?'

'That,' said Arkady, 'is the cause of all my troubles with the railway people.' It was one thing to persuade a surveyor that a heap of boulders was the eggs of the Rainbow Snake, or a lump of reddish sandstone was the liver of a speared kangaroo. It was something else to convince him that a featureless stretch of gravel was the musical equivalent of Beethoven's Opus 111.

By singing the world into existence, Arkady said, the Ancestors had been poets in the original sense of *poesis*, meaning 'creation'. No Aboriginal could conceive that the created world was in any way imperfect. His religious life had a single aim: to keep the land the way it was and should be. The man who went 'walkabout' was making a ritual journey. He trod in the footprints of his Ancestor. He sang the Ancestor's stanzas without changing a word or note—and so recreated the Creation.

'Sometimes,' said Arkady, 'I'll be driving my "old men" through the desert, and we'll come to a ridge of sandhills, and suddenly they'll all start singing. "What are you mob singing?" I'll ask, and they'll say, "Singing up the country, boss. Makes the country come up quicker."'

Aboriginals could not believe the country existed until they could see and sing it—just as in the Dreamtime the country had not existed until the Ancestors sang it.

'So the land,' I said, 'must first exist as a concept in the mind? Then it must be sung? Only then can it be said to exist?'

'True.'

'In other words, "to exist" is "to be perceived"?'

'Yes.'

'Sounds suspiciously like Bishop Berkeley's Refutation of Matter.'

'Or Pure Mind Buddhism,' said Arkady, 'which also sees the world as an illusion.'

'Then I suppose these 300 miles of steel, slicing through innumerable songs, are bound to upset your old men's mental balance.'

'Yes and no,' he said. 'They're very tough, emotionally, and very pragmatic. Besides, they've seen far worse than a railway.' Not only did they believe that all the 'living things' had been made in secret beneath the earth's crust, but also that all the white man's gear—his aeroplanes, his guns, his Toyota Land Cruisers—and every invention that will ever be invented, were slumbering below the surface, waiting their turn to be called.

'Perhaps,' I suggested, 'they could sing the railway back into the created world of God?'

'You bet,' said Arkady, and grinned.

It was after five. The waitress was clearing up the left-overs. Arkady looked up and asked, abruptly: 'What's your interest in all this? What do you want here?'

'I came here to test an idea,' I said.

'A big idea?'

'Probably a very obvious idea. But one I have to get out of my system.'

'And?'

He made me nervous with his sudden shift of mood. I began to explain how I had once tried, unsuccessfully, to write a book about nomads.

'Pastoral nomads?'

'No,' I said. 'Nomads. *Nomos* is Greek for "pasture". A nomad moves from pasture to pasture.'

I went to Africa, I continued, to the Sudan. I sailed down the Dongola Reach in a trading felucca. I went to the 'Ethiopians', a euphemism for brothel. I had a narrow escape from a rabid dog. At an under-staffed clinic I acted the role of anaesthetist for a caesarean birth. Next I joined up with a geologist who was surveying for minerals in the Red Sea hills.

This was nomad country, the nomads being the Beja: Kipling's 'fuzzy-wuzzies', who didn't give a damn for either the Pharaohs of Egypt or the British at Omdurman. The men were tall and lean, and wore sand-coloured cottons folded in an X across the chest. With shields of elephant hide and 'Crusader' swords dangling from their belts, they would come into the villages to trade their meat for grain. They looked down on the villagers as though they were some kind of animal.

In the early light of dawn, as the vultures flexed their wings along the rooftops, the geologist and I would watch the men at their daily grooming. They anointed each other's hair with scented goat's grease and then teased it out in corkscrew curls, making a buttery parasol which, like a turban, prevented their brains from going soft. By evening, when the grease had melted, the curls bounced back to form a solid pillow.

Our camel-man was a joker called Mahmoud, whose mop of hair was even bigger than the others. He began by stealing the geological hammer. Then he left his knife for us to steal. Then, with hoots of laughter, we swapped them back, and in this way we became great friends. When the geologist went back to Khartoum, Mahmoud took me off into the desert to look for rock-paintings.

We had three camels, two for riding and one for water-skins, yet usually we preferred to walk. He went barefoot; I was in boots. I never saw anything like the lightness of his step and, as he walked, he sang: usually a song about a girl from the Wadi Hammamat who was lovely as a green parakeet. The camels were his only property. He had no flocks and wanted none. He was immune to everything that we would call 'progress'.

We found our rock-paintings: red ochre pin-men scrawled on the overhang of a rock. Nearby there was a long, flat boulder with a cleft up one end and its surface pocked with cup-marks. This, said Mahmoud, was the dragon with its head cut off by Ali. He asked me, with a wicked grin, whether I was a Believer. In two weeks I never saw him pray.

Later, when I went back to England, I found a photo of a 'fuzzy-wuzzy' carved in relief on an Egyptian tomb of the Twelfth Dynasty at Beni Hassan: a pitiful, emaciated figure, like the pictures of victims in the Sahel drought, and recognizably the same as Mahmoud.

The Pharaohs had vanished; Mahmoud and his people had lasted. I felt I had to know the secret of their timeless and irreverent vitality.

I quit my job in the London 'art world' and went back to the dry places; alone, travelling light.

The names of the tribes I travelled among are unimportant; Rguibat, Quashgai, Taimanni, Turkomen, Bororo, Tuareg—people whose journeys, unlike my own, had neither beginning nor end. I slept in black tents, blue tents, skin tents, yurts of felt and windbreaks of thorns. One night, caught in a sandstorm in the Western Sahara, I understood Muhammad's dictum: *A journey is a fragment of Hell.*

The more I read, the more convinced I became that nomads had been the crankhandle of history, if for no other reason than that the great monotheisms had, all of them, surfaced from the pastoral milieu . . .

Arkady was looking out of the window.

Arkady lived in a rented studio apartment above a row of lock-up garages, in the lot behind the supermarket. As he unlocked the door, a cool draught blew in our faces. There was a note shoved through on to the mat. He switched on the light, and read.

'Not before time,' he mumbled.

'What's that?' I asked.

He explained how one of the Kaititj elders, an old man called Alan Nakumurra, had been holding up the survey for the last four weeks. He was the last male survivor of his clan and 'traditional owner' of the country north of Middle Bore Station. The railway surveyors had been anxious to peg out this particular stretch of track. Arkady had put them off till Alan could be found.

'Where did he go?'

'Where do you think?' he laughed. 'He went walkabout.'

'What happened to the others of his clan?'

'Shot,' said Arkady, 'by police patrols in the twenties.'

He put through a call to his boss. He talked business for a minute or two and then said there was this Pom in town who wanted to go 'out bush' with the survey team . . . No, not a journalist . . . Yes, as Poms went, relatively harmless . . . No, not a photographer . . . No, not interested in watching rituals . . . No, not tomorrow . . . The day after . . .

There was a pause. You could almost hear the man thinking on the far end of the line. Then Arkady smiled and gave a 'thumbs-up' sign. 'You're on,' he said.

Flynn

Seldom in its missionary endeavours can the Catholic Church in Australia have suffered from so difficult a case as that of Father Flynn.

He was a foundling, dumped by an unknown mother at the store of an Irishman at Fitzroy Crossing. At the age of six, he was sent to a Benedictine mission, where he refused to play with other black children, learned to serve at Mass and had the habit of asking questions about dogma in a soft reverential brogue. One day, he reeled off pat the name of every Pope, from St Peter to Pius XIII. The Fathers taught him Latin and encouraged him to take Holy Orders.

Flynn was ordained in 1969. He went to Rome. He had an audience with the Holy Father, which lasted approximately one and a quarter minutes. On his return to Australia, the Order decided he should be the first Aboriginal to take charge of a mission on his own.

The place they chose was Roe River in the Kimberleys. And to equip himself for the task, Flynn was sent to learn from one of the old-timers, Father Villaverde, at another Benedictine outpost: Boongaree.

Father Villaverde was a leathery Extremeñan from Trujillo. For fifty years he had suffered flood, famine, disease, mutiny, a Japanese bombardment and many other onslaughts of the Devil.

Boongaree was an hour's walk from the coast. Roe River, Flynn's mission, on the other hand, lay 150 miles up country and could be cut off by the 'wets' for three months or more. They were not missions in the usual sense but cattle-stations, which the Order had picked up for a song in 1946. They had proved to be a very sound investment.

Coming as he did from the birthplace of the Pizarros, Father Villaverde felt obliged to cast himself in the role of conquistador. He said it was useless to try to impress the heathen with acts of love, when all they understood was force. He forbade them to hunt or even to garden. The only hope for their economic salvation was to foster an addiction to horse flesh.

He would snatch small boys from their mothers and set them on a bucking saddle. Nothing gave him greater joy than to charge through the bush at the head of his troop of young daredevils. On Saturday afternoons, he would preside over a sports meeting, with sprinting, wrestling, spear-throwing and boomerang-throwing—and in each event he took part himself. A natural athlete—although in his seventies—he rejoiced at the chance of showing off his superior, European physique. The blacks, who knew how to humour him, would hold back their strength, allow him to win, crown him with a victor's wreath and carry him shoulder-high to his quarters.

He banned all anthropologists, journalists and other snoopers. He prohibited 'traditional' ceremonies. Above all, with a kind of priestly envy, he resented his lads going off to look for wives. Once they got away, to Broome or Fitzroy Crossing, they picked up foul language, foul diseases and a taste for drink. So, having done everything to prevent them going, he did everything to prevent them coming back.

The blacks believed he was deliberately trying to run down their numbers.

Father Villaverde hated Flynn on sight and put him through every kind of ordeal. He made him wade up to his neck in flood water, castrate bullocks and scrub the latrines. He accused him of eyeing the Spanish nursing sisters at Mass, whereas it was they—poor village girls sent out in batches from a convent near Badajoz—who had, of course, been eyeing him.

One day, as the Spaniards were showing a Texan cattle king around the mission, the Texan's wife insisted on photographing a white-bearded elder, who sat cross-legged and unbuttoned in the dust. The old man was furious. He spat a neat gob of phlegm, which landed at the lady's feet. But she, rising to the occasion, apologized, ripped the film from her camera and, bending forward with the air of Lady Bountiful, asked, 'Is there anything I can send you from America?'

'There is,' he snapped. 'Four Toyota Land Cruisers!'

Father Villaverde was shocked. To this authentic *caballero*, the internal combustion engine was an anathema. Someone must have been stirring up trouble. His suspicions fell on Father Flynn.

A month or so later, he intercepted a letter from the Department of Aboriginal Affairs in Canberra, thanking the Boongaree Council for their request for a Land Cruiser: the matter would receive consideration.

'And what,' shrieked Father Villaverde, 'is the Boongaree Council?'

Flynn folded his arms, waited for the tirade to blow over, and said, 'We are.'

From that day on, there was open war.

At the next Saturday's sports meeting, just as Father Villaverde had hurled his winning throw, Flynn, in a white soutane, strode out from behind the chapel carrying a spear which had been rubbed with red ochre. He beckoned the spectators to clear a space and, with an apparently effortless flick, sent the weapon soaring into the air.

The length of the throw was over twice that of the Spaniard—who took to his bed in rage.

I forget the name of the three tribes camped around the mission. The point to remember is that Tribe A was the friend and ally of Tribe B, and both were blood enemies of the men of Tribe C—who, outflanked and deprived of their source of women, were in danger of dying out.

The three camps lay equidistant from the mission buildings: each tribe facing the direction of its former homeland. Fights would break out only after a period of taunts and accusations of sorcery. Yet, by tacit agreement, none of the allies would gang up on its common enemy. All three recognized the mission itself as neutral ground.

Father Villaverde preferred to condone these periodic bouts of bloodshed: as long as the savages persisted in their ignorance of the Gospel, they were bound to go on fighting each other. Besides, the role of peacemaker suited his vanity. At the sound of screams, he would rush to the scene, stride through the clashing spears and, with the gesture of Christ calming the waters, say, 'Stop!'—and the warriors would shamble off home.

The leading lawman of Tribe C had the unforgettable name of Cheekybugger Tabagee. An expert tracker in his youth, he had guided prospecting expeditions through the Kimberleys. He now hated every white man and, in thirty years, had not addressed one word to the Spaniards.

Cheekybugger was built on a colossal scale, but he was old, arthritic and covered with the scabs of a skin disease. His legs were useless. He would sit in the half-shade of his humpy and let the dogs lick his sores.

He knew he was dying and it enraged him. One by one, he had watched the young men go, or go to pieces. Soon there would be no one—either to sing the songs or to give blood for ceremonies.

In Aboriginal belief, an unsung land is a dead land: since, if the songs are forgotten, the land itself will die. To allow that to happen was the worst of all possible crimes, and it was with this bitter thought that Cheekybugger decided to pass his songs to the enemy—thereby committing his people to perpetual peace, which, of course, was a far graver decision than conniving at perpetual war.

He sent for Flynn and asked him to act as mediator.

Flynn went from camp to camp, argued, exhorted and finally arrived at a formula. The snag was one of protocol.

Cheekybugger had begun the negotiations: in law, it was he who must deliver the songs in person and hand over his tjuringa, the sacred stone disk serving as a modern title-deed. The question was how. He couldn't walk. He would not be carried. He scoffed at the offer of a horse. In the end it was Flynn who hit on the solution: by borrowing a wheelbarrow from the Malay cook who worked the kitchen garden.

The procession set off between two and three of a blistering blue afternoon, when the cockatoos were silent and the Spaniards snoring through their siesta. Cheekybugger went ahead in the wheelbarrow, pushed by his eldest son. Across his knee, wrapped in newspaper, lay his tjuringa, which he now proposed to lend to the enemy. The others followed in single file.

At some point beyond the chapel, two men—from Tribes A and B—stepped from the bushes and escorted the party to the place of 'business'.

Flynn lagged behind, his eyes half-closed, with the air of a man in a trance.

Around sunset, one of the nursing sisters took a short cut

through the bush and heard the drone of voices and the *tak . . . tak . . .* of boomerangs being clacked together. She hurried to tell Father Villaverde.

He rushed out to break up the meeting. Flynn walked out from behind a tree and warned him to stay away.

After the fight, people said that Flynn had simply clamped his hands around his attacker's wrists and held them. This, however, did not prevent Father Villaverde from writing letter after letter to his superiors, claiming unprovoked assault and demanding that this acolyte of Satan be drummed from the body of the Church.

Father Villaverde was advised not to send the letters. Already, Aboriginal pressure groups were lobbying for an end to the missions. Flynn had not taken part in a heathenish rite: he had only acted as peacemaker. What if the press got wind of the affair? What if it came out that an elderly Spaniard had been stirring up tribal warfare?

Father Villaverde gave in, against his better judgement, and in October 1976, two months before the 'wets', Flynn left to take charge of Roe River. The previous incumbent refused to meet him and left for Europe on sabbatical. The rains came—and there was silence.

Some time during Lent, the Catholic Bishop of the Kimberleys radioed Boongaree to confirm or deny a rumour that Flynn had 'gone native'—to which Father Villaverde answered, 'He *is* native!'

On the first day fit for flying, the Bishop flew with Father Villaverde to Roe River in his Cessna, where they inspected the damage 'like two conservative politicians at the scene of a terrorist bomb.'

The chapel was in disarray. Buildings had been burned for firewood. The stock-pens were empty and there were charred beef bones everywhere. Father Villaverde said, 'Our work in Australia is at an end.'

Flynn then overplayed his hand. He believed the Land Rights movement was advancing faster than it was. He counted on the assurance of certain left-wingers that missions all over the country would be handed over to the blacks. He refused to compromise. Father Villaverde trumped him.

The affair had touched the Church at its most brittle point: the financial. It was not generally known that both Boongaree and Roe River had been financed with capital raised originally in Spain. A bank in Madrid held the title deeds as collateral. To forestall any attempt at confiscation, both missions were sold, secretly, to an American businessman and absorbed into the assets of a multi-national corporation.

The press campaigned for their return. The Americans threatened to close an unprofitable smelter north of Perth with a loss of 500 jobs. The unions intervened. The campaign subsided. The Aboriginals were dispersed, and Dan Flynn—as he styled himself—went to live with a girl in Broome.

Before moving into her apartment, Flynn wrote a letter, in faultless Latin, requesting the Holy Father to release him from his vows.

The couple moved to Alice Springs and were active in Aboriginal politics.

The ex-Benedictine was holding court to half a dozen people in the darker part of a garden party to which Arkady had brought me. The moonlight shone on Flynn's brow ridges; his face and beard were swallowed up in the darkness. His girl-friend sat at his feet. From time to time, she would stretch her lovely long neck across his thigh and he would reach out a finger and tickle her. When Arkady crouched beside the chair and explained what I wanted, I heard Flynn mutter: 'Christ, not another!'

I had to wait a full five minutes before he deigned to turn his head in my direction. Then he asked in a flat, ironic voice: 'Is there anything I can do to help you?'

'There is,' I said, nervously. 'I'm interested in the Songlines.'

'Are you?'

I was so daunted by his presence that I was sure that anything I said would sound silly. I tried to interest him in various theories on the evolutionary origins of language.

'There are linguists,' I said, 'who believe the first language was in song.'

He looked away and stroked his beard.

I described how gypsies communicate over colossal distances by singing secret verses down the telephone.

'Do they?'

Before being initiated, I went on, a young gypsy boy had to memorize the songs of his clan, the names of his kin, as well as hundreds and hundreds of international phone numbers.

'Gypsies,' I said, 'are probably the best phone-tappers in the world.'

'I cannot see,' said Flynn, 'what gypsies have to do with our people.'

'Because gypsies,' I said, 'also see themselves as hunters. The world is their hunting-ground. Settlers are "sitting game". In fact, the gypsy word for "settler" is the same as the word for "meat".'

Flynn turned to face me.

'You know what our people call the white man?' he asked.

'Meat.'

'And you know what they call a welfare cheque?'

'Also meat.'

'Bring a chair,' he said. 'I want to talk to you.'

I sat down beside him.

'Sorry I was a bit sharp,' he said. 'You should see the nutters I have to deal with.'

White men, he began, made the common mistake of assuming that, because the Aboriginals were wanderers, they could have no system of land tenure. This was nonsense. Aboriginals, it was true, could not imagine territory as a block of land hemmed in by frontiers: rather they saw it as an interlocking network of 'lines' or 'ways through'.

'All our words for "country",' he said, 'are the same as the words for "line".'

For this there was one simple explanation. Most of outback Australia was arid scrub or desert where rainfall was always patchy; one year of plenty might be followed by seven years of lean. To move in such a landscape was survival; to stay in the same place, suicide. Yet to feel 'at home' in that country depended on being able to leave it. Everyone hoped to have at least four 'ways out', along which he could travel in a crisis. Every tribe—like it or not—had to cultivate relations with its neighbour.

'So if A had fruits,' said Flynn, 'and B had duck, and C had an ochre quarry, there were formal rules for exchanging these commodities, and formal routes along which to trade.'

What the Whites used to call the 'walkabout' was, in practice, a kind of bush telegraph-cum-stock-exchange, spreading messages between peoples who never saw each other, who might be unaware of the other's existence.

'This trade,' he said, 'was not trade as you Europeans know it. Not the business of buying and selling for profit! Our people's trade was always symmetrical.'

Aboriginals in general had the idea that all 'goods' were potentially malign and would work against their possessors unless they were forever in motion. The 'goods' did not have to be edible or useful. People liked nothing better than to barter useless things, or things they could supply for themselves: feathers, sacred objects, belts of human hair.

'I know,' I interrupted. 'Some people traded their umbilical cords.'

'I see you've done your reading.'

Trade goods, he continued, should be seen rather as the bargaining counters of a gigantic game, in which the whole continent was the gaming-board and all its inhabitants were players. 'Goods' were tokens of intent: to trade again, meet again, fix frontiers, intermarry, sing, dance, share resources and share ideas.

A shell might travel from hand to hand, from the Timor Sea to the Bight, along 'roads' handed down since time began. These 'roads' would follow the line of unfailing water-holes. The water-holes, in turn, were ceremonial centres where men of different tribes would meet.

'For what you call coroborees?'

'*You* call them coroborees,' he said. 'Not us.'

'All right,' I nodded. 'Are you saying that a trade route always runs along a songline?'

'The trade-route *is* the songline,' said Flynn. 'Because songs, not things, are the principal medium of exchange. Trading in "things" is the secondary consequence of trading in song.'

Before the whites came, he went on, no one in Australia was landless, since everyone inherited, as his or her private property, a stretch of the Ancestor's song and the stretch of country over which the song passed. A man's verses were his title-deeds to territory. He could lend them to others. He could borrow other verses in return. The one thing he couldn't do was sell or get rid of them.

Supposing the elders of a Carpet Snake clan decided it was time to sing their song cycle from beginning to end. Messages would be sent out, up and down the track, summoning song-owners to assemble at the Big Place. One after the other, each 'owner' would then sing his stretch of the Ancestor's footprints, and always in the correct sequence.

'To sing a verse out of order,' Flynn said sombrely, 'was a dreadful crime. It usually meant the death penalty.'

Wherever you had a Big Place, he continued, the chances were that other Dreamings would converge on it. So at one of your 'coroborees' you might have four different totemic clans, from any number of different tribes, all of whom would swap songs, dances, sons and daughters, and grant each other 'rights of way' through the country.

'When you've been around a bit longer,' he said, 'you'll hear the expression "acquiring ritual knowledge".'

All this meant was that the man was extending his song map. He was widening his options, exploring the world through song.

'Imagine two Blacks,' he said, 'meeting for the first time in an Alice pub. One will try one Dreaming. The other will try another. Then finally something'll click . . .'

The next point, he said, was to understand that every song cycle went leap-frogging through language barriers, regardless of tribe or frontier. A Dreaming-track might start in the north-west, near Broome; thread its way through twenty languages or more; and go on to hit the sea near Adelaide.

'And yet,' I said, 'it's still the same song.'

'Our people,' Flynn said, 'say they recognize a song by its "taste" or "smell" . . . by which, of course, they mean the tune. The tune *always* stays the same, from the opening bars to the finale.'

'Does that mean,' I asked, 'that a young man on walkabout could sing his way across Australia providing he could hum the right tune?'

'In theory, yes,' Flynn agreed.

'Like an international frontier,' I said. 'The road signs change language, but it's still the same road.'

'More or less,' said Flynn. 'But it doesn't get the beauty of the system. Here there are no frontiers, only roads and stops.' A 'stop' was the 'handover point' where the song passed out of your ownership; where it was no longer yours to look after and no longer yours to lend. You'd sing to the end of your verses, and there lay the boundary.

Suppose you took a tribal area like that of the Central Aranda? Suppose there were 600 Dreamings weaving in and out of it? That would mean 1200 handover points dotted around the perimeter. Each stop had been sung into position by a Dreamtime Ancestor: its place on the song map was thus unchangeable. But since each was the work of a *different* Ancestor, there was no way of linking them sideways to form a modern political frontier.

An Aboriginal family, he said, might have five full brothers, each of whom belonged to a different totemic clan, each with different allegiances inside and outside the tribe. To be sure, Aboriginals had fights and vendettas and blood feuds—but always to redress some imbalance or sacrilege. The idea of invading their neighbour's land would never have entered their heads.

'What this boils down to,' I said, hesitantly, 'is something quite similar to bird-song. Birds call their territorial boundaries, and ensure their even spacing over the habitat.'

Arkady, who had been listening with his forehead on his kneecaps, looked up and shot me a glance: 'I was wondering when you'd rumble to that one.'

Lizard

When I dropped in on Arkady at the office he said, 'I've got good news for you.'

A radio message had come in from Cullen, an Aboriginal out-station about 350 miles away on the West Australian border. Two clans were having a quarrel about mining royalties. They had called on Arkady to mediate. 'We can get through the railway business in a couple of days. Then we'll head out west across country.'

T he road was a straight band of tarmac and on either side there were strips of red dirt with paddy melon growing over them. The melons were the size of cricket balls. Every few miles, we passed the gates of a cattle-station, or a wind-pump with cattle clustered round it. There were a lot of dead beasts, legs in the air, ballooned up with gas and the crows on top of them. The rains were two months late.

'Marginal country,' said Arkady. Almost all the best pastoral leases had been bought up by foreigners: Vesteys, Bunker Hunt, and the like. No wonder Territorians felt cheated! 'The country's against them,' he said. 'The politicians are against them. The multinationals are against them. The Abos are against them. Surely this country's only good for Abos?' He described how once, while they were tracing a songline near Mount Wedge, the pastoralist had driven up and, waving a shotgun, had hollered, 'Get off my land! Get them coons off my land!' So Arkady, who had already written the man five letters without receiving a reply, explained the provisions of the Land Rights Act, whereby 'traditional owners' were allowed to visit their sites.

This made the pastoralist hopping mad: 'There ain't no sacred sites on my land,' he yelled. 'Oh yes, there are,' said one of the Aboriginals present.' 'Oh, no, there aren't.' 'You're standing on one, mate.'

The road curved to cross a creek-bed and, on the far side, where Arkady pointed away to the east, was a switchback of pale brown hills. They stood up like cardboard scenery from the plain.

'You see the small hill, there? That was where the railway people wanted to make a cutting. It would have saved at least two miles of track.'

The hills lay on the northern edge of Aranda country: yet when Arkady sent word round the usual channels, no one wanted to claim them. He had been on the point of assuming there were no 'owners' when an Aranda mob showed up in his office . . . and said they were.

He drove five of the men to the hills where they moped around miserably, clearly afraid. Again and again he asked, 'What are the songs of this place?' or, 'What's the dreaming-story here?' They clamped their mouths and wouldn't say a word.

'I couldn't think what was up,' he said. 'So I told them about the cutting, and that really set them off. They all began blubbering, "Blackfella die! Whitefella die! All people die! End of Australia! End of world! Finish!"'

'Well, obviously,' said Arkady, '*that* had to be something big. So I asked the elder, who's shaking from head to foot, "What *have* you got down there?" And he cups his hand around my ear and whispers: "MAGGOT POWER!"'

The song that lay along the line of hills told of a Dreamtime Ancestor who failed to perform the correct ritual for controlling a bush-fly breeding cycle. Swarms of maggots overran the Burt Plain, stripping it bare of vegetation. The Ancestor, however, rounded them up and crammed them back beneath the spur of rock where, ever since, they'd been breeding and breeding underground. The old men said that, if they cut into the hillside, there'd be a gigantic explosion. A cloud of flies would spiral upwards and cover the whole earth and kill every man and animal with poison.

'The Bomb?'

'The Bomb,' said Arkady, grimly. 'Some of my friends learned a lot about the Bomb. *After* it went off.'

Before the British H-Bomb test at Maralinga, the Army posted KEEP OUT! signs, in English, for Aboriginals to read. Not everyone saw them or could read English.

'They went through it,' he said.

'The cloud?'

'The cloud.'

'How many died?'

'No one knows,' he said.

The road ran on towards a white house in a clump of trees with a spread of buildings beyond it. This was Middle Bore Station. There were chestnut horses grazing in a field of bone-white grass. Although it was late in the afternoon, most of the people were still asleep. A woman sat sorting bush-tucker under a tree and, when Arkady greeted her, she looked down and stared at her toes.

We picked our way past the 'humpies', zigzagging through clumps of spinifex towards the wheel-less body of a Volkswagen van. There was a green tarpaulin stretched over the door and a length of plastic hose dribbling into a patch of water-melon. Chained to the van was the usual sharp-muzzled hound.

'Alan?' Arkady raised his voice above the yapping.

No reply.

'Alan, are you there? . . . Christ,' he said under his breath, 'let's hope he's not gone off again.'

We waited a while longer and a long black hand appeared around the edge of the tarpaulin. This was followed, after an interval, by a wiry, silver-bearded man wearing a pale grey stetson, dirty white pants and a purple shirt printed with guitars. He was barefoot. He stepped into the sunlight, looked clean through Arkady, and majestically lowered his head.

Old Alan was *kirda*: that is to say, he was the 'owner' or 'boss' of the land we were going to survey. He was responsible for its upkeep, for making sure its songs were sung and its rituals performed on time.

Arkady unrolled the survey map, weighting the corners with stones to stop them lifting in the blasts of wind. He pointed to various hills, roads, bores, fences—and the probable route of the railway. Alan looked on with the composure of a general at a staff meeting. From time to time, he would stretch a questioning finger to some feature on the map, and then withdraw it. Then he splayed both first and second fingers into a V and ran them up and down the sheet, like dividers, his lips working silently, at speed. He was, as Arkady told me later, measuring off a songline.

We set off to the east in the Land Cruiser, where the country was a flat and treeless waste entirely lacking in cover. Alan kept raising a finger to a solitary bump on the horizon. It was almost dark by the time we reached a small rocky hill, its boulders bursting with the white plumes of spinifex in flower, and a black fuzz of leafless mallee bush. The hill, said Arkady, was the 'resting place' of the Lizard Ancestor.

While Arkady unpacked, I went off to hack some firewood, then lit the fire, using bark and grass for tinder. We cooked our steaks over it, but the meat turned out charred and tough, and we had very little appetite. The firelight lapped their faces. The moon came up. We could just discern the profile of the hill. We sat in silence until Arkady, judging the moment was right, turned to Alan and asked quietly in English: 'So what's the story of this place, old man?'

Alan gazed into the fire. The skin stretched taut over his cheekbones and shone. Then, almost imperceptibly, he tilted his head towards a man in a blue shirt, who had said little since we arrived at the camp. The man got to his feet and began to mime (with words of pidgin thrown in) the travels of the Lizard Ancestor.

It was a song of how the Lizard and his lovely young wife had walked from northern Australia to the Southern Sea, and of how a southerner had seduced the wife and sent him home with a substitute.

I don't know what species of lizard he was supposed to be. All I do know is that the man in the blue shirt made the most lifelike lizard you could ever hope to imagine. He was male and female, seducer and seduced. He was glutton, he was cuckold, he was weary traveller. He would claw his lizard-feet sideways, then freeze and cock his head. He would lift his lower lid to cover the iris, and flick out his lizard-tongue. He would puff his neck into goitres of rage; and at last, when it was time for him to die, he writhed and wriggled, his movements growing fainter and fainter like the dying swan's.

Then his jaw locked, and that was the end. The performance had lasted not more than three minutes.

The death of the lizard touched us and made us sad. But the old men who had gathered round the fire had been in stitches since the wife-swapping episode and went on hooting and cackling long after the man-in-blue sat down. Even the resigned and beautiful face of old Alan composed itself into a smile. Then one by one they yawned, and spread out their swags, and curled up and went to sleep.

'They must have liked you,' Arkady said. 'It was their way of saying thanks for supper.'

We lit a hurricane-lamp and sat on a couple of camping-chairs away from the fire.

What we had witnessed, he said, was not of course the *real* Lizard song, but a 'false front', or sketch performed for strangers. The real song would have named each water-hole the Lizard-Man drank from, each tree he cut a spear from, each cave he slept in, covering the whole long distance of the way.

Arkady had understood the pidgin far better than I. This is the version I then jotted down:

> The Lizard and his wife set off to walk to the Southern Sea. The wife was young and beautiful and had skin far lighter than her husband. They crossed swamps and rivers until they stopped at a hill—the hill at Middle Bore—and there they slept the night. In the morning they passed the camp of some dingoes, where a mother was sucking a brood of pups. 'Ha!' said the Lizard. 'I'll remember those pups and eat them later.'
>
> The couple walked on, past Oodnadatta, past Lake Eyre, and came to the sea at Port Augusta. A sharp wind was blowing off the sea, and the Lizard felt cold and started to shiver. He saw, on a headland nearby, the camp-fire of some Southerners and said to his wife: 'Go over to those people and borrow a fire stick.'
>
> She went. But one of the Southerners, lusting after her lighter skin, made love to her—and she agreed to stay with him. He made his own wife paler by smearing her from head to foot with yellow ochre and sent her, with the fire stick, to the solitary traveller. Only when the ochre began to rub off did the Lizard realize he was victim of a kidnap. He stamped his feet. He puffed himself up in fury, but, being a stranger in a distant country, he was powerless to take revenge. Miserably, he turned for home with his uglier, substitute wife. On the way he stopped to kill and eat the dingo puppies but these had a bad effect on his digestion and made him sick. On reaching the hill at Middle Bore, he lay down and died . . .

Arkady and I sat mulling over this story of an antipodean Helen. The distance from here to Port Augusta, as the crow flew, was roughly 1,100 miles, about twice the distance—so we calculated—from Troy to Ithaca. We tried to imagine an *Odyssey* with a verse for every twist and turn of the hero's ten-year voyage.

I looked at the Milky Way and said: 'One might as well count the stars.'

Round Table

Two days later, we saw a herd of camels, soaked in the downpour, and then through the mist we began to see the rounded hump of Mount Cullen, rearing up above the level of the plain. As we came up closer, the colour of the mountain turned from grey to purple: the colour of sodden, red sandstone. A mile or two beyond, there was a sheer, faceted escarpment, raised into a peak at one end, and then tapering away towards the north.

This, said Arkady, was Mount Liebler. On a saddle between these two mountains lay the settlement of Cullen.

We drove along the airstrip, past the caravans of the white advisers, towards a building of galvanized metal sheet. There was a petrol pump outside it. The sun had come out and it was hot and sticky. Packs of dogs were squabbling over a few scraps of offal. There was no one about.

Dispersed among the bushes were a number of 'humpies', but most of the Pintupi preferred to live in windbreaks of thorn. We did see a few bits of washing.

'Who would guess,' said Arkady, 'that this is a flourishing community of four hundred souls?'

Titus Tjilkamata, the man Arkady had come to see, lived about twenty-five miles south-west of Cullen settlement, in a shanty beside a soakage.

He was apparently in such a foul mood that Arkady, who had been bracing himself for the ordeal, suggested I stay behind, until he'd 'taken the temperature.' He enlisted the support of Titus's 'manager', a soft-spoken man with a limp and the nickname 'Limpy'. The two of them set off in the Land Cruiser. I looked in on Rolf, the minuscule man at the store.

Rolf was reading Proust. 'I've got someone here you should meet,' he said.

He handed a toffee to a small boy and told him to run and fetch Joshua. About ten minutes later, a middle-aged man appeared in the doorway, all leg and no body, very dark-skinned in a black cowboy hat.

'Ha!' said Rolf. 'Mr Wayne himself.'

'Boss!' said the Aboriginal, in a gravelly American accent.

'Listen, you old scrounger. This is a friend of mine from England. I want you to tell him about the Dreamings.'

'Boss!' he repeated.

Joshua was a famous Pintupi 'performer' who could always be counted on to give a good show. He had performed in Europe and the United States. On flying into Sydney for the first time, he mistook the lights for stars—and asked why the plane was flying upside down.

I followed him home along a winding path through the spinifex. He had no hips to speak of, and his trousers kept falling down to reveal a pair of neat, callused buttocks.

'Home' lay on the highest point of the saddle between Mount Cullen and Mount Liebler. It consisted of a gutted station-wagon which Joshua had rolled on to its roof so he could lie under the bonnet in the shade. The cab was wrapped in black plastic sheet. A bundle of hunting spears was poking out of one window.

We sat down cross-legged in the sand. I asked him if he'd mind pointing out some local Dreamings.

'Ho! Ho!' He broke into a wheezy cackle. 'Many Dreamings! *Many*!'

'Well, who,' I asked, waving towards Mount Liebler, 'is that?'

'Ho! Ho!' he said. 'That one a Big One. A Walk One. A Perenty One.'

The perenty, or lace-monitor, is the largest lizard in Australia. It can reach a length of eight feet or more, and has a burst of speed to run down a horse. Joshua stuck his tongue in and out like a lizard's and, twisting his fingers into claws, dug them crabwise into the sand to imitate the perenty's walk.

I looked up again at the cliff-line of Mount Liebler and found I could 'read' into the rock the lizard's flat, triangular head, his shoulder, his foreleg and hind leg, and the tail tapering away towards the north.

'Yes,' I said. 'I can see him. So where was this Perenty Man coming from?'

'Come long way,' said Joshua. 'Come long, long way. Some way up Kimberley.'

'And where's he going on to?'

He raised his hand towards the south.

Having established that the Perenty songline followed a north-south axis, I then swivelled round and pointed to the bulbous bulk of Mount Cullen. 'Well, who's this one?'

'Women,' Joshua whispered. 'Two women.'

He told the story of how the Two Women had chased the Perenty Man up and down the country until, at last, they cornered him here and attacked his head with digging-sticks. The Perenty Man, however, had dug himself into the earth, and got away. A hole on the summit of Mount Liebler, not unlike a meteorite crater, was all that remained of the head wound.

Out towards the south, the country was green after the rain. There were isolated rocks jutting out of it, like islands in a blue-green sea. 'Tell me, Joshua,' I asked, 'what Dreamings are those rocks over there?'

Joshua listed Fire, Spider, Wind, Grass, Porcupine, Snake, Old Man, Two Men, and an unidentifiable animal 'like a dog but a white one.'

His own Dreaming, the Porcupine (or echidna), came down from the direction of Arnhem Land, through Cullen itself and on towards Kalgoorlie.

I looked back again towards the settlement, at the scatter of metal roofs and the spinning sails of the wind-pump. There are several springs at the foot of Mount Cullen. There must always have been plenty of water.

'So Porcupine's coming up this way?' I said.

'Same one, Boss.' Joshua smiled. 'You seeing him good.'

He traced the line of the Porcupine track across the airstrip, past the school and the wind-pump, then along the foot of the Perenty cliff before it swooped down on to the plain.

'Can you sing him for me?' I asked. 'Can you sing him coming up this way?'

He glanced round to make sure no one was in earshot and then, in his chesty voice, he sang a number of the Porcupine couplets, keeping time by flicking his finger-nail against a piece of cardboard sheet.

'Thank you,' I said.

'Boss.'

'Tell me another story.'

'You like them stories?'

'I like them.'

'OK, Boss!' He tilted his head from side to side. 'Story 'bout the Big Fly One.'

'Dragon-fly?' I asked.

'Bigger one.'

'Bird?'

'Bigger.'

Aboriginals, when tracing a songline in the sand, will draw a series of lines with circles in between. The line represents a stage in the Ancestor's journey (usually a day's march). Each circle is a 'stop', 'water-hole', or one of the Ancestor's campsites.

But the story of the Big Fly One was beyond me. It began with a few straight sweeps, then it wound into a kind of rectangular maze, and finally ended in a series of wiggles. As he traced each section, Joshua kept calling a refrain, in English: 'Ho! Ho! They got the money over there.'

I must have been very dim-witted that morning, because it took me ages to realize that this was a Qantas Dreaming. Joshua had flown to London. The 'maze' was London Airport: the Arrivals gate, Health, Immigration, Customs, and then the ride into the city on the Underground. The 'wiggles' were the twists and turns of the taxi, from the tube station to the hotel.

In London, Joshua had seen all the usual sights—the Tower of London, changing of the guard and so on—but his real destination had been Amsterdam.

The ideogram for Amsterdam was even more perplexing. There was a circle. There were four smaller circles around it; and there were wires from each of these circles that led to a rectangular box.

Eventually, it dawned on me that this was some kind of round-table conference at which he, Joshua, had been one of four participants. The others, in a clockwise direction, had been 'a white one, a father one; a thin one, a red one; a black one, a fat one.'

It struck me that the 'wires' were microphone cables, but Joshua shook his head vigorously. He knew all about microphones. They *had* microphones, on the table.

'No! No!' he shouted, pointing to his temples. These wires had been attached to their heads.

'What the hell? Electrodes or something?'

'Hey!' he cackled. 'You got him.'

The picture I pieced together—true or false I can't begin to say—was of a 'scientific' experiment at which an Aboriginal had sung his Dreaming song, a Catholic monk had sung a Gregorian chant, a Tibetan lama had sung his mantras, and an African had sung something else: all four of them singing their heads off, to test the effect of different song styles on the rhythmic structure of the brain.

The episode struck Joshua, in retrospect, as so unbelievably funny that he had to hold his stomach for laughing.

So did I.

We laughed ourselves into hysterics and lay gasping for breath on the sand.

Arkady came back in the late afternoon looking tired and worried. He showered, wrote up some notes and lay on his bunk. The visit to Titus had not gone well. No, that is not true. He and Titus had got on very well, but what Titus had to tell him was a depressing story.

Titus's father was Pintupi, his mother was Loritja, and he was forty-seven or forty-eight years old. He had been born not far from his shanty, but around 1942—attracted by the white man's jam, tea and flour—his parents had migrated out of the desert and taken refuge at the Lutheran mission on Horn River. The pastors spotted in Titus a child of outstanding intelligence, and took him for education.

Even as late as the fifties, the Lutherans ran their schools on the lines of a Prussian academy—and Titus was a model pupil. There are pictures of him at his desk, his hair neatly parted, in grey flannel shorts and spit-and-polished shoes. He learned to speak fluent English and German. He learned calculus. He mastered all kinds of mechanical skills. As a young lay preacher, he once astonished his teachers by delivering a sermon, in German, on the theological consequences of the Edict of Worms.

Twice a year, in June and again in November, he would get out his double-breasted suit, board the train for Adelaide and spend a few weeks catching up with modern life. In the public library he would read the back numbers of *Scientific American*. One year, he took a course in petrochemical technology.

The 'other' Titus was the ultra-conservative song-man who lived, half-naked, with his dependants and his dogs; who hunted with a spear and never a rifle; who spoke six or seven Aboriginal languages and was famous, up and down the western desert, for his judgements on tribal law.

Titus had welcomed the Land Rights Act as a chance for his people to get back on to their country—and their only hope of getting rid of alcoholism. He detested the activities of the mining companies.

Under the Act, the government reserved the right to all minerals under the ground and to grant licences for prospecting. If the companies wished to make soundings in Aboriginal country, they were at least obliged to consult the 'traditional owners' and, if mining operations started, to pay them a royalty.

Titus, after weighing up the pros and cons, took the line that money from minerals was bad money—bad for whites and bad for blacks. It had corrupted Australia and given it false values and false standards of living. When a company got permission to put seismic lines through his country, he gave them the scorn of his passive non-co-operation.

This attitude was not calculated to win him friends among either white business men or ambitious blacks in Alice. It was also the reason for the present dispute.

Around 1910, Titus's grandfather, in the course of diplomacy with what is now the Amadeus Mob, had exchanged two sets of unmarked tjuringas—thus giving rights of access to each other's hunting-ground. Since the tjuringas had never been returned, the agreement was still in force.

One day, just as the mining company despaired of dealing with Titus, a deputation from the Amadeus settlement turned up in Alice to say that they, not he, were the 'owners' of the country and its songs—and were therefore entitled to mining royalties. What they had done was to tamper with the tjuringas, engraving them with their own totemic designs. They had, in other words, forged the title-deeds to Titus's birthright.

Titus, who knew of Arkady by reputation only, had sent a message for help.

Arkady, at his briefing in Alice, had been assured that this was simply a squabble about money. But Titus, it turned out, didn't give a hoot for money. The crisis was much more dangerous since, by altering the tjuringas, the Amadeus Mob had attempted to re-write the Creation. Titus told Arkady how, at nights, he heard his Ancestors howling for vengeance—and how he felt forced to obey them.

Arkady, for his part, realized the urgency of somehow getting the offenders to 'withdraw' their sacrilege, and could only think of playing for time. He suggested Titus take a holiday in Alice, but Titus said grimly, 'I'll stay.'

'Then promise me one thing,' Arkady said. 'Do nothing until I get back to you.'

'I promise.'

Arkady was sure Titus meant to keep the promise. But what he found so shocking was the idea that, from now on, Aboriginals themselves were going to twist their own law in order to line their pockets.

'And if that's going to be the future,' he said, 'I might as well give up.'

That evening I looked out to see, hanging over Mount Liebler, a solid black barrage of cloud with bolts of lightning fizzling at the edges.

A few minutes later, the storm broke in solid sheets of water.

'Christ,' said Arkady, 'we'll be bogged in here for weeks.'

It poured again in the night. Next morning, before light, Arkady shook me awake. 'We got to get going,' he said. 'Quick.' He had been listening to the weather forecast. There was worse weather on the way.

'Must we?' I said, sleepily.

'I must. You stay, if you want.'

'No, I'll come.'

We drove off through the puddles along the airstrip and joined the road that comes from the Gibson Desert. The dawn was murky and sunless. We came off a ridge of higher ground . . . and the road disappeared into a lake.

'Well, that,' said Arkady, 'is that.'

It was pouring by the time we got back to Cullen.

Arkady spent the rest of the morning on the radio. The reception was terrible. All the roads to Alice were closed and would be for at least ten days. There were two seats on the mail plane—if the pilot would only make a detour.

Around noon there was a message that the plane would try to land.

'You coming?' asked Arkady.

'No,' I said. 'I'll stay.'

After Arkady had left I started rearranging the caravan as a place to work in.

There was a plyboard top which pulled out over the second bunk to make a desk. There was even a swivelling office chair. I unpacked some exercise pads and, with the obsessive neatness that goes with the beginning of a project, I made three neat stacks of the notebooks I had been keeping for twenty years and had brought out with me from England. The notebooks had been part of the work I had done on my nomad book. At that moment, I felt that the 'nomadic' phase of my life might be passing, and I knew that before the malaise of settlement crept over me I would have to reopen those notebooks.

From the Notebooks

Above all, do not lose your desire to walk: every day I walk myself into a state of well-being and walk away from every illness; I have walked myself into my best thoughts, and I know of no thought so burdensome that one cannot walk away from it . . . by sitting still, and the more one sits still, the closer one comes to feeling ill . . . Thus if one just keeps on walking, everything will be all right.

Søren Kierkegaard, letter to Jette (1847)

Solvitur ambulando. 'It is solved by walking.'

One commonly held delusion is that men are the wanderers and women the guardians of hearth and home. This can, of course, be so. But women, above all, are the guardians of continuity: if the hearth moves, they move with it.

It is the gypsy women who keep their men on the road. Similarly, in the gale-lashed waters of the Cape Horn archipelago, it was the women of the Yaghan Indians who kept their embers alight in the bottom of their bark canoes. The missionary Father Martin Gusinde compared them to the 'Ancient Vestals' or to 'fidgety birds of passage who were happy and inwardly calm only when they were on the move.'

In central Australia, women are the driving force behind the return to the old ways of life. As one woman said to a friend of mine, 'Women are ones for country.'

> Useless to ask a wandering man
> Advice on the construction of a house.
> The work will never come to completion.

After reading this text, from the Chinese *Book of Odes*, I realized the absurdity of trying to write a book on nomads.

Psychiatrists, politicians, tyrants are forever assuring us that the wandering life is an aberrant form of behaviour; a neurosis; a form of unfulfilled sexual longing; a sickness which, in the interests of civilization, must be suppressed.

Nazi propagandists claimed that gypsies and Jews—peoples with wandering in their genes—could find no place in a stable Reich.

In the East, they still preserve the once universal concept: that wandering re-establishes the original harmony which once existed between man and the universe.

There is no happiness for the man who does not travel. Living in the society of men, the best man becomes a sinner. For Indra is the friend of the traveller. Therefore wander!

Aitareya Bráhmana

73

You cannot travel on the path before you have become the Path itself.

Gautama Buddha

Walk on!

His last word to his disciples

In Islam, and especially among the Sufi Orders, *siyahat* or 'errance'—the action or rhythm of walking—was used as a technique for dissolving the attachments of the world and allowing men to lose themselves in God.

The aim of a dervish was to become a 'dead man walking': one whose body stays alive on the earth yet whose soul is already in Heaven. A Sufi manual, the *Kashf-al-Majhub*, says that, towards the end of his journey, the dervish becomes the Way not the wayfarer, i.e. a place over which something is passing, not a traveller following his own free will.

Arkady, to whom I mentioned this, said it was quite similar to an Aboriginal concept: 'Many men afterwards become country, in that place, Ancestors.'

By spending his whole life walking and singing his Ancestor's songline, a man eventually became the track, the Ancestor and the song.

The Wayless Way, where the Sons of God lose themselves and, at the same time, find themselves.

Meister Eckhart

In the early Christian Church there were two kinds of pilgrimage: the first was 'to wander for God' (*ambulare pro Deo*) in imitation of Christ or of Father Abraham who quit the City of Ur and went to live in a tent. The second was the 'penitential pilgrimage', in which criminals guilty of 'enormous crimes' (*peccata enormia*) were required, in accordance with a fixed set of tariffs, to assume the role of travelling beggar—with hat, purse, baton and badge—and work out their salvation on the road.

The idea that walking dissolved crimes of violence goes back to the wanderings forced on Cain to atone for the murder of his brother.

Nomos is Greek for 'pasture', and 'the Nomad' is a chief or clan elder who presides over the allocation of pastures. *Nomos* thus came to mean 'law', 'fair distribution', 'that which is allotted by custom'—and so the basis of all Western law.

The verb *nemein*—'to graze', 'to pasture', 'to range' or 'to spread'—has a second sense as early as Homer: 'to deal', 'to apportion' or 'to dispense'—especially of land, honour, meat or drink. *Nemesis* is the 'distribution of justice' and so of 'divine justice'. *Nomisma* means 'current coin': hence 'numismatics'.

In the *Muqaddimah* or 'Universal History' of Ib'n Khaldūn, a philosopher who surveyed the human condition from a nomadic viewpoint, we read:

> The Desert People are closer to being good than settled peoples because they are closer to the First State and are more removed from all the evil habits that have infected the hearts of settlers.

By 'desert people' Ib'n Khaldūn means the bedouin, such as those he once recruited as mercenaries from the heart of the Sahara, in the days of his warlike youth.

Years later, when he had gazed into the slanting eyes of Tamerlane and witnessed the piles of skulls and smouldering cities, he, too, like the Old Testament prophets, felt the fearful anxiety of civilization, and looked back with longing to life in the tents.

Ib'n Khaldūn based his system on the intuition that men decline, morally and physically, as they drift towards cities.

The rigours of the desert, he suggested, had preceded the softness of cities. The desert was thus a reservoir of civilization, and desert peoples had the advantage over settlers because they were more abstemious, freer, braver, healthier, less bloated, less craven, less liable to submit to rotten laws, and altogether easier to cure.

Le Désert est monothéiste. Renan's aphorism implies that blank horizons and a dazzling sky will clear the mind of its distractions and allow it to concentrate on the Godhead. But life in the desert is not like that!

To survive at all, the desert dweller—Tuareg or Aboriginal—must develop a prodigious sense of orientation. He must forever be naming, sifting, comparing a thousand different 'signs'—the tracks of a dung beetle or the ripple of a dune—to tell him where he is; where the others are; where rain has fallen; where the next meal is coming from; whether if plant X is in flower, plant Y will be in berry, and so forth.

It is a paradox of the monotheistic faiths that, although they arose within the ambit of the desert, the desert people themselves regard the Almighty with an indifference that is decidedly cavalier. 'We will go up to God and salute him,' said a bedouin to Palgrave in the 1860s, 'and if he proves hospitable, we will stay with him; if otherwise, we will mount our horses and ride off'.

Muhammad said, 'No man becomes a prophet who was not first a shepherd.' But, as he had to confess, the Arabs of the desert were 'the most hardened in infidelity and hypocrisy.'

Until recently, a bedouin who migrated within sight of Mecca would not think it worthwhile, even once in a lifetime, to circumambulate the shrines. Yet the Hadj, or 'Sacred Journey', was itself a 'ritual' migration—to detach men from their sinful homes and reinstate, if temporarily, the equality of all men before God.

The concept has its equivalent in the Central Australian languages where *tjurna djugurba* means 'the footprints of the Ancestor' and 'the Way of the Law.'

It would seem there exists, at some deep level of the human psyche, a connection between 'path-finding' and 'law'.

The Norwegian anthropologist, Frederick Barth, writes of how the Basseri, another tribe of Iranian nomads, were, in the 1930s, forbidden by Reza Shah to move from their winter grazing ground.

In 1941, the Shah was deposed, and they were free once again to make the 300-mile journey to the Zagros. Free they were, but they had no animals. Their fine-fleeced sheep had suffocated on the southern plains: yet they set off all the same.

They became nomads again, which is to say, they became human again. 'The supreme value to them,' wrote Barth, 'lay in the freedom to migrate, not in the circumstances that make it economically viable.'

To the Arabian bedouin, Hell is a sunlit sky and the sun a strong, bony female—mean, old and jealous of life—who shrivels the pastures and the skin of humans.

The moon, by contrast, is a lithe and energetic young man, who guards the nomad while he sleeps, guides him on night journeys, brings rain and distils the dew on plants. He has the misfortune to be married to the sun. He grows thin and wasted after a single night with her. It takes him a month to recover.

When Barth came to account for the dearth of ritual among the Basseri—or of *any* rooted belief—he concluded that the Journey itself *was* the ritual, that the road to summer uplands *was* the Way, and that the pitching and dismantling of tents were prayers more meaningful than any in the mosque.

A white explorer in Africa, anxious to press ahead with his journey, paid his porters for a series of forced marches. But they, almost within reach of their destination, set down their bundles and refused to budge. No amount of extra payment would convince them otherwise. They said they had to wait for their souls to catch up.

The Bushmen, who walk immense distances across the Kalahari, have no idea of the soul's survival in another world. 'When we die, we die,' they say. 'The wind blows away our footprints, and that is the end of us.'

That man is a migratory species is, in my opinion, born out by an experiment made at the Tavistock Clinic in London and described by Dr John Bowlby in his *Attachment and Loss*.

Every normal baby will scream if left alone, and the best way of silencing these screams is for the mother to take it in her arms and rock or 'walk' it back to contentment. Bowlby rigged up a machine which imitated, exactly, the pace and action of a mother's walk, and found that, providing the baby was healthy, warm and well-fed, it stopped crying at once. 'The ideal movement,' he wrote, 'is a vertical one with a traverse of three inches.' Rocking at slow speeds, such as thirty cycles a minute, had no effect: but once you raised the pace to fifty and above, every baby ceased to cry and almost always stayed quiet.

Day in, day out, a baby cannot have enough walking. And if babies instinctively demand to be walked, the mother, on the African savannah, must have been walking too: from camp to camp on her daily foraging round, to the waterhole and on visits to the neighbours.

The question occurs to me—and quite seriously—how many shoe soles, how many ox-hide soles, how many sandals Alighieri wore out in the course of his poetic work, wandering about on the goat paths of Italy.

The *Inferno* and especially the *Purgatorio* glorify the human gait, the measure and rhythm of walking, the foot and its shape. The step, linked to the breathing and saturated with thought: this Dante understands as the beginning of prosody.

Osip Mandelstam, Conversations about Dante,
trans. Clarence Brown

Before coming to Australia I'd often talk about the Songlines, and people would inevitably be reminded of something else.

'Like the ley-lines? they'd say: referring to ancient stone circles, menhirs and graveyards, which are laid out in lines across Britain. They are of great antiquity but are visible only to those with eyes to see.

Sinologists were reminded of the 'dragon-lines' of *feng-shui*, or traditional Chinese geomancy: and when I spoke to a Finnish journalist, he said the Lapps had 'singing stones', which were also arranged in lines.

To some, the Songlines were like the Art of Memory in

reverse. In Frances Yates's wonderful book, one learned how classical orators, from Cicero and earlier, would construct memory palaces: they would fasten sections of their speech on to imaginary architectural features and then, after working their way round every architrave and pillar, they could memorize colossal lengths of speech. The features were known as *loci* or 'places'. But in Australia the *loci* were not a mental construction, but had existed for ever, as events of the Dreamtime.

Other friends were reminded of the Nazca 'lines', which are etched into the meringue-like surface of the central Peruvian Desert and are, indeed, some kind of totemic map.

No. These were not the comparisons I was looking for. Not at this stage. I was beyond that.

Trade means friendship and co-operation; and for the Aboriginal the principal object of trade was song. Song, therefore, brought peace. Yet I felt the Songlines were not necessarily an Australian phenomenon, but universal: that they were the means by which man marked out his territory, and so organized his social life. All other successive systems were variants—or perversions—of this original model.

The main Songlines in Australia appear to enter the country from the north or the north-west—from across the Timor Sea or the Torres Strait—and from there weave their way southwards across the continent. One has the impression that they represent the routes of the first Australians—and that they have come from *somewhere else*.

How long ago? Fifty thousand years? Eighty or a hundred thousand years? The dates are insignificant compared to those from African prehistory.

And here I must take a leap into faith: into regions where I would not expect anyone to follow.

I have a vision of the Songlines stretching across the continents and ages; that wherever men have trodden they have left a trail of song (of which we may, now and then, catch an echo); and that these trails must reach back, in time and space, to an isolated pocket in the African savannah, where the First Man, opening his mouth in defiance of the terrors that surrounded him, shouted the opening stanza of the World Song, 'I AM!'

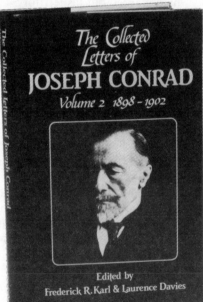

BILL BUFORD
AN INTERVIEW
WITH RYSZARD
KAPUŚCIŃSKI

Bill Buford: Your first book to be published in English was *The Emperor,* and that appeared only four years ago. But you had been writing for nearly thirty years before your two translators, an American and a Pole, took it upon themselves to translate your book and submit it to an American publisher. What do you feel we should know about those years before the writing of *The Emperor?*

Ryszard Kapuściński: You know, for years, I have been building up a small collection of books, newspapers and photographs about Pinsk. I would like to show it to you. Pinsk, you see, is the town where I was born and where I lived until I was eight, when the entire area, originally part of Poland, came under Russian control.

Buford: The collection is material for an autobiography?

Kapuściński: I don't know, maybe. No: it's merely part of a landscape, my landscape, the landscape that I came from. It is the landscape of a flat, a very flat, country, a marshland, and there are two things that are important to me about Pinsk.

First: that here in this very provincial town, this town of dirt roads, cut off from everything, was in fact an extraordinary cosmopolitan gathering. Many of the founders of the State of Israel came from my town. There were Jews, Poles, Byelorussians, Ukrainians, Armenians, and every kind of religion, from Judaism to Catholicism to Islam, and we all lived together. The people were called Poleshuks, meaning merely 'people born in the district of Polesie,' and they were a people without a nation and without, therefore, a national identity.

And, second, while Pinsk was very international—or, if you like, very 'nation-less'—it was also very poor.

Buford: How?

Kapuściński: Poor in the most elementary things. During the war we ate very primitive pastry—flour and water. That was our diet. We never had shoes: we covered our feet with bark. I remember

Photo: Derry Moore

83

my father telling me about the army after the First World War. There were three regiments in Pinsk, but only enough shoes for one. So on Sundays, only one regiment at a time could attend Mass: once the Mass had ended, the regiment would exit, take off their shoes and give them to the members of the next regiment waiting outside.

Buford: This accounts no doubt for the fascination with footwear evident sometimes in your work.

Kapuściński: I am obsessed with footwear. It was the dream of my youth always to have a pair of shoes. A shoe, you see, was a matter of prestige, of great pride.

Buford: I recall your account of the 'Soccer War', the conflict between Honduras and El Salvador, over a qualifying match for the World Cup. You were almost killed dragging yourself along the ground trailing a Honduran conscript who, abandoning all thoughts about the battle around you, began compulsively robbing boots off the dead soldiers to take back home to his family. Even so, I'm not sure if I understand how it is that Pinsk, this landscape of yours, is meant to influence your writing.

Kapuściński: Because Pinsk, even though borrowing so much from Europe, was not part of Europe. It was not until I was seven years old that I saw my first train. I didn't have a telephone until I was thirty, and I am still learning how to use it. People are always having to stop me as I'm half-way through the door on my way to deliver a message to someone who might live miles away because it simply doesn't occur to me to dial a number. I'm made uneasy by technology, I don't trust it, I'm uncomfortable around it. But I am not uncomfortable in the Third World. I have always re-discovered my home, re-discovered Pinsk, in Africa, in Asia, in Latin America. In Ethiopia I am at home. Amid poverty I am at home. I know what the life means. The society of Polesie was, really, a feudal one, a tribal society: it prepared me for Africa.

You know, sometimes I am asked if I will leave Poland, if I will emigrate. And my reply, half-joking, is always the same: there is no need to emigrate, I already have. I am an emigrant from Pinsk, from this other world.

Buford: You left Pinsk, then, in 1940, hiding from the Germans in one direction and the Russians in the other. What was it like when you finally came to Warsaw, once the war had ended?

Kapuściński: We were all very happy that the war was over. We were re-united with our father. But otherwise we were very uncertain. We had no idea what the future would be like. And Warsaw was such a terrible disaster, with most of the buildings burned to the ground. I remember walking. Every road in every direction was crowded with people. No money, no food. Just miles and miles of people walking, walking, walking, carrying their small bundles of things. We found a small place, a burnt-out building, a ruin, and that became our home.

Buford: And how, amid conditions in which the paramount concern was securing your survival, did you succeed in getting an education?

Kapuściński: Eventually a secondary school was established. It was worse than our home: it was four walls. There was no glass in the windows, no floor, and the walls themselves were blackened from the fires. There were fifty boys in the class, and between us we had one book which the teacher would read and pass round, and which each of us would take turns reading. But, you know, it was the same in Pinsk. I remember that only one book could be found in our class during the war, Stalin's *The Problems of Leninism,* and that was the book from which we learned to read. It was the book from which we learned the alphabet—the Russian alphabet.

Buford: Why did you choose to study history?

Kapuściński: Actually it had been my ambition to study philosophy, but at the time there were no philosophy courses. Traditional philosophy had been dismissed as bourgeois, and, while there were lecturers in philosophy, the only philosophy they could teach was bourgeois philosophy, and the university was therefore prohibited from hiring them. A Marxist philosophy hadn't developed yet.

Buford: How much were you aware of the machinations of the government at the time? Of how its members had been trained in Moscow during the war, or of the rigged election in 1947?

Kapuściński: Well, I was an activist at the time. We were all activists. Kolakowski, other writers, intellectuals—some of them later emigrated in fact. I can't think of anyone who wasn't. I myself had joined one of the communist youth organizations in 1948.

Buford: Because communism was seen as an unequivocally good thing?

Kapuściński: Yes. Of course. Among young people, a very good thing. We all thought we were doing the right thing, and we were very committed, very enthusiastic. We were full of hope.

Buford: And what was it you hoped to achieve? What were you hoping a Communist government would bring? That the land would be re-distributed or—

Kapuściński: Everything. Everything good. Yes, yes, we were full of confidence. You must remember how young we were. It is hard to explain this to young people in Poland today, because they are so much more informed that we ever thought possible: they have access to history, to information, to news. We had none of this. We had no tradition and no books; we were poor—really, very, very poor—and inexperienced and uneducated. And the little education that we did have came from Stalinist texts. Don't forget that I entered university in 1950: the height of the Stalinist era, in which everything was pure, uncompromised Stalinism.

Buford: An interest in philosophy, a grounding in history: these are not the obvious disciplines for training a war correspondent. Were you tempted by academia?

Kapuściński: I had actually been asked to stay on at the university to teach, but for me scholarship was tedious, a burden. By then I had done quite a bit of writing. I had had my first poem published in *Slowo Powszechne,* a Catholic daily, and had had a number of poems published in the leading literary magazine. On finishing university in 1955, I was twenty-three years old, and I began working for *Sztandar Mlodych,* a youth journal, at the most militant time in its history. It was the age of investigative reporting.

Buford: And the most important piece to emerge in that time was in fact written by you.

Kapuściński: That would be 'This Too is the Truth of Nowa Huta.' Somehow, our paper succeeded in getting my article passed, and it was extremely polemical. Nowa Huta was the showcase steel factory being built near Cracow. It was meant to be our economic triumph. But I had worked there as a student. I had friends there. I knew what the conditions were like, and they were appalling: the plant was mismanaged and the supervisors were frequently drunk. The moment the article appeared, there was a great uproar, and I had to go into hiding.

Buford: Hiding?

Kapuściński: Yes, the workers, who were my friends, protected me. Eventually I was apprehended, fired from the paper and punished.

Buford: What kind of punishment?

Kapuściński: It is complicated. The uproar, in any event, continued, until finally a commission was appointed to investigate my allegations. It confirmed everything I said, and I was awarded the Golden Cross of Merit. I was still twenty-three.

The experience was an exciting one for me. It illustrated that writing was about risk—about risking everything. And that the value of the writing is not in what you publish but in its consequences. If you set out to describe reality, then the influence of the writing is upon reality.

Buford: I find this all a little curious. At the age of twenty-three, you wrote an article, extremely political in its implications, dealing specifically with a Polish subject, which had such an impact that it actually changed government policy. You were then to go on to write a series of stories, some of the most elegant you've written, about life in rural Poland, *The Polish Bush,* that became an immediate bestseller. But you seem to have spent the rest of your writing career avoiding Poland. Why?

Kapuściński: It's not that I've avoided Poland. It's just that there are others writing about Poland, and they do it very well. My subject is a different one, for I became fascinated by something else.

Shortly after I was reinstated, I approached the editor of the paper. I had won a prize, and I asked if I could go abroad. I wanted to get out of Warsaw. I wanted to see the world. He asked me where I wanted to go, and I said I wanted to see something different, something exotic.

Buford: Like?

Kapuściński: Like Czechoslovakia.

Buford: Czechoslovakia?

Kapuściński: Yes, because for me Czechoslovakia was the big world, was foreign, was far away. Instead, the editor sent me to India.

Buford: Had the paper ever sent a correspondent abroad?

Kapuściński: Never.

Buford: No foreign correspondents?

Kapuściński: I was the first.

You mustn't forget that for my generation the outside world did not exist. There was no outside world, or, if there was, we knew little about it. A place like India wasn't a country. Africa wasn't a continent. They were fairy-tales. And I wanted, really, nothing more than the opportunity to see what the world was like.

Buford: And after India?

Kapuściński: After India, there was Pakistan and Afghanistan. My reports were liked, and so I was then sent to the Far East, to Japan and China, where for a time I worked as the resident foreign correspondent for the paper, and eventually to Africa. It was exciting because I was discovering the world. It is for this reason that years later, in 1968, while compiling a number of pieces that would eventually be published as *The Soccer War,* I insisted they be arranged in the historical order in which they were written. It was important to me to illustrate the experiences by which a foreigner enters a new world—especially the world of Africa. He is, for instance, at first frightened, then surprised—and then he discovers the pleasure, the fun, the exhilaration.

I also remember, while compiling that book, that during my time in Latin America I was always missing my Africa.

Buford: Why?

Kapuściński: I'm not sure. In part, because Africa was my youth, and, perhaps in saying I miss my Africa, I am actually saying that I am missing my youth. It was in Africa that I really came into my own as a correspondent, for I had very different responsibilities from those of your traditional correspondent.

For a start, I was by then working for PAP, the Polish Press Agency. And I chose to work for a press agency for very specific reasons, because in every other respect working for an agency is pure slavery.

Buford: 'Hardened cynical men,' as you describe them in *The Emperor,* 'who have seen everything and lived through everything, and who are used to fighting a thousand obstacles that most people could never imagine just to do their jobs.'

Kapuściński: No other journalist—working for a paper or magazine or television—has to put up with the horrors of a press agency writer. One day I will write about them, my friends, these anonymous markers of events, these terrible victims of information, working day and night in the worst of all possible conditions. But I took on this job voluntarily, because I knew that working for a press agency I would see more things, meet more people. A mercenary, a revolutionary, a general is not going to waste his time on a journalist from an obscure newspaper in Poland that he has never heard of—even if it were possible for that obscure newspaper to send a correspondent to see him. But he might grant an interview to a journalist who is reporting to the entire country.

And I also knew that, working for the agency, I could travel more than if working for someone else. Poland is a poor country. It cannot afford many foreign correspondents. Reuters, Associated Press or Presse France have a correspondent in nearly every African country; working for Poland, I was asked to be the correspondent for the entire continent. I could not only go wherever I wanted, but it was my job to go wherever I wanted: if there was trouble, I was meant to be there to see it. I am often asked how was it possible that I could have seen so much as a journalist. I have personally witnessed twenty-seven revolutions. It seems impossible, but that is precisely what my job required: I was responsible for fifty countries; I was bound to come across something at least once a month, in at least one of those countries. I was full of stories.

Buford: I get a sense that you must have been quite an operator.

Kapuściński: You had to be; you had to be because the job required it and because, working for a poor agency, your greatest resource was never money—it was information: contacts: who you knew, what you knew.

A journalist working for a wealthy agency can hire a car or an aeroplane at a moment's notice, but I never could. So, for instance, when trouble erupted in Zanzibar, I had to get there, but had no transport. Unlike the journalists from the big agencies, however, I knew some people involved in the revolution. They were my friends. One of the big agency journalists asked for my help: he had the aeroplane but no permission to land. So I made a deal: 'Okay, Felix, I have no money to hire a plane. But if you take me with you, I'll arrange the clearance you need to be able to land.'

Buford: I know you don't want to talk about Amin right now, because he is the subject of the book you are writing, but I wonder how it was that you came to meet him?

Kapuściński: That was in 1962. I was in Kampala and had contracted cerebral malaria and was very, very ill. I was unconscious for three weeks, when one day, just when I was starting to recover, I looked up and there he was at my bedside.

Buford: You were, I understand, the model for the journalist in Andrzej Wajda's film *Rough Treatment.* And Wajda describes you as a man who can't sit still. You depart and then you return, tell a few stories and then disappear again. To what extent were you using your travels to collect material for the writing you would later do?

Kapuściński: No, you don't understand. I was there in Africa because I found it so compelling. I was aware that I was seeing something unique, for I was there at an important historical moment: the liberation of Africa—when African nations everywhere were declaring their independence.

I wish I could convey what Africa was like. I have experienced nothing like it. Africa has its own personality. Sometimes it is a sad personality, sometimes impenetrable, but always unrepeatable. Africa was dynamic. It was aggressive, on the attack. And I liked that. Afterwards, now, finding myself in quiet surroundings, amid conditions of stability, in Europe, I become bored.

Otherwise I wasn't in Africa to collect experience. I was merely a journalist, working for an agency. It is true that I saw myself as a writer, but I always had—as a poet, having been a published poet for years.

Buford: You're living in a country which, on the whole, seems to believe that it has a Marxist government imposed upon it against its will; on the other hand, you have witnessed a number of revolutions, with which you have often shown a great deal of sympathy, that were in the name of Marxism. Do you feel a genuine revolution is possible? Have you not seen too much to believe in the hope that a revolution offers?

Kapuściński: It was in the nineteenth century that faith in science invited an analogous faith in history: that history had laws, that it could be known, that it followed a pattern. What we believe now—certainly what I believe—is very different. History is impossible to penetrate, and that is its great richness.

Yes, there can be revolutions, revolutions that begin in the name of justice, and bring about some version of just reform. Salazar in Portugal, for instance. And there are others which do not succeed. But I am much more interested in the mystery of history, why a revolution ever takes place in the first place. In Ethiopia, the revolution began because of the increases in the price of petrol. But the price of petrol had been increasing for years. Why suddenly a revolution?

Buford: Is it easy to point to the parallels between the political situations described in your books and the political situation in Poland: the corrupt court of Haile Selassie suggests the corrupt bureaucracy of Warsaw; the mad, irrational modernization of the Shah recalls Gierek and the uncontrolled spending of the seventies. In your travels through Africa, were you aware of the Polish parallels?

Kapuściński: In Africa, you find a population fighting for its independence, and trying to preserve its traditions to establish its national identity. But I wasn't looking for parallels.

Buford: Are you aware that readers here in Poland see the parallels, and read your books almost as allegories?

Kapuściński: No, they are not allegories. But there are bound to be parallels, of course.

Buford: What kind of relationship do you have with your readers in Poland? Or, to put it another way, is the experience of being a writer in Poland different from what you believe it would be if you were living in western Europe?

Kapuściński: Yes, yes, I think it's a very different experience. I'll give you an example. Not so long ago I was asked to a town outside Warsaw to give a reading. It was scheduled to begin at five o'clock, and I arrived about half an hour early. But it was impossible to get in. The hall was packed. In fact, it was so packed that no one, with so many people squeezed up against the door-frame, was able to get out. By the time I succeeded in reaching the podium, I had been crushed and pressed and pulled by so many bodies that all my buttons had popped off. My shirt was torn, and I had lost my glasses. At around five-thirty, I began reading.

Buford: It's ironic that western writers, especially Americans, have always envied the writer living under a politically repressive regime, who enjoys what George Steiner has described as the 'muse of censorship'. Your work does not presuppose a muse of this sort at all. Even so, you have what few western writers could ever hope to enjoy: stories to tell, and a readership that's desperate to hear them. You could almost be described as a story-teller of the most traditional sort: a voyager returning with the stories of his voyage.

I am curious about how you made the transition from being a press agency journalist to a writer. What made you want to write books?

Kapuściński: Again, my work as an agency journalist is important, because all my books developed from the experiences I had. My responsibility was always to cover an event: to locate the geopolitical story, and as quickly as possible send a cable down the line with its details. It was straightforward journalism, nothing more, nothing less. But once I had sent the cable, I was always left with a feeling of inadequacy. I had only covered the political event, and not really conveyed the deeper, and, I felt, truer nature of what was going on. And this sense of dissatisfaction remained with me each time I returned to Poland.

You can always find two versions of my work. The first version is what I do when I'm in the field: it's all in the cables, the stories filed. The second version is what I write later, and that expresses what I actually felt, what I lived through, the reflections surrounding the simple news story.

You know, a press cable is a very conservative medium for conveying news. We are always limited: by the number of words, by the time we can get on the machine, by the money, by the information that the newspapers back home want to receive. But the realities we face, especially in the Third World, are so much richer, more complicated, than a newspaper will ever allow us to report.

Buford: What kind of story was not getting expressed in a newspaper?

Kapuściński: It is not the story that is not getting expressed: it's what surrounds the story. The climate, the atmosphere of the street, the feeling of the people, the gossip of the town, the smell; the thousand, thousand elements of reality that are part of the event you read about in 600 words in your morning paper.

You know, sometimes the critical response to my books is

amusing. There are so many complaints: Kapuscinski never mentions dates, Kapuscinski never gives us the name of the minister, he has forgotten the order of events. All that, of course, is exactly what I avoid. If those are the questions you want answered, you can visit your local library, where you will find everything you need: the newspapers of the time, the reference books, a dictionary.

Buford: Your sense of inadequacy as a reporter is analogous to the sense of inadequacy many modernist novelists felt when they said that the demands of the traditional plot or story inhibited the expression of the real story—the things surrounding the story.

Kapuściński: Yes, that is what I am trying to express.

Buford: How, then, are you different from a novelist?

Kapuściński: Ah, you have just touched upon an important point in my thinking.

Twenty years ago, I was in Africa, and this is what I saw: I went from revolution to *coup d'état*, from one war to another; I witnessed, in effect, history in the making, real history, contemporary history, our history. But I was also surprised: I never saw a writer. I never met a poet or a philosopher—even a sociologist. Where were they? Such important events, and not a single writer anywhere?

Then I would return to Europe and I would find them. They would be at home, writing their little domestic stories: the boy, the girl, the laughing, the intimacy, the marriage, the divorce—in short, the same story we've been reading over and over again for a thousand years. You know, the other day I was reading about the novels that won the annual French prizes. It was incredible. None of these books had anything to do with our world, our reality—nothing. There was one about an unwanted child, and another about a boy, a girl, the laughing, the intimacy—

Buford: Is it then that you find contemporary literature too self-referential, too obsessed with its own formal workings to—

Kapuściński: No, it is simply that so much of our literature is so very traditional, even when seen as being avant-garde. And if avant-garde, it is only avant-garde because of its style—as if assembled in a workshop. It is never avant-garde for its subject; it is never caught actually looking out at the world. The writer is always looking over his shoulder, noting the position of his predecessor. Contemporary literature is a very private affair.

Buford: I am reminded of Joseph Brodsky's essay on the Russian novel in which he says that the twentieth century will never produce a genuinely 'Russian' novel, because so much of the literary imagination is dominated by the state—either in obeisance to it, or even in necessary resistance to it. Your work probably comes the closest to being freed from the constraints of the state. Its allegiances are to history.

Kapuściński: I don't know. I'm not forming a manifesto and certainly don't want to appear dogmatic. But I do feel that we are describing a new kind of literature. I feel sometimes that I am working in a completely new field of literature, in an area that is both unoccupied and unexplored.

Buford: The literature of political experience?

Kapuściński: The literature of personal . . . no, that's not right. You know, sometimes, in describing what I do, I resort to the Latin phrase *silva rerum*: the forest of things. That's my subject: the forest of things, as I've seen it, living and travelling in it. To capture the world, you have to penetrate it as completely as possible.

Buford: —But using story to make sense of this forest of things, to give it shape and coherence? For your writing certainly relies on narrative.

Kapuściński: Yes, story is the beginning. It is half of the achievement. But it is not complete until you, as the writer, become part of it. As a writer, you have experienced this event

on your own skin, and it is your experience, this feeling along the surface of your skin, that gives your story its coherence: it is what is at the centre of the forest of things.

The traditional trick of literature is to obscure the writer, to express the story through a fabricated narrator describing a fabricated reality. But for me, what I have to say is validated by the fact that I was there, that I witnessed the event. There is, I admit, a certain egoism in what I write, always complaining about the heat or the hunger or the pain I feel, but it is terribly important to have what I write authenticated by its being lived. You could call it, I suppose, personal reportage, because the author is always present. I sometimes call it literature by foot.

Buford: How is this different from New Journalism—the work of Hunter S. Thompson, Joan Didion or Tom Wolfe, who also put a premium on the first-person reporter?

Kapuściński: That's an important question. And while I knew nothing about New Journalism when I was in Africa, I can see now that New Journalism was the beginning, in liquidating the border between fact and fiction. But New Journalism was ultimately just journalism describing the strangeness of America. I think we have gone beyond all that. It is not a New Journalism, but a New Literature.

Why am I a writer? Why have I risked my life so many times, come so close to dying? Is it to report the weirdness? To earn my salary? Mine is not a vocation, it's a mission. I wouldn't subject myself to these dangers if I didn't feel that there was something overwhelmingly important—about history, about ourselves—that I felt compelled to get across. This is more than journalism.

ANDRE DEUTSCH NEW FICTION

William T. Vollmann
YOU BRIGHT AND RISEN ANGELS
Comic, exaggerated and frankly bizarre, William T. Vollmann's first novel is a wild, freewheeling and ambitious depiction of cosmic battle between young revolutionaries and hide-bound reactionaries. Dealing with powerful human feelings, it raises even the most commonplace material to visionary heights.
£11.95

David Gurr
THE RING MASTER
The story of the rise of Hitler seen from the inside: the transformation of a vast Wagnerian dream into a nightmare reality of horror and perversion. By playing outrageous games with the history of the Third Reich, David Gurr shows how myth can take us to the heart of truth.
£11.95

Hunter Steele
LORD HAMLET'S CASTLE
Was Hamlet mad, pretending, or both? Was he in love with Ophelia? Or with his mother? Was he cowardly? Sicklied o'er? Or merely outconspired? In this dazzling, provocative novel, Hunter Steele gives answers to many such questions and evokes the frozen, doomy grandeur of Elsinore, throwing new light on the familiar story.
£9.95

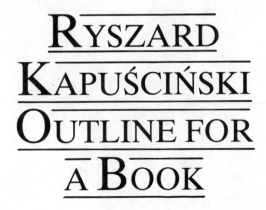

1

I have come home from Africa, jumping from a tropical roasting-pit and dropping into a snow-bank.

'You're so tanned. Have you been in Zakopane?'

Will the Polish imagination never stretch further than Zakopane? I'm working on *Polityka*. My current editor Mieczysław F. Rakowski is sending me into the provinces: Yes, you are to continue living in the bush, but in our own, native Polish bush.

Somewhere along the way, perhaps in Olecko or Ornet, I read that a great, almost global, conflict has broken out in the Congo. This is July, 1960. The Congo—the most unknown and inaccessible country of Africa—has declared its independence and everything is happening at once: the army has revolted, the settlers are trying to leave, paratroopers have arrived from Belgium, the anarchy, the hysteria, the slaughter. I buy a ticket and return by train to Warsaw.

2

I ask my editor to send me to the Congo. I'm already caught up in it. I've already got the fever.

3

The trip is impossible. Everyone from the socialist countries is being thrown out of the Congo. On a Polish passport there would be no way of getting there. As a consolation, the travel committee allots me some hard currency and a ticket for a trip to Nigeria. But what's Nigeria to me? Nothing's going on there.

4

I walk around depressed and heart-broken. Suddenly a glimmer of hope. Somebody mentions that in Cairo there's a Czech journalist who wants to force his way into the Congo through the jungle. Officially, I leave for Nigeria; secretly, I've had the airline ticket rewritten for Cairo and fly out of Warsaw.

5

In Cairo I find the Czech, Jarda Bouczek. We sit in his apartment. Beyond the window roars the gigantic hot city, a stone oasis cut in half by the navy-blue Nile. Jarda wants to get to the Congo by way of Sudan, which means travelling by air to Kartoum, then by air to Juba, and in Juba we will have to buy a car: what will happen after Juba is a big question. The goal is Stanleyville, the capital of the eastern province of the Congo, where the Lumumba government has taken refuge (Lumumba himself has already been arrested and his friend Antoine Gizenga leads the government). I watch as Jarda's index finger journeys up the Nile, pauses briefly for a tourist stopover (here there is nothing but crocodiles, here the jungle begins), turns to the southwest, and comes to rest on the banks of the Congo river where the name 'Stanleyville' can be seen beside a little circle with a dot in it. I tell Jarda that I want to join the expedition and that I have official instructions to go to Stanleyville (which is a lie). He agrees, but adds that I might pay for this journey with my life (which later turns out to be close to the truth). He shows me a copy of his will, which he has deposited with his embassy. I am to do the same.

6

After a thousand problems getting a Sudanese visa, I change my Warsaw-Cairo-Lagos ticket for a Warsaw-Khartoum-Juba ticket at the United Arab Airlines office and fly to the Sudan. Jarda stays behind in Cairo, awaiting another Czech. They will catch up with me in Khartoum and we will fly on together. Khartoum is provincial and nightmarishly hot; I am dying of boredom and the heat.

7

Jarda arrives with his colleague, Duszan, another journalist. We wait a few days for the plane, and finally fly to Juba in the southern Sudan—a small garrison-settlement in the midst of an unlikely wasteland. Nobody wants to sell us a car, but in the end we find a dare-devil (in Juba, too, the opinion prevails that anyone who travels to the Congo is as good as dead) who agrees, for a large sum of money, to drive us to the border, more than one hundred and twenty miles away.

8

The next day we reach the border, guarded by a half-naked policeman with a half-naked girl and a little boy. They don't give us any trouble, and everything looks like it will turn out to be rather enjoyable, when, ten or so miles on, we are stopped in the village of Aba by a patrol of Congolese gendarmes. In Cairo, Pierre Mulele, the minister of Lumumba's government, and later the leader of the Simba uprising (murdered), had given us visas to the Congo—written out by hand on an ordinary sheet of paper. But the name Mulele means nothing to the gendarmes. Their grim, closed faces—obscured in the depths of their helmets—are unfriendly. They order us to return to the Sudan. Go back, they say, because it's dangerous here and the further you go the more dangerous it becomes. As if they are the sentries of a hell. We can't go back to the Sudan, Jarda tells them, because we don't have return visas (which is true). The bargaining starts. I've brought along several cartons of cigarettes and the Czechs have a box of costume jewellery. We bribe the gendarmes with a few trinkets (beads, clip-on earrings). They permit us to continue and the leader appoints a sergeant Seraphim to escort us. In Aba we rent a car with a local driver. It is an old, enormous, entirely decrepit Ford. But old, enormous, entirely decrepit Fords are by nature unfailing and in them you can drive across the whole continent of Africa and a good bit more.

9

At daybreak we start towards Stanleyville: 600 miles of muddy dirt road, driving the whole time through a sombre green tunnel in a stench of decomposing leaves, entangled branches and roots. We are passing deeper and deeper into the greatest jungle in Africa, into an uncanny world of rotting, proliferating, monstrously exaggerated botany. We are driving through a tropical wilderness that fills me with awe.

Along the way we are stopped by gendarmerie patrols, drunk or hungry, indifferent or aggressive—the rebellious, undisciplined army which, gone wild, has taken over the country, robbing and raping. When stopped we push Seraphim out of the car and watch what happens. If Seraphim falls into an embrace we breathe easy: he has come across another from his tribe. But if he is slapped across the face and poked with the butt of a rifle, our skin crawls: the same thing—or worse, perhaps—awaits us. What is it—our stupidity or passion or ambition or foolishness or the obligation we've imposed upon ourselves—that keeps us going along this road, on which it is so easy to die? As we drive on I feel that with each mile another barrier has dropped behind us, another gate slammed shut, and turning back becomes more and more impossible. After two days, we roll into Stanleyville.

10

That same man was here yesterday. He arrived in a muddy car, accompanied by three others. The car stopped in front of the bar. The man entered to drink a beer, leaving the others to wander around the town. The bar was empty; the man sat alone drinking. The bartender put on a record. Bill Haley sang 'See you later, alligator.'

'We don't need that,' said the man at the table. The bartender took the record off. The other three came in.

'Ready?' the man drinking beer asked.

'Ready,' they said, and the four of them left. There were people standing in the square, watching, as the four approached: the tall, slender man in front, behind him the three stout ones, with long arms.

The girls started nudging each other: they liked the thin one. The thin one smiled at them, then at everyone, and began speaking.

We didn't know who he was. We usually knew everyone who came to speak, but this one we hadn't seen before. In the past, it was the white who used to speak. He would swab his forehead with a handkerchief and mumble various things. The ones standing close to him had to listen and then repeat what he said to the others standing further away. In the mumbling there was always something about taxes and public works. He was an administrator, so he couldn't talk about anything else. Sometimes Mami came, our king, the king of the Bangs. Mami had a lot of beads and bracelets that gave off a hollow sound. Mami didn't have any power, but he used to say that power would return to the Bangs. Then the Bangs would take revenge on the Angra, who had pushed them away from the banks of the fish-filled Aruwimi River. Mami would shake his fist, and you could hear that hollow jangling.

But this man spoke differently. He told us that our tribe was not alone. There was a whole family of tribes and that family was called *la nation congolaise.* All must be brothers; there lies strength. He spoke for a long time, until night fell and the darkness came. The darkness took away all the faces. You couldn't see anything except this man's words. Those words were bright. We could see them distinctly.

He asked, 'Any questions?'

Everybody was quiet. The speeches always used to end this way, and whoever asked a question was beaten afterwards. It was quiet. Finally somebody cried out, 'You! What's your name?'

'Me?' the man laughed. 'My name's Lumumba, Patrice Lumumba.'

We were sitting in the room one evening when Kambi came in. He had a face I hope I never see again.

'Patrice Lumumba,' he said, in a flat voice, 'is dead.'

I thought the floor would collapse, felt that we would crash two stories to the ground. I looked at Kambi. He wasn't crying, he wasn't shaking his fist, he wasn't cursing. He was standing there helplessly. It is a common sight here: standing helplessly. You are a minister, and you don't know what to do. Your party has shattered, and you don't know how to put it back together. You are waiting for help, and help hasn't come.

Kambi sat down and repeated over and over, mechanically, like a rosary: 'It was the Belgians, it was the Belgians, it was the Belgians . . .'

I listened for the sounds of the city. I was listening for the shooting, for the revenge. But Stanleyville was dark, dead and mute. There were no fires. Nobody was unsheathing his knife.

'Kambi, did you ever see Lumumba?'

No. Kambi never saw him. But he listened to him. He had

brought a tape recorder, which he plugged in, and the tape began, one of Lumumba's speeches in parliament. Kambi listened to his tape constantly, as if to a tape of music. He leaned his forehead on his arm and closed his eyes.

Our hotel windows are open, and the words of Patrice spill out into the street. But the street is empty. Patrice is speaking to the empty street, but he can't see that: there is only his voice.

Patrice is calm, even dry, beginning without a sign of emotion. At first he informs, presenting the situation. He is speaking clearly, with a strong accent, enunciating each syllable diligently, like an actor mindful of the cheap seats. Suddenly his voice soars, vibrates, becomes piercing, tense, almost hysterical. Patrice attacks the forces of intervention. You can hear a light pounding: he is striking his hand against the lectern to accentuate the force of his reasoning. The attack is violent, but brief.

The tape falls silent except for the wavy rhythm of the mechanism. Kambi has been holding his breath, and now he gasps for air.

Again Patrice. His voice quiet, slow, with pauses between the words. A bitter tone, a disillusioned one. The words are catching in his throat. He is speaking to a large and noisy hall, quarrelsome like a renaissance congress of nobles. In a moment the carpet knights will be shouting.

They don't shout.

The hall falls quiet. Patrice has them in his hand again. He explains, persuades. His voice drops to a whisper. Kambi leans over the reels. He listens to the confidences of the leader. Whisper, whisper, the rustle of the tape and whisper. The sound of breathing. You cannot hear the hall. The hall is silent, the street empty, the Congo invisible. The tape keeps running. Kambi listens. The voice regains its tone, strength, energy. The agitator is standing on the platform now. His last chance: to convince them, win them over, sweep them away. He stakes everything on that last chance. The tape spins: a maddening invasion of words, *l'unité, l'unité,* a crush of arguments, of phrases—there is no turning back; we have to reach it, it, where our Uhuru is, our hope, our manioc, our Congo, victory, *l'indépendance.*

Now the flame is burning.
The tape flies off the reel.

Lumumba. It is worth seeing how Africa listens to its leaders. You have to see the crowd on the way to a rally, in a holiday mood, excited, with fever in its eyes. And you need strength to endure the moment of screaming that greets the appearance of one of these speakers. It's good to stand in the crowd. To applaud together with them, laugh and feel angry. Then you can feel their patience and strength, their fervour and power. A rally in Africa is like a harvest festival, joyous and full of dignity. The witch doctors cast spells, the imams read the Koran, the orchestras play jazz. The wind snaps the colourful crêpe, women vendors sell rattles and the great names talk politics from the rostrum.

The awakened Africa needs great names. As symbols, as cement, as compensation. For centuries the history of the continent has been anonymous. In the course of 300 years traders shipped millions of slaves. Who can name even one? For centuries they fought the white invasion. Who can name one warrior? What name recalls the suffering of the black generations? What name speaks of the bravery of exterminated tribes? Asia had Confucius and Buddha, Europe Shakespeare and Napoleon. No name that the world would know emerges from the African past. More—no name that Africa itself would know.

And now almost every year of the great march of Africa, as if making up for the irreversible delay, new names are inscribed in history. None of them has laboriously climbed the ladder of government promotions, pinching votes and bowing to patrons. A liberation struggle has carried them to the top: they are children born of the longings not only of their own countries, but of the whole continent. Thus, each becomes a sort of pan-African leader. Each of them will long to make his capital the Mecca of Black Africa.

But Lumumba will not make it. Everything in the biography of the man comes down to the formula: he will not make it.

The Congo is gigantic. Small clusters of people live scattered across a great jungle and a vast savannah, unacquainted, knowing little about each other. Ten people per square mile.

107

The Congo is as big as India. It took Gandhi twenty years to cover India. Lumumba tried to cover the Congo in six months.

And here, as in India, you must cover the whole country. Call on every village, stop in every small town and speak, speak, speak. People want to see their leader; they want to hear him at least once. Because what if he's the leader of some bad cause, some godless affair? You have to see for yourself, let him speak out and then decide whether he's a leader or not. In other countries leaders have the press, radio, film and television at their fingertips. They have personnel.

Lumumba has none of this. Everything is Belgian. But say he had a newspaper. How many people would be able to read it? Say he had a radio station: how many houses have radios? Instead he has to criss-cross the country. Like Mao, like Gandhi, like Nkrumah and Castro. Old photographs show all of them in simple peasant attire. Mao tightening his belt around a padded coat, Mahatma's skinny legs sticking out of his *dhoti*, Kwame throwing an ornamented *kente* over his shoulder and Fidel standing there in a threadbare partisan's shirt.

But Lumumba is always elegant. The whiteness of his shirt, the starched collar, his cufflinks, the stylish knot of his tie, his glasses in expensive frames. This is not the popular touch. This is the *style évolue* of the would-be European. When Nkrumah travels to Europe he demonstratively puts his African costume on. When Lumumba travels to an African village he demonstratively puts on European dress. Perhaps this is not even a demonstration of anything. But it is read that way.

Anyway, he doesn't spend a lot of time in the villages. Patrice is not the peasant-leader type. Or working-class. He is a product of the city, and the African city is not as a rule an agglomeration of the proletariat, but of bureaucrats and petits-bourgeois. Patrice sprang from the city, not from the village. Not from peasants, but from those who were peasants yesterday. There's the difference. A person coming straight from the jungle to the Boulevard Albert in Leo reels around like a drunk. The constrast is too great, the jump too violent. Back there, he lived quietly in his tribe and everything was comprehensible. Whether he liked it or not, the tribal organization gave him one thing: a balanced life. He knew that if he found himself in situation X, he should resolve it by method Y. Such was the custom. But in the city a man finds himself alone. In the city there is the boss, the landlord, the grocer. One pays you, and the others have to be paid. And there are more people to be paid than people paying, and that's where the trouble starts. Nobody gives a damn about anybody else. Work lets out. You have to go somewhere. People go to the bars.

Lumumba's career begins in the bars: there are 500 of them in the clay-hut districts of Leo. The African bar has nothing in common with, for instance, the Bar Łowicki back home in Warsaw. In the Łowicki a guy stands in line, gets a shot of vodka, munches a pickle, and disappears. If there's to be a second shot, he has to stand in line again. A crowd, haste—cultural life is out of the question.

My favourite bar in Africa is called 'Alex'. Often the names are more suggestive: 'Why Not?', 'You'll Get Lost', or 'Only You'. Recently, more high-flown signs have been hung out, like 'Independence', 'Freedom' or 'The Struggle'. 'Alex' is a small one-storey shack decorated like an inn for a country wedding—gaudy and extravagant. It stands in the shade of the palms, among billboards advertising Coca-Cola, Martell and Shell. In the morning it's virtually empty, but in the evening it draws a swarm of people. They sit on tin chairs at tin tables and drink beer.

There has to be beer. A lot of bottles and a lot of glasses. The bottle caps ring out as they hit the floor. Out of them the black pussy-cats make belts, which they wrap around their hips. The pussy-cats walk and the caps jangle. This jangling is considered arousing.

There has to be jazz. And raspy rock, raspy Armstrong. The records are so worn that they no longer contain any melody: only that rasping. But the bar dances. It makes no difference that everyone is sitting down. Look at their feet, their shoulders, their hands. You can talk, argue and flirt, do business, read the Bible, or snooze. The body always dances. The belly undulates, the head sways—the whole bar sways like that until late at night.

It is a second home. In their own homes they cannot sit around because it's cramped, grey, poverty-stricken. The women are quarrelling, the kids are peeing in the corner, there are no bright crêpe dresses and Armstrong isn't singing. Home is constraint; the bar, freedom. A white informer will not go to a bar because a white person can be spotted a mile away. So you can talk about everything. The bar is always full of words. The bar deliberates, argues and pontificates. The bar will take up any subject, argue about it, dwell on it, try to get at the truth. Everybody will come around and put in their two cents' worth. The subject doesn't matter. The important thing is to participate, speak up. An African bar is the Roman Forum, the main square in a medieval market town, Robespierre's Parisian wine cellar. Reputations, adulatory or annihilating, are born here. Here you are lifted on to a pedestal or tumbled to the pavement with a crash. If you delight the bar you will go on to a great career; if the bar laughs at you, you might as well go back to the jungle. In the fumes of foaming beer, in the pungent scent of the girls, in the incomprehensible roiling of the tom-toms, names, dates, opinions and judgements are exchanged. The bar weighs a problem, ponders it, brings forth the pros and cons. Someone is gesticulating, a woman is nursing a baby, laughter explodes around someone's table. Gossip, fever and crowding. Here they are settling the price for a night together, there they are putting together a revolutionary programme; at the next table somebody is recommending a good witch doctor, and further on somebody is saying that there is going to be a strike. A bar like this is everything you could want: a club and a pawn shop, a boardwalk and a church porch, a theatre and a school, a dive and a rally, a bordello and a party cell.

You have to take account of the bars: Lumumba understands this perfectly. He stops in for a beer, too. Patrice doesn't like keeping his mouth shut. He feels that he has something to say and he wants to get it out. Patrice is an inspired speaker, a genius. He begins with casual conversations in the bar. Nobody knows him here: a strange face. He's not a Bangal or a Bakong. What's more, he doesn't back any of the tribes. There's only one Congo, this stranger says. The Congo is a great subject; you can talk about it endlessly without repeating yourself. Such things are good listening. And the bar starts to listen—for the first time it hushes, settles down, falls silent. It pricks up its ears, ruminates, compares points of view. Our country is enormous, Patrice explains. It is rich and beautiful. If the Belgians would leave, it could be a superpower.

How can we oppose the Belgians? With unity. The Bangals should stop letting snakes into the huts of the Bakongos. That only leads to quarrels and not to *Fraternité*. No freedom in that—and your women don't even have enough to buy a bunch of bananas. This isn't life.

Patrice speaks simply. You have to. He came from the village, too; he knows these people, torn out of their routines, shaken and disoriented, off the rails, looking for some sort of support in the incomprehensible new world of the city, some oar to grab hold of, a chance to catch their breath before plunging back into this whirl of faces, into the confusion of the market, into everyday drudgery. When you talk to these people you can see how everything inside their heads is tangled up in the most fantastic way. Refrigerators and poisoned arrows, de Gaulle and Ferhat Abbas, fear of the witch doctor and wonder at the sputnik. When the Belgians sent their expeditionary force to the Congo, they ordered the infantrymen to change into paratroopers' uniforms. I kept wracking my brains—why were they all paratroopers? Then it dawned on me: because paratroopers are feared here. In Africa they are frightened of anybody who drops out of the sky. Anybody who does is not just anybody. There's something in it, although it's better not to go into such things too deeply.

Patrice is a son of his people. At times he too can be naïve and mystical; he too has a predisposition to jump from one extreme to another, from explosions of happiness to mute despair. Lumumba is a fascinating character because he is extraordinarily complex. Nothing about the man submits to definition. Every formulation is too tight. Restless, a chaotic enthusiast, a sentimental poet, an ambitious politician, an animated soul, amazingly tough and submissive all at once, confident to the last that he is right, deaf to the words of others, enraptured—by his own splendid voice.

Lumumba enchants the bars. From the very moment he walks in. He conquers them totally. Patrice always speaks with conviction, and people want to be convinced. They want to discover some new faith, because the tribal faith has become shaky. We used to say, 'Comrade, don't just agitate among us, give us something we can feel.' Lumumba knows how to give the bars something they can feel. He teaches, demonstrates, proves. The people say yes and applaud. *Il a raison,* they shout—He's right! And today in the Congo, when his name is mentioned, they say again with melancholy reflection: *Oui, il avait raison.* Yes, he was right.

11

The army moved out at dusk. We heard the roar of engines and eight big trucks drove through the square. The soldiers stood leaning on the handrails, helmeted, with rifles slung across their backs. It's not the custom here for the army to sing. They drove in silence through the empty city, through streets emptied by the curfew. There were perhaps 300 of them. The trucks turned on to the road out of town—we could still hear the roar of the engines— and then everything disappeared into silence, jungle, the gloaming of the suddenly falling night.

I wanted very badly to go with them. I wanted to see the war which I had forced my way into the Congo for in the first place. But we had found no war, only a brawl, absurd quarrels and heavy-handed imperialistic intrigue. There was nothing for us to do here. There were days when we didn't set foot outside the hotel because there was nowhere to go. And there was no reason to. Everything seemed either inconceivable or obvious. Even conversations were senseless. The Mobutu supporters considered the Lumumba supporters animals, and the Lumumba partisans regarded the Mobutu supporters as scoundrels. How many times can you listen to this sort of thing? The one with the most patience was Fedyashin. Fedyashin was always getting people to talk, and then coming back to us with some new revelation: 'You know, this young fellow says they have a lot of followers in Kindu.' I don't know what was wrong with me, but this seemed not of the slightest interest.

That's why I wanted to go with the army. The army is a concrete reality. The army was now beginning an offensive. In the heart of the continent, 300 soldiers were starting off towards a war. But I couldn't be among them. I had a wolf ticket. You get that ticket when you cross a certain parallel. When you reach a place where you find out that you have white skin. This is a discovery, a sensation, a shock. I had lived for years without being aware of that skin. A hundred children play in the courtyard of the town house I live in back home, and not one of them has ever given his skin a thought. They only know that if it's dirty, that's bad. But if it's clean and white—good! Well, they're wrong. It's bad. Very bad. Because white skin is the wolf ticket.

People ask why the blacks beat the whites in the Congo. Why, indeed. Because the whites used to beat the blacks. It's a closed circle of revenge. What is there to explain? People give in to that psychosis and it deforms and kills them. In the jungles of the Eastern Province I found a Polish émigré. For a hundred kilometres around he was the only white left. He was gravely ill. Sitting hunched over, he would repeat mechanically, 'I can't take it, I can't take it.' He had been raised in the colonial world: a black man would be walking along, and a white gentleman and his lady would be returning from a party—the black wouldn't get out of the way, the car would stop, and the gentleman would hit the black in the face. If the black was walking too slowly—in the face. If he sat down—in the face. Mumbled—in the face. Drank—in the face. The blacks have strong teeth, but they can get tired of it all, of taking it and taking it, even on a robust jaw. Thus the world has changed and now the émigré sits and trembles: his fillings are not very strong.

Now the strong teeth were on the offensive, and the rotten teeth were hiding in the corners. I too would have gone to the front, but for my wolf ticket. I thought of going and explaining: 'I'm from Poland. At the age of sixteen, I joined a youth organization. On its banners were slogans about the brotherhood of the races and the common struggle against colonialism. I was an activist. I organized solidarity rallies with the peoples of Korea, Vietnam and Algeria—with all the peoples of the world. I stayed up all night painting banners. You never even saw our banners—they were huge, enormous, really caught your eye. I have been with you wholeheartedly every moment of my life. I've always regarded colonialists as the lowest vermin. I'm with you and I'll prove it with deeds.'

We set out to do just that. To go with the offensive. With relief we left our stuffy hotel rooms and started across the city. It was hot, awfully hot, but nothing could hold us back. The downtown part ended and we entered a native quarter. Beyond lay the army camp and headquarters. That was our goal. We didn't get far. An officer suddenly stopped us. He looked at us threateningly and asked us something. We couldn't understand the language. The officer was slightly built; we could have taken care of him easily, but a crowd of onlookers appeared at once, trapping us inside a tight circle. This was no joke. The officer swore and pointed his finger at us, and we stood there helpless and mute, our language incomprehensible to his ears. He asked more questions—the soldier was becoming furious. I thought to myself, this is where we get it. But what could we do? We stood and waited. A boy on a bicycle rode out of a side street. He stopped and pushed through towards us. He understood French; he could interpret. We told him we were from Poland and Czechoslovakia. He translated. The people in the crowd looked at each other, searching for a sage who would know what those names meant. The officer didn't know, which made him angrier still. More shouts; we stood as meek as sheep. Each of us wanted to say that we were full of feelings of friendship and that we stood in solidarity with the struggle of the people, of which our desire to take part in the offensive was proof—but the officer kept on screaming and we couldn't get a word in. He must have been insisting that we were Belgians; I don't know what he was after. Finally Jarda found a way out. Jarda lived in Cairo, so he had a driver's licence printed in Arabic. He took it out to show the officer, the crowd looked on eagerly, and he said: 'It's from Nasser.'

The magic of this word serves all over Africa. 'A-ha.' The officer understood. 'So you're from Nasser. What a shame, that so many people in this world look like Belgians.'

'It's not our fault,' I said in Polish, 'not our fault at all.'

The officer shook our hands, about-turned and walked away. The people departed and we were left alone. We could have kept going, but somehow everything had lost its sparkle. In fact, we had no reason to feel resentful. In Poland there are a lot of people who don't know that countries such as Gabon and Bechuanaland really exist. A Belgian history book I once leafed through—written for Congolese schools—was written in such a way that you could think Belgium was the only country in the world. The only one.

We were back to sitting around in the hotel. Jarda listened to the radio. Duszan read a book. I practised shadow-boxing.

Translated from the Polish by William R. Brand

The truck is racing through the dusk, its headlamps, like pupils, searching for the finishing line. It's close: Jeziorany, twenty kilometres. Another half hour, and we'll be there. The truck is pushing hard, but it's touch and go. The old machine wasn't meant for such a long haul.

On the flat-bed lies a coffin.

Atop the black box is a garland of haggard angels. It's worst on bends: the box slides and threatens to crush the legs of those sitting on the side rails. They curse, desecrating the coffin's decomposing contents.

The road bends into blind curves, climbing. The engine howls, rises a few notes, hiccups, chokes and stops. Another breakdown. A smeared figure alights from the cab. That's Zieja, the driver. He crawls under the truck, looking for the damage. Hidden underneath, he swears at the perverse world. He spits when hot grease drips on to his face. Finally he drags himself out into the middle of the road and brushes off his clothes. '*Kaput*,' he says. 'It won't start. You can smoke.'

To hell with smoking. We feel like crying.

Just two days ago I was in Silesia at the Aleksandra-Maria coal mine. The story called for an interview with the director of the workers' dormitory. I found him in his office explaining something to six youngsters. And I listened in.

This was the problem. During blasting a block of coal had fallen and crushed a miner. They managed to dig out the body, but he had died instantly. No one had known the dead man well. He had been working in the mine for barely two weeks. His identity was established. Name: Stefan Kanik. Age: eighteen. His father lived in Jeziorany, in Mazuria. The management contacted the local authorities there by telephone. It turned out that the father was paralysed and could not travel to the funeral. The Jeziorany authorities asked if the remains couldn't be transported to the home town. The management agreed, provided a truck and assigned the director of the workers' dormitory to find six people to escort the coffin.

These are the ones who have been summoned.

Five agree, one refuses. He doesn't want to lose any overtime. So there's a gap.

Can I go as the sixth?

The director shakes his head: a reporter as a pallbearer?

This empty road, this wreck of a truck, this air without a wisp of breeze.

This coffin.

Zieja wipes his oily hands with a rag. 'So what next?' he asks. 'We were supposed to be there this evening.'

We are stretched out on the edge of a ditch, on grass coated with a patina of dust. Our backs ache, our legs hurt, our eyes sting. Sleep, uninvited, introduces itself: warm, companionable, ingratiating.

'I think we all deserve a little nap,' says Wiśnia and curls up into a ball.

'And so?' Zieja says, surprised. 'Are we just going to go to sleep? But what about that other one?'

He shouldn't have mentioned it. Embarrassed by the question, sleep becomes awkward, backs away. We have been lying, tormented by our fatigue, and now feel anxious and uncertain, stare dully into a sky swimming with a school of silver stars.

We have to decide on something. 'What? Perhaps you'll tell me.'

Woś says: 'Let's stay here till morning. In the morning one of us can go to town and borrow a tractor. There's no need to hurry. This isn't a bakery.'

Jacek says: 'We can't wait till morning. It would be better to get this over with quickly, as quickly as possible.'

Kostarski says: 'You know, what if we just picked him up and carried him? He was a little guy, and a good part of him is still underneath that block of coal. It's not much of a load. We'll be finished by noon.'

It's a crazy idea, but it's one everyone likes. Put your shoulder to the wheel. It's early evening, and there aren't more than fifteen kilometres to go. We'll make it for sure. Besides, there is something else. Crouching at the edge of the ditch, having overcome the first temptation of sleep, more and more we begin to feel that with this coffin literally hanging above our heads we are keeping a vigil, here in the deep darkness, amid shadows and bushes and the silent, deaf horizon: the tension of waiting for the dawn would be unbearable. It would be better to go, better to lug him! Take some sort of action, move, talk, destroy the silence of the black box, prove that you belong to the realm of the living—in which he, nailed in, stiff, is an intruder, an alien, resembling nothing at all.

At the same time we find ourselves looking upon the task ahead—this arduous carrying—as a sort of offering to be presented to the deceased, so that he will leave us in peace, freeing us of his stubborn, insistent presence.

This march with the coffin on our backs has got off to a rough start. Seen from the viewpoint beneath it, the world has shrivelled to a small segment: the pendulum legs of the man ahead, a black slice of ground, the pendulum of your own legs. With his vision confined to this meagre prospect, a man instinctively summons imagination to his aid. Yes, the body may be bound, but the mind remains free.

'Anybody that came along now and ran into us would sure make tracks.'

'Know what? The moment he starts moving, we drop him and take off.'

'I just hope it doesn't rain. If it rains, he'll be waterlogged, and then he'll be very, very heavy.'

But there is no sign of rain. The evening is warm and the enormous, clear sky soars above an earth that is asleep now except for the sound of the crickets and the rhythm of our steps.

'Seventy-three, seventy-four, seventy-five'—Kostarski is counting. At 200 steps we change. We switch sides, left to right. Then the other way around. The edge of the coffin, hard and sharp, digs into our shoulders. We turn off the paved road on to a forest track, taking a short cut that passes near the shore of the lake. After an hour we haven't done more than three kilometres.

'Why is it,' Wiśnia wonders, 'that someone dies and instead of being buried in the ground he hangs around and wears everybody else out. Not only that. They all wear themselves out just so that he can hang around. Why?'

'I read somewhere,' Jacek says, 'that in the war, when the snow melted on the Russian battlefields, the hands of the dead would start to show, sticking straight up. You'd be going along the road and all you'd see would be the snow and these hands. Can you imagine, nothing else? A man, when he's finished, doesn't want to drop out of sight. It's people who hide him from their sight. To be left in peace, they hide him. He won't go on his own.'

'Just like this one of ours,' says Woś. 'He'd follow us round the world. All we have to do is take him along. I think we could even get used to it.'

'Why not?' Gruber quips from the back of the coffin. 'Everyone's always bearing some burden. A career for one, rabbits for another, a wife for a third. So why shouldn't we have him?'

'Don't speak ill of him, or he'll kick you in the ear,' Woś warns.

'He's not dangerous,' Gruber says softly. 'He's behaved himself so far. He must have been OK.'

But in fact we don't know what he was like. None of us ever saw him. Stefan Kanik, eighteen, died in an accident. That's all. Now we can add that he weighed around sixty kilos. A young, slender boy. The rest is a mystery, a guess. And now this riddle—boxed up, unseen, unknown—this shape, this alien, this stiff, rules six living men, monopolizes their thoughts, wears out their bodies, and, in silence, accepts their votive sacrifice.

'If he was a good guy, then you don't mind lugging him,' says Woś, 'but if he was a son of a bitch, into the water with him.'

What was he like? Can you establish such facts? Yes, certainly! We've been lugging him for about five kilometres and we've poured out a barrel of sweat. Haven't we invested a great deal of labour, of nerves, of our own peace of mind, into this remnant? This effort, a part of ourselves, passes on to the stiff, raises his worth in our eyes, unites us with him, makes him our brother across the barrier between life and death. The feeling of mutual strangeness dwindles. He has become ours. We won't plop him into the water. Sentenced to our burden, we will fulfill, to the very end, our appointed mission.

The forest trail leads to the edge of the lake. There is a little clearing. Woś calls for a rest and starts to make a bonfire.

The flame shoots up immediately, impudent and playful. We settle down in a circle and pull off our shirts, now wet and sour-smelling. In the glow of the fire we can see each other's sweating face, glistening torso and red, swollen shoulders. The heat spreads from the bonfire in waves. We back away, leaving the coffin by the fire.

'We'd better move that piece of furniture before it starts to roast and begins stinking,' Woś says.

We pull the coffin back, push it into the bushes, where Pluta breaks off some branches and covers it up.

We sit down again. We are still breathing heavily, fighting sleep and a feeling of unease, baking ourselves in the warmth and revelling in a light miraculously conjured from the darkness. We begin to fall into a state of inertia, abandon, numbness. The night has encapsulated us, closed us off from the world, from any other existence.

Just at that moment we hear Wiśnia's high, terrifying whisper: 'Quiet. Something's coming!'

A sudden, unbearable spasm of terror. Icy pins stab into our backs. Against our will, we glance towards the bushes, in the direction of the coffin. Jacek can't take it: he presses his head into the grass and, exhausted, sleep-starved, suddenly afraid, he begins to weep. This brings us all to our senses. Woś comes to himself first and falls upon Jacek, pulling at him and then pummelling him. He beats him fiercely, until the boy's weeping turns to groans, to a low, drawn-out sigh. Woś backs off at last, leans on a stump and ties his shoe.

In the meantime the voices that Wiśnia detected become distinct: they are approaching. We can hear snatches of melody, laughter, shouts. We listen attentively. Amid this dark wilderness our caravan has found traces of mankind. The voices are quite close now. Finally we pick out the silhouettes. Two, three, five.

They're girls. Six, seven.

Eight girls.

The girls—at first afraid, uncertain—end up staying. As the conversation gets off the ground, they start settling down around the fire next to us, so close that we could reach out and put our arms around them. It feels good. After everything we've been through, after a day of hard travelling, an exhausting march, the nerve-wracking tension, after all of this, or perhaps in spite of all this, it feels good.

'Are you coming back from a hike, too?' they ask.

'Yes,' Gruber says, lying. 'Beautiful evening, isn't it?'

'Beautiful. I'm just starting to appreciate it. Like everyone.'

'Not everyone,' Gruber says. 'There are some who don't appreciate anything. Now or ever. Never.'

We're all watching the girls closely. In colourful dresses, their shoulders bare and sun-bronzed—in the flickering light golden and brown by turns—their eyes seemingly indifferent but in fact provocative and vigilant at the same time, accessible and unreachable, they stare into the flames and appear to be surrendering to the strange and somewhat pagan mood that a night-time, forest-bonfire evokes in people. Looking upon these unexpected visitors, we feel that, despite the numbness, sleepiness and exhaustion, we are slowly being filled by an inner warmth: and, while wanting it, we sense the danger that comes with it. The edifice that holds in place the purpose and justification for making this extraordinary effort on behalf of a dead man is suddenly tottering. Why bother? Who needs it, when an opportunity like this presents itself? Only negative feelings link us to the dead man: in our new mood we could break away from the stiff so completely that any further toil of carrying the coffin would strike us as downright idiocy. Why make fools of ourselves?

Woś, however, has remained gloomy after the incident with Jacek, and has not joined in the flirting. He draws me aside.

'There's going to be trouble,' he whispers. 'One or the other of them is sure to go off after a skirt. And if we're a man short, we won't be able to carry the coffin. Then what?'

From this remove, our legs almost touching the sides of the coffin, we watch the scene in the clearing. Gruber will go for sure. Kostarski, Pluta—no. And Jacek? He's a question mark. He is, at heart, a shy boy, and wouldn't initiate a thing unless the girl made the first move: he'd turn tail at her first 'no.' Yet because his character affords him few chances, he would grab avidly if one presented itself.

'It's a dead cert Jacek goes,' Woś says.

'Let's get back to the fire,' I tell him. 'We're not going to solve anything here.'

We return. Pluta has thrown on some more wood. 'Remember,

it was autumn,' the girls are singing. We feel good, and we feel uneasy. No one has breathed a word about the coffin, but the coffin is still there. Our awareness of its existence, of its paralysing participation, makes us different from the girls.

Stefan Kanik, eighteen. Someone who is missing and who at the same time is the most present. Reach out and you can put your arm around a girl; take a few steps and you can lean over the coffin—we are standing between life at its most beautiful and death at its most cruel.

The stiff came to us unknown, and for that reason we can identify him with every boy we have known. Yes, that was the one, that one for sure. He was standing in the window in an unbuttoned checked shirt, watching the cars drive past, listening to the babble of conversations, looking at the passing girls—the wind blowing out their full skirts, uncovering the whiteness of their starched slips, so stiff that you could stand them up on the floor like haystacks. And then he went out into the street and met his own girl and walked with her, buying her lifesavers and the most expensive lemon soda—'Moorish Delight'—and then she bought him strawberries and they went to the movie *Holiday with Monica,* where an actress with a difficult name undresses in front of an actor with a difficult name, which his girl had never done in front of him, not even once. And afterwards he kissed her in the park, watching from out of the corner of his eye from behind her head, through her careless loose hair, to make sure that a policeman wasn't coming who would take down his name and send him to school, or would want twenty *zloty* when they didn't have more than five between them. And afterwards the girl would say, 'We have to go now,' but she wouldn't get up from the park bench; she would say, 'Come on, it's late,' and she would cuddle against him more tightly, and he would ask, 'Do you know how butterflies kiss?' and move his eyelids close to her cheek and flutter them, which must have tickled her, because she would laugh.

Perhaps he would meet her many more times, but in our minds that naïve and banal image was the only and the final one, and afterwards we saw only what we had never wanted to see, ever, until the last day of our lives.

And when we pushed away that other, bad vision, we felt good again and everything was a joy to us: the fire, the smell of trampled grass, that our shirts had dried, the sleep of the earth, the taste of cigarettes, the forest, the rested legs, the stardust, life—life most of all.

In the end, we went on. The dawn met us. The sun warmed us. We kept walking. Our legs buckled, our shoulders went numb, our hands swelled, but we managed to carry it to the cemetery—to the grave—our last harbour on earth, at which we put in only once, never again to sail forth—this Stefan Kanik, eighteen, killed in a tragic accident, during blasting, by a block of coal.

Translated from the Polish by William R. Brand

PICADOR
OUTSTANDING INTERNATIONAL WRITING

Hardback Published 9 January

£8.95

THE ENCHANTER
Vladimir Nabokov *(Trans. Dmitri Nabokov)*

His long lost novel in print for the first time – 'A minor masterpiece. It is a first treatment of the theme that was to make such an impact 15 years later in *Lolita' Daily Telegraph*

'Quite a discovery . . . After this, 1987 will be all downhill' *Observer*

First British Publication Published 30 January

£2.95

THE JAGUAR SMILE
A Nicaraguan Journey
Salman Rushdie

Salman Rushdie went to Nicaragua in July 1986 not knowing what to expect. What he found was overwhelming. Discover the Nicaragua behind the headlines

First Publication Published 13 March

£2.95

THE WIND BLOWS AWAY OUR WORDS
Doris Lessing

Doris Lessing turns to non-fiction bringing the plight of Afghanistan to our attention. Seven years after the Russian invasion she went to see the conditions of the 4,000,000 refugees. Her account should not be missed.

Available now

£3.50

And Don't Forget

BREAKFAST IN HELL
A Doctor's Experiences of the Ethiopian Famine
Myles Harris

'Not an easy meal; but it should be carefully digested by any who still think money alone will truly help the hungry'*Frederick Forsyth*

'Evelyn Waugh couldn't have done it better' *Tom Wolfe*

ED GRAZDA
PHOTOGRAPHS FROM
THE NORTH-WEST
FRONTIER

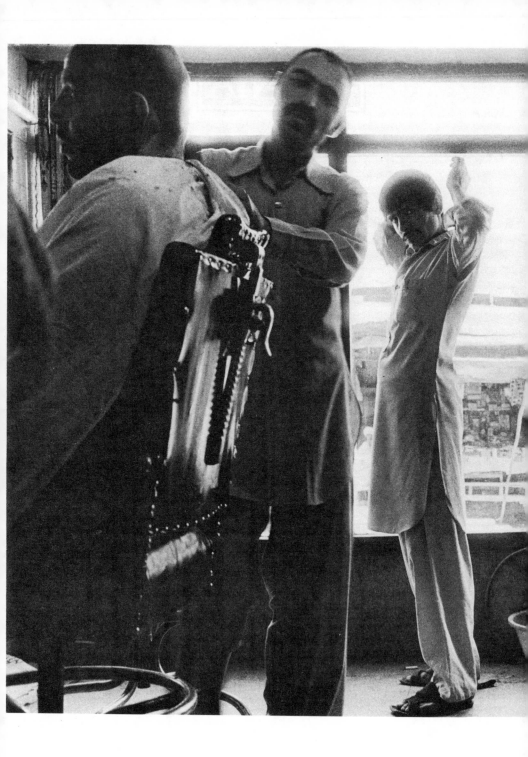

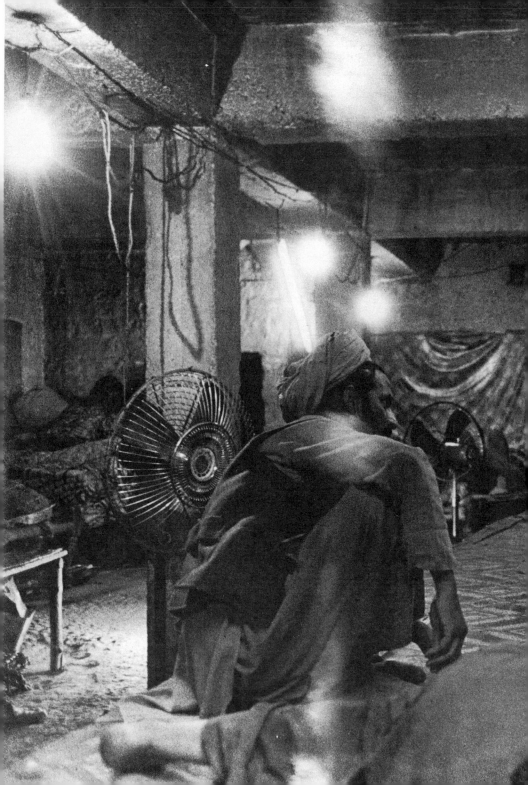

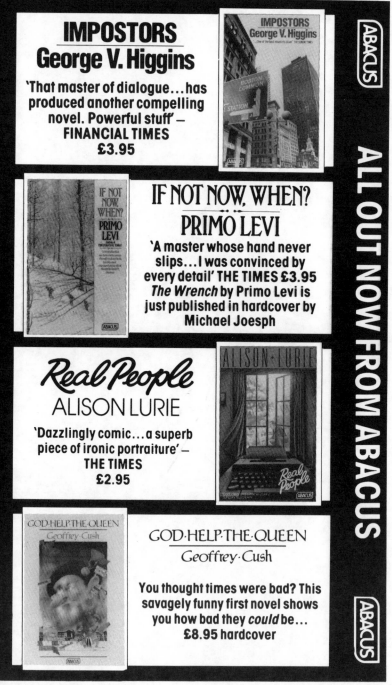

RICHARD FORD
GREAT FALLS

T his is not a happy story. I warn you.

My father was a man named Jack Russell, and when I was a young boy in my early teens, we lived with my mother in a house to the east of Great Falls, Montana, near the small town of Highwood and the Highwood Mountains and the Missouri River. It is a flat, treeless benchland there, all of it used for wheat farming, though my father was never a farmer, but was brought up near Tacoma, Washington, in a family that worked for Boeing.

He—my father—had been an Air Force sergeant and had taken his discharge in Great Falls. And instead of going home to Tacoma, where my mother wanted to go, he had taken a civilian's job with the Air Force, working on planes, which was what he liked to do. And he had rented the house out of town from a farmer who did not want it left standing empty.

The house itself is gone now—I have been to the spot. But the double row of Russian olive trees and two of the outbuildings are still standing in the milkweeds. It was a plain, two-storey house with a porch on the front and no place for the cars. At the time, I rode the school bus to Great Falls every morning, and my father drove in, while my mother stayed home.

My mother was a tall, pretty woman, thin, with black hair and slightly sharp features that made her seem to smile when she wasn't smiling. She had grown up in Wallace, Idaho, and gone to college a year in Spokane, then moved out to the coast, which is where she met Jack Russell. She was two years older than he was, and married him, she said to me, because he was young and wonderful looking, and because she thought they could leave the sticks and see the world together—which I suppose they did for a while. That was the life she wanted, even before she knew much about wanting anything else or about the future.

When my father wasn't working on airplanes, he was going hunting or fishing, two things he could do as well as anyone. He had learned to fish, he said, in Iceland, and to hunt ducks up on the DEW line—stations he had visited in the Air Force. And during the time of this—it was 1960—he began to take me with him on what he called his 'expeditions'. I thought even then, with as little as I knew, that these were opportunities other boys would dream of having but probably never would. And I don't think that I was wrong in that.

It is a true thing that my father did not know limits. In the spring, when we would go east to the Judith River Basin and camp up on the banks, he would catch a hundred fish in a weekend, and sometimes more than that. It was all he did from morning until night, and it was never hard for him. He used yellow corn kernels stacked on to a # 4 snelled hook, and he would rattle this rig-up along the bottom of a deep pool below a split shot sinker, and catch fish. And most of the time, because he knew the Judith River and knew how to feel his bait down deep, he could catch fish of good size.

It was the same with ducks, the other thing he liked. When the northern birds were down, usually by mid-October, he would take me and we would build a cattail and wheat-straw blind on one of the tule ponds or sloughs he knew about down the Missouri, where the water was shallow enough to wade. We would set out his decoys to the leeward side of our blind, and he would sprinkle corn on a hunger-line from the decoys to where we were. In the evenings when he came home from the base, we would go and sit out in our blind until the roosting flights came and put down among the decoys—there was never calling involved. And after a while, sometimes it would be an hour and full dark, the ducks would find the corn, and the whole raft of them—sixty, sometimes—would swim in to us. And at the moment he judged they were close enough, my father would say to me, 'Shine, Jackie,' and I would stand and shine a seal-beam car light out on to the pond, and he would stand up beside me and shoot all the ducks that were there, on the water if he could, but flying and getting up as well. He owned a Model 11 Remington with a long-tube magazine that would hold ten shells, and, with that many, and shooting straight over the surface rather than down on to it, he could kill or wound thirty ducks in twenty seconds' time. I remember distinctly the report of that gun and the flash of it over the water into the dark air, one shot after another, not even so fast, but measured in a way to hit as many as he could.

What my father did with the ducks he killed, and the fish, too, was sell them. It was against the law then to sell wild game, and it is against the law now. And though he kept some for us, most he would take—his fish laid on ice, or his ducks still wet and bagged in the burlap corn sacks—down to the Great Northern Hotel, which was still open then on Second Street in Great Falls, and sell them to the Negro caterer who bought them for his wealthy customers and for the dining-car passengers who came through. We would drive in my father's Plymouth to the back of the hotel—always this was after dark—to a concrete loading ramp and lighted door that were close enough to the yards that I could sometimes see passenger trains waiting at the station, their car lights yellow and warm inside, the passengers dressed in suits, all bound for some place far away from Montana—Milwaukee or Chicago or New York City, unimaginable places to me, a boy fourteen years old, with my father in the cold dark, selling illegal game.

The caterer was a tall, stooped-back man in a white jacket, who my father called 'Professor Ducks' or 'Professor Fish', and the Professor referred to my father as 'Sarge'. He paid a quarter per pound for trout, a dime for whitefish, a dollar for a mallard duck, two for a speckle or a blue goose, and four dollars for a Canada. I have been with my father when he took away a hundred dollars for fish he'd caught and, in the fall, more than that for ducks and geese. When he had sold game in that way, we would drive out Tenth Avenue and stop at a bar called The Mermaid which was by the air base, and he would drink with some friends he knew there, and they would laugh about hunting and fishing while I played pin-ball and wasted money in the juke-box.

It was on such a night as this that the unhappy things came about. It was in late October. I remember the time because Halloween had not been yet, and in the windows of the houses that I passed every day on the bus to Great Falls, people had put pumpkin lanterns, and set scarecrows in their yards in chairs.

My father and I had been shooting ducks in a slough on the Smith River, upstream from where it enters on the Missouri. He had killed thirty ducks, and we'd driven them down to the Great Northern and sold them there, though my father had kept two back in his corn sack. And when we had driven away, he suddenly said, 'Jackie, let's us go back home tonight. Who cares about those hard-dicks at The Mermaid. I'll cook these ducks on the grill. We'll do something different tonight.' He smiled at me in an odd way. This was not a thing he usually said, or the way he usually talked. He liked The Mermaid, and my mother—as far as I knew—didn't mind it if he went there.

'That sounds good,' I said.

'We'll surprise your mother,' he said. 'We'll make her happy.'

We drove out past the air base on Highway 87, past where there were planes taking off into the night. The darkness was dotted by the green and red runway beacons, and the tower light swept the sky and trapped planes as they disappeared over the flat landscape toward Canada or Alaska and the Pacific.

'Boy-oh-boy,' my father said—just out of the dark. I looked at him, and his eyes were narrow, and he seemed to be thinking about something. 'You know, Jackie,' he said, 'your mother said something to me once I've never forgotten. She said, "Nobody dies of a broken heart." This was somewhat before you were born. We were living down in Texas and we'd had some big blow-up, and that was the idea she had. I don't know why.' He shook his head.

He ran his hand under the seat, found a half-pint bottle of whiskey, and held it up to the lights of the car behind us to see what there was left of it. He unscrewed the cap and took a drink, then held the bottle out to me. 'Have a drink, son,' he said. 'Something oughta be good in life.' And I felt that something was wrong. Not because of the whiskey, which I had drunk before and he had reason to know about, but because of some sound in his voice, something I didn't recognize and did not know the importance of, though I was certain it was important.

I took a drink and gave the bottle back to him, holding the whiskey in my mouth until it stopped burning and I could swallow it a little at a time. When we turned out the road to Highwood, the lights of Great Falls sank below the horizon, and I could see the small white lights of farms then, burning at wide distances in the dark.

'What do you worry about, son?' my father said. 'Do you worry about girls? Do you worry about your future sex life? Is that some of it?' He glanced at me, then back at the road.

'I don't worry about that,' I said.

'Well, what then?' my father said. 'What else is there?'

'I worry if you're going to die before I do,' I said, though I hated saying that, 'or if Mother is. That worries me.'

'It'd be a miracle if we didn't,' my father said, with the half-pint held in the same hand he held the steering-wheel. I had seen him drive that way before. 'Things pass too fast in your life, Jackie. Don't worry about that. If I were you, I'd worry we might not.' He smiled at me, and it was not the worried, nervous smile from before, but a smile that meant he was pleased. And I don't remember him ever smiling at me that way again.

We drove on out behind the town of Highwood and on to the flat field-roads toward our house. I could see, out on the prairie, a moving light where the farmer who rented our house to us was disking his field for winter wheat. 'He's waited too late with that business,' my father said and took a drink, then threw the bottle right out the window. 'He'll lose that,' he said. 'The cold'll kill it.' I did not answer him, but what I thought was that my father knew nothing about farming, and if he was right it would be an accident. He knew about planes and hunting game, and that seemed all to me.

'I want to respect your privacy,' he said then, for no reason at all that I understood. I am not even certain he said it, only that it is in my memory that way. I don't know what he was thinking of. Just words. But I said to him, I remember well, 'It's all right. Thank you.'

We did not go straight out the Geraldine Road to our house. Instead my father went down another mile and turned, went a mile and turned back again so that we came home from the other direction. 'I want to stop and listen now,' he said. 'The geese should be in the stubble.' We stopped and he cut the lights and engine, and we opened the car windows and listened. It was eight o'clock at night and it was getting colder, though it was dry. But I could hear nothing, just the sound of air moving lightly through the cut field, and not a goose sound. Though I could smell the whiskey on my father's breath and on mine, could hear the motor ticking, could hear him breathe, hear the sound we made sitting side by side on the car seat, our clothes, our feet, almost our hearts beating. And I could see out in the night the yellow lights of our house, shining through the olive trees south of us like a ship on the sea. 'I hear them, by God,' my father said, his head stuck out the window. 'But they're high up. They won't stop here now, Jackie. They're high flyers, those boys. Long gone geese.'

There was a car parked off the road, down the line of wind-break trees beside a steel thresher the farmer had left out to rust. You could see moonlight off the tail-light chrome. It was a Pontiac, a two-door hard-top. My father said nothing about it, and I didn't either, though I think now for different reasons.

The floodlight was on over the side door of our house, and lights were on inside, upstairs and down. My mother had a pumpkin on the front porch, and the wind chime she had hung by the door was tinkling. My dog, Major, came out of the quonset shed and stood in the car lights when we drove up.

'Let's see what's happening here,' my father said, opening the door and stepping out quickly. He looked at me inside the car, and his eyes were wide and his mouth drawn tight.

We walked in the side door and up the basement steps into the kitchen, and a man was standing there—a man I had never seen before, a young man with blond hair, who might've been twenty or twenty-five. He was tall and was wearing a short-sleeved shirt and beige slacks with pleats. He was on the other side of the breakfast table, his fingertips just touching the wooden table top. His blue eyes were on my father, who was dressed in hunting clothes.

'Hello,' my father said.

'Hello,' the young man said, and nothing else. And for some reason I looked at his arms, which were long and pale. They looked like a young man's arms, like my arms. His short sleeves had each been neatly rolled up, and I could see the bottom of a small green tattoo edging out from underneath. There was a glass of whiskey on the table, but no bottle.

'What's your name?' my father said, standing in the kitchen under the bright ceiling light. He sounded like he might be going to laugh.

'Woody,' the young man said and cleared his throat. He looked at me, then he touched the glass of whiskey, just the rim of the glass. He wasn't nervous, I could tell that. He did not seem to be afraid of anything.

'Woody,' my father said and looked at the glass of whiskey. He looked at me, then sighed and shook his head. 'Where's Mrs Russell, Woody? I guess you aren't robbing my house, are you?'

Woody smiled. 'No,' he said. 'Upstairs. I think she went upstairs.'

'Good,' my father said, 'that's a good place.' And he walked straight out of the room, but then came back and stood in the doorway. 'Jackie, you and Woody step outside and wait on me,' he said. 'Just stay there and I'll come out.' He looked at Woody then in a way I would not have liked him to look at me, a look that meant he was studying Woody. 'I guess that's your car,' he said.

'That Pontiac.' Woody nodded.

'OK,' my father said. 'Right.' Then he went out again and up the stairs. At that moment the phone started to ring in the living-room and I heard my mother say, 'Who's that?' And my father say, 'It's me. It's Jack.' And I decided I wouldn't go answer the phone. Woody looked at me, and I understood he wasn't sure what to do. Run, maybe. But he didn't have run in him. Though I thought he would probably do what I said if I would say it.

'Let's just go outside,' I said.

And he said, 'All right.'

Woody and I walked outside and stood in the light of the flood lamp above the side door. I had on my wool jacket, but Woody was cold and stood with his hands in his pockets, and his arms bare, moving from foot to foot. Inside, the phone was ringing again. Once I looked up and saw my mother come to the window and look down at Woody and me. Woody didn't look up or see her, but I did. I waved at her, and she waved back at me and smiled. She was wearing a powder-blue dress. In another minute the phone stopped ringing.

Woody took a cigarette out of his shirt pocket and lit it. Smoke shot through his nose into the cold air, and he sniffed, looked around the ground and threw his match on the gravel. His blond hair was combed backwards and neat on the sides, and I could smell his aftershave on him, a sweet, lemon smell. And for the first time I noticed his shoes. They were two-tones, black with white tops and black laces. They stuck out below his baggy pants and were long and polished and shiny, as if he had been planning on a big occasion. They looked like shoes some country singer would wear, or a salesman. He was handsome, but only like someone you would see beside you in a dime store and not notice again.

'I like it out here,' Woody said, his head down, looking at his shoes. 'Nothing to bother you. I bet you'd see Chicago if the world was flat. The Great Plains commence here.'

'I don't know,' I said.

Woody looked up at me, cupping his smoke with one hand. 'Do you play football?'

'No,' I said. I thought about asking him something about my mother. But I had no idea what it would be.

'I *have* been drinking,' Woody said, 'but I'm not drunk now.'

Then the wind rose, and from behind the house I could hear Major bark once from far away, and I could smell the irrigation ditch, hear it hiss in the field. It ran down from Highwood Creek to the Missouri, twenty miles away. It was nothing Woody knew about, nothing he could hear or smell. He knew nothing about anything that was here. I heard my father say the words, 'That's a real joke,' from inside the house, then the sound of a drawer being opened and shut, and a door closing. Then nothing else.

Woody turned and looked into the dark toward where the glow of Great Falls rose on the horizon, and we both could see the flashing lights of a plane lowering to land there. 'I once passed my brother in the Los Angeles airport and didn't even recognize him,' Woody said, staring into the night. 'He recognized *me*, though. He said, "Hey, bro, are you mad at me, or what?" I wasn't mad at him. We both had to laugh.'

Woody turned and looked at the house. His hands were still in his pockets, his cigarette clenched between his teeth, his arms taut. They were, I saw, bigger, stronger arms than I had thought. A vein went down the front of each of them. I wondered what Woody knew that I didn't. Not about my mother—I didn't know anything about that and didn't want to—but about a lot of things, about the life out in the dark, about coming out here, about airports, even about me. He and I were not so far apart in age, I knew that. But Woody was one thing, and I was another. And I wondered how I would ever get to be like him, since it didn't necessarily seem so bad a thing to be.

'Did you know your mother was married before?' Woody said.

'Yes,' I said. 'I knew that.'

'It happens to all of them, now,' he said. 'They can't wait to get divorced.'

'I guess so,' I said.

Woody dropped his cigarette into the gravel and toed it out

with his black-and-white shoe. He looked up at me and smiled the way he had inside the house, a smile that said he knew something he wouldn't tell, a smile to make you feel bad because you weren't Woody and never could be.

It was then that my father came out of the house. He still had on his plaid hunting coat and his wool cap, but his face was as white as snow, as white as I have ever seen a human being's face to be. It was odd. I had the feeling that he might've fallen inside, because he looked roughed up, as though he had hurt himself somehow.

My mother came out the door behind him and stood in the floodlight at the top of the steps. She was wearing the powder-blue dress I'd seen through the window, a dress I had never seen her wear before, though she was also wearing a car coat and carrying a suitcase. She looked at me and shook her head in a way that only I was supposed to notice, as if it was not a good idea to talk now.

My father had his hands in his pockets, and he walked right up to Woody. He did not even look at me. 'What do you do for a living?' he said, and he was very close to Woody. His coat was close enough to touch Woody's shirt.

'I'm in the Air Force,' Woody said. He looked at me and then at my father. He could tell my father was excited.

'Is this your day off, then?' my father said. He moved even closer to Woody, his hands still in his pockets. He pushed Woody with his chest, and Woody seemed willing to let my father push him.

'No,' he said, shaking his head.

I looked at my mother. She was just standing, watching. It was as if someone had given her an order, and she was obeying it. She did not smile at me, though I thought she was thinking about me, which made me feel strange.

'What's the matter with you?' my father said into Woody's face, right into his face—his voice tight, as if it had gotten hard for him to talk. 'Whatever in the world is the matter with you? Don't you understand something?' My father took a revolver pistol out of his coat then, and put it up under Woody's chin, into the soft pocket behind the bone, so that Woody's whole face rose, but his arms stayed at his sides, his hands open. 'I don't know what to do with you,' my father said. 'I don't have any idea what to do with you. I just don't.' Though I thought that what he wanted to do was hold

Woody there just like that until something important took place, or until he could simply forget about all this.

My father pulled the hammer back on the pistol and raised it tighter under Woody's chin, breathing into Woody's face—my mother in the light with her suitcase, watching them, and me watching them. A half a minute must've gone by.

And then my mother said, 'Jack, let's stop now. Let's just stop.'

My father stared into Woody's face as if he wanted Woody to consider doing something—moving or turning around or anything on his own to stop this—that my father would then put a stop to. My father's eyes grew narrowed, and his teeth were gritted together, his lips snarling up to resemble a smile. 'You're crazy, aren't you?' he said. 'You're a goddamn crazy man. Are you in love with her, too? Are you, crazy man? Are you? Do you say you love her? Say you love her! Say you love her so I can blow your fucking brains in the sky.'

'All right,' Woody said. 'No. It's all right.'

'He doesn't love me, Jack. For God's sake,' my mother said. She seemed so calm. She shook her head at me again. I do not think she thought my father would shoot Woody. And I don't think Woody thought so. Nobody did, I think, except my father himself. But I think he did, and was trying to find out how to.

My father turned suddenly and glared at my mother, his eyes shiny and moving, but with the gun still on Woody's skin. I think he was afraid, afraid he was doing this wrong and could mess all of it up and make matters worse without accomplishing anything.

'You're leaving,' he yelled at her. 'That's why you're packed. Get out. Go on.'

'Jackie has to be at school in the morning,' my mother said in just her normal voice. And without another word to any one of us, she walked out of the flood lamp light carrying her bag, turned the corner at the front porch steps and disappeared toward the olive trees that ran in rows back into the wheat.

My father looked back at me where I was standing in the gravel, as if he expected to see me go with my mother toward Woody's car. But I hadn't thought about that—though later I would. Later I would think I should have gone with her, and that things between them might've been different. But that isn't how it happened.

'You're sure you're going to get away now, aren't you, Mister?' my father said into Woody's face. He was crazy himself, then. Anyone would've been. Everything must have seemed out of hand to him.

'I'd like to,' Woody said. 'I'd like to get away from here.'

'And I'd like to think of some way to hurt you,' my father said and blinked his eyes. 'I feel helpless about it.' We all heard the door to Woody's car close in the dark. 'Do you think that I'm a fool?' my father said.

'No,' Woody said. 'I don't think that.'

'Do you think you're important?'

'No,' Woody said. 'I'm not.'

My father blinked again. He seemed to be becoming someone else at that moment, someone I didn't know. 'Where are you from?'

And Woody closed his eyes. He breathed in, then out, a long sigh. It was as if this was somehow the hardest part, something he hadn't expected to be asked to say.

'Chicago,' Woody said. 'A suburb of there.'

'Are your parents alive?' my father said, all the time with his blue magnum pistol pushed under Woody's chin.

'Yes,' Woody said. 'Yessir.'

'That's too bad,' my father said. 'Too bad they have to know what you are. I'm sure you stopped meaning anything to them a long time ago. I'm sure they both wish you were dead. You didn't know that. But I know it. I can't help them out, though. Somebody else'll have to kill you. I don't want to have to think about you anymore. I guess that's it.'

My father brought the gun down to his side and stood looking at Woody. He did not back away, just stood, waiting for what I don't know to happen. Woody stood a moment, then he cut his eyes at me uncomfortably. And I know that I looked down. That's all I could do. Though I remember wondering if Woody's heart was broken and what any of this meant to him. Not to me, or my mother, or my father. But to him, since he seemed to be the one left out somehow, the one who would be lonely soon, the one who had done something he would someday wish he hadn't and would have no one to tell him that it was all right, that they forgave him, that these things happen in the world.

Woody took a step back, looked at my father and at me again as if he intended to speak, then stepped aside and walked away toward the front of our house, where the wind chime made a noise in the new cold air.

My father looked at me, his big pistol in his hand. 'Does this seem stupid to you?' he said. 'All this? Yelling and threatening and going nuts? I wouldn't blame you if it did. You shouldn't even see this. I'm sorry. I don't know what to do now.'

'It'll be all right,' I said. And I walked out to the road. Woody's car started up behind the olive trees. I stood and watched it back out, its red tail-lights clouded by exhaust. I could see their two heads inside, with the headlights shining behind them. When they got into the road, Woody touched his brakes, and for a moment I could see that they were talking, their heads turned toward each other, nodding. Woody's head and my mother's. They sat that way for a few seconds, then drove slowly off. And I wondered what they had to say to each other, something important enough that they had to stop right at that moment and say it. Did she say, *I love you*? Did she say, *This is not what I expected to happen*? Did she say, *This is what I've wanted all along*? And did he say, *I'm sorry for all this,* or *I'm glad,* or *None of this matters to me*? These are not the kinds of things you can know if you were not there. And I was not there and did not want to be. It did not seem like I should be there. I heard the door slam when my father went inside, and I turned back from the road where I could still see their tail-lights disappearing, and went back into the house where I was to be alone with my father.

Things seldom end in one event. In the morning I went to school on the bus as usual, and my father drove in to the air base in his car. We had not said very much about all that had happened. Harsh words, in a sense, are all alike. You can make them up yourself and be right. I think we both believed that we were in a fog we couldn't see through yet, though in a while, maybe not even a long while, we would see lights and know something.

In my third period class that day a messenger brought a note for me that said I was excused from school at noon, and I should meet my mother at a motel down Tenth Avenue South, a place not so far from my school, and we would eat lunch together.

It was a grey day in Great Falls that day. The leaves were off the trees and the mountains to the east of town were obscured by a low sky. The night before had been cold and clear, but today it seemed as if it would rain. It was the beginning of winter in earnest. In a few days there would be snow everywhere.

The motel where my mother was staying was called the Tropicana, and was beside the city golf course. There was a neon parrot on the sign out front, and the cabins made a *U* shape behind a little white office building. Only a couple of cars were parked in front of cabins, and no car was in front of my mother's cabin. I wondered if Woody would be here, or if he was at the air base. I wondered if my father would see him there, and what they would say.

I walked back to cabin 9. The door was open, though a DO NOT DISTURB sign was hung on the knob outside. I looked through the screen and saw my mother sitting on the bed alone. The television was on, but she was looking at me. She was wearing the powder-blue dress she had had on the night before. She was smiling at me, and I liked the way she looked at that moment, through the screen, in shadows. Her features did not seem as sharp as they had before. She looked comfortable where she was, and I felt like we were going to get along, no matter what had happened, and that I wasn't mad at her—that I had never been mad at her.

She sat forward and turned the television off. 'Come in, Jackie,' she said, and I opened the screen door and came inside. 'It's the height of grandeur in here, isn't it?' My mother looked around the room. Her suitcase was open on the floor by the bathroom door, which I could see through and out the window on to the golf course, where three men were playing under the milky sky. 'Privacy can be a burden, sometimes,' she said, and reached down and put on her high-heeled shoes. 'I didn't sleep very well last night, did you?'

'No,' I said, though I had slept all right. I wanted to ask her where Woody was, but it occurred to me at that moment that he was gone now and wouldn't be back, that she wasn't thinking in terms of him and didn't care where he was or ever would be.

'I'd like a nice compliment from you,' she said. 'Do you have one of those to spend?'

'Yes,' I said. 'I'm glad to see you.'

'That's a nice one,' she said and nodded. She had both her shoes on now. 'Would you like to go have lunch? We can walk across the street to the cafeteria. You can get hot food.'

'No,' I said. 'I'm not really hungry now.'

'That's OK,' she said and smiled at me again. And, as I said before, I liked the way she looked. She looked pretty in a way I didn't remember seeing her, as if something that had had a hold on her had let her go, and she could be different about things. Even about me.

'Sometimes, you know,' she said, 'I'll think about something I did. Just anything. Years ago in Idaho, or last week, even. And it's as if I'd read it. Like a story. Isn't that strange?'

'Yes,' I said. And it did seem strange to me, because I was certain then what the difference was between what had happened and what hadn't, and knew I always would be.

'Sometimes,' she said, and she folded her hands in her lap and stared out the little side window of her cabin at the parking lot and the curving row of other cabins. 'Sometimes I even have a moment when I completely forget what life's like. Just altogether.' She smiled. 'That's not so bad, finally. Maybe it's a disease I have. Do you think I'm just sick and I'll get well?'

'No. I don't know,' I said. 'Maybe. I hope so.' I looked out the bathroom window and saw the three men walking down the golf course fairway carrying golf clubs.

'I'm not very good at sharing things right now,' my mother said. 'I'm sorry.' She cleared her throat, and then she didn't say anything for almost a minute while I stood there. 'I *will* answer anything you'd like me to answer, though. Just ask me anything, and I'll answer it the truth, whether I want to or not. OK? I will. You don't even have to trust me. That's not a big issue for us. We're both grown-ups now.'

And I said, 'Were you ever married before?'

My mother looked at me strangely. Her eyes got small, and for a moment she looked the way I was used to seeing her—sharp-faced, her mouth set and taut. 'No,' she said. 'Who told you that? That isn't true. I never was. Did Jack say that to you? Did your father say that? That's an awful thing to say. I haven't been that bad.'

'He didn't say that,' I said.

'Oh, of course he did,' my mother said. 'He doesn't know just to let things go when they're bad enough.'

'I wanted to know that,' I said. 'I just thought about it. It doesn't matter.'

'No, it doesn't,' my mother said. 'I could've been married eight times. I'm just sorry he said that to you. He's not generous sometimes.'

'He didn't say that,' I said. But I'd said it enough, and I didn't care if she believed me or didn't. It was true that trust was not a big issue between us then. And in any event, I know now that the whole truth of anything is an idea that stops existing finally.

'Is that all you want to know, then?' my mother said. She seemed mad, but not at me, I didn't think. Just at things in general. And I sympathized with her. 'Your life's your own business, Jackie,' she said. 'Sometimes it scares you to death it's so much your own business. You just want to run.'

'I guess so,' I said.

'I'd like a less domestic life, is all.' She looked at me, but I didn't say anything. I didn't see what she meant by that, though I knew there was nothing I could say to change the way her life would be from then on. And I kept quiet.

In a while we walked across Tenth Avenue and ate lunch in the cafeteria. When she paid for the meal I saw that she had my father's silver-dollar money clip in her purse and that there was money in it. And I understood that he had been to see her already that day, and no one cared if I knew it. We were all of us on our own in this.

When we walked out on to the street, it was colder and the wind was blowing. Car exhausts were visible and some drivers had their lights on, though it was only two o'clock in the afternoon. My mother had called a taxi, and we stood and waited for it. I didn't know where she was going, but I wasn't going with her.

'Your father won't let me come back,' she said, standing on the curb. It was just a fact to her, not that she hoped I would talk to him or stand up for her or take her part. But I did wish then that I had never let her go the night before. Things can be fixed by staying. But to go out into the night and not come back hazards life. And everything can get out of hand.

My mother's taxi came. She kissed me and hugged me very hard, then got inside the cab in her powder-blue dress and high heels and her car coat. I smelled her perfume on my cheeks as I stood watching her. 'I used to be afraid of more things than I am now,' she said, looking up at me, and smiled. 'I've got a knot in my stomach, of all things.' And she closed the cab door, waved at me, and rode away.

I walked back toward my school. I thought I could take the bus home if I got there by three. I walked a long way down Tenth Avenue to Second Street, beside the Missouri River, then over to town. I walked by the Great Northern Hotel, where my father had sold ducks and geese and fish of all kinds. There were no passenger trains in the yard and the loading dock looked small. Garbage cans were lined along the edge of it, and the door was closed and locked.

As I walked toward school I thought to myself that my life had suddenly turned, and that I might not know exactly how or which way for possibly a long time. Maybe, in fact, I might never know. It was a thing that happened to you—I knew that—and it had happened to me in this way now. And as I walked on up the cold street that afternoon in Great Falls, the questions I asked myself were these: why wouldn't my father let my mother come back? Why would Woody stand in the cold with me outside my house and risk being killed? Why would he say my mother had been married before, if she hadn't been? And my mother herself—why would she do what she did?

In five years my father had gone off to Ely, Nevada, to ride out the oil strike there, and been killed by accident. And in the years since then I have seen my mother from time to time—in one place or another, with one man or other—and I can say, at least, that we know each other. But I have never known the answer to these questions, have never asked anyone their answers. Though possibly it—the answer—is simple: it is just low-life, some coldness in us all, some helplessness that causes us to misunderstand life when it is pure and plain, makes it seem like a border between two nothings, and makes us no more or less than animals who meet on the road—watchful, unforgiving, and adrift without patience or desire.

TLS/Cheltenham Literature Festival
POETRY COMPETITION 1987
for an unpublished poem of up to fifty lines, in English

JUDGES

GRACE NICHOLS, PETER PORTER,
CHRISTOPHER REID and,

from *The Times Literary Supplement*, Jeremy Treglown
(Editor) and Lindsay Duguid (Commentary Editor)

ABOUT FIFTY SHORTLISTED POEMS PUBLISHED
ANONYMOUSLY IN THE *TLS* FOR A READERS' BALLOT

PRIZES

Readers' choices   £500   £250   £100
Judges' choices   £500   £250   £100
and subsequent publication in the *TLS*

Closing date for entries July 31

For details and entry forms, send a stamped addressed envelope
or International Reply Coupons to: Poetry Competition,
Town Hall, Cheltenham, GL50 1QA, England.

Organized as part of the
Cheltenham Festival of Literature,
October 4–18.

PREVIOUS WINNERS INCLUDE

JOHN FULLER, SEAMUS HEANEY,
DEREK MAHON, EDWIN MORGAN,
RICHARD MURPHY, SYLVIA PLATH,
CRAIG RAINE.

RAYMOND CARVER
MENUDO

Raymond Carver

I can't sleep, but when I'm sure my wife Vicky is asleep, I get up and look through our bedroom window, across the street, at Oliver and Amanda's house. Oliver has been gone for three days, but his wife Amanda is awake. She can't sleep either. It's four in the morning, and there's not a sound outside—no wind, no cars, no moon even—just Oliver and Amanda's place with the lights on, leaves heaped up under the front windows.

A couple of days ago, when I couldn't sit still, I raked our yard—Vicky's and mine. I gathered all the leaves into bags, tied off the tops, and put the bags alongside the curb. I had an urge then to cross the street and rake over there, but I didn't follow through. It's my fault things are the way they are across the street.

I've only slept a few hours since Oliver left. Vicky saw me moping around the house, looking anxious, and decided to put two and two together. She's on her side of the bed now, scrunched on to about ten inches of mattress. She got into bed and tried to position herself so she wouldn't accidentally roll into me while she slept. She hasn't moved since she lay down, sobbed, and then dropped into sleep. She's exhausted. I'm exhausted too.

I've taken nearly all of Vicky's pills, but I still can't sleep. I'm keyed up. But maybe if I keep looking I'll catch a glimpse of Amanda moving around inside her house, or else find her peering from behind a curtain, trying to see what she can see over here.

What if I do see her? So what? What then?

Vicky says I'm crazy. She said worse things too last night. But who could blame her? I told her—I had to—but I didn't tell her it was Amanda. When Amanda's name came up, I insisted it wasn't her. Vicky suspects, but I wouldn't name names. I wouldn't say who, even though she kept pressing and then hit me a few times in the head.

'What's it matter *who*?' I said. 'You've never met the woman,' I lied. 'You don't know her.' That's when she started hitting me.

I feel *wired*. That's what my painter friend Alfredo used to call it when he talked about friends of his coming down off something. *Wired*. I'm wired.

This thing is nuts. I know it is, but I can't stop thinking about Amanda. Things are so bad just now I even find myself thinking about my first wife, Molly. I loved Molly, I thought, more than my own life.

158

I keep picturing Amanda in her pink night-gown, the one I like on her so much, along with her pink slippers. And I feel certain she's in the big leather chair right now, under the brass reading lamp. She's smoking cigarettes, one after the other. There are two ashtrays close at hand, and they're both full. To the left of her chair, next to the lamp, there's an end table stacked with magazines—the usual magazines that nice people read. We're nice people, all of us, to a point. Right this minute, Amanda is, I imagine, paging through a magazine, stopping every so often to look at an illustration or a cartoon.

Two days ago, in the afternoon, Amanda said to me, 'I can't read books any more. Who has the time?' It was the day after Oliver had left, and we were in this little café in the industrial part of the city. 'Who can concentrate any more?' she said, stirring her coffee. 'Who reads? Do you read?' (I shook my head.) 'Somebody must read, I guess. You see all these books around in store windows, and there are those clubs. Somebody's reading,' she said. 'Who? I don't know anybody who reads.'

That's what she said, apropos of nothing—that is, we weren't talking about books, we were talking about our *lives*. Books had nothing to do with it.

'What did Oliver say when you told him?'

Then it struck me that what we were saying—the tense, watchful expressions we wore—belonged to the people on afternoon TV programs that I'd never done more than switch on and then off.

Amanda looked down and shook her head, as if she couldn't bear to remember.

'You didn't admit who it was you were involved with, did you?'

She shook her head again.

'You're sure of that?' I waited until she looked up from her coffee.

'I didn't mention any names, if that's what you mean.'

'Did he say where he was going, or how long he'd be away?' I said, wishing I didn't have to hear myself. This was my neighbor I was talking about. Oliver Porter. A man I'd helped drive out of his home.

'He didn't say where. A hotel. He said I should make my arrangements and be gone—*be gone,* he said. It was like biblical the way he said it—out of his house, out of his *life*, in a week's time. I guess he's coming back then. So we have to decide something real important, real soon, honey. You and I have to make up our minds pretty damn quick.'

It was her turn to look at me now, and I know she was looking for a sign of life-long commitment. 'A week,' I said. I looked at my coffee, which had gotten cold. A lot had happened in a little while, and we were trying to take it in. I don't know what long-term things, if any, we'd thought about those months as we moved from flirtation to love, and then afternoon assignations. In any case, we were in a serious fix now. Very serious. We'd never expected—not in a hundred years—to be hiding out in a café, in the middle of the afternoon, trying to decide matters like this.

I raised my eyes, and Amanda began stirring her coffee. She kept stirring it. I touched her hand, and the spoon dropped out of her fingers. She picked it up and began stirring again. We could have been anybody drinking coffee at a table under fluorescent lights in a run-down café. Anybody, just about. I took Amanda's hand and held it, and it seemed to make a difference.

Vicky's still sleeping on her side when I go downstairs. I plan to heat some milk and drink that. I used to drink whisky when I couldn't sleep, but I gave it up. Now it's strictly hot milk. In the whisky days I'd wake up with this tremendous thirst in the middle of the night. But, back then, I was always looking ahead: I kept a bottle of water in the fridge, for instance. I'd be dehydrated, sweating from head to toe when I woke, but I'd wander out to the kitchen and could count on finding that bottle of cold water in the fridge. I'd drink it, all of it, down the hatch, an entire quart of water. Once in a while I'd use a glass, but not often. Suddenly I'd be drunk all over again and weaving around the kitchen. I can't begin to account for it—sober one minute, drunk the next.

The drinking was part of my destiny—according to Molly, anyway. She put a lot of stock in destiny.

I feel wild from lack of sleep. I'd give anything, just about, to be able to go to sleep, and sleep the sleep of an honest man.

Why do we have to sleep anyway? And why do we tend to sleep less during some crises and more during others? For instance, that time my dad had his stroke. He woke up after a coma—seven days and nights in a hospital bed—and calmly said 'Hello' to the people in his room. Then his eyes picked me out. 'Hello, son,' he said. Five minutes later, he died. Just like that—he died. But, during that whole crisis, I never took my clothes off and didn't go to bed. I may have catnapped in a waiting-room chair from time to time, but I never went to bed and *slept.*

And then a year or so ago I found out Vicky was seeing somebody else. Instead of confronting *her*, I went to bed when I heard about it, and stayed there. I didn't get up for days, a week maybe—I don't know. I mean, I got up to go to the bathroom, or else to the kitchen to make a sandwich. I even went out to the living-room in my pajamas, in the afternoon, and tried to read the papers. But I'd fall asleep sitting up. Then I'd stir, open my eyes and go back to bed and sleep some more. I couldn't get enough sleep.

It passed. We weathered it. Vicky quit her boyfriend, or he quit her, I never found out. I just know she went away from me for a while, and then she came back. But I have the feeling we're not going to weather this business. This thing is different. Oliver has given Amanda that ultimatum.

Still, isn't it possible that Oliver himself is awake at this moment and writing a letter to Amanda, urging reconciliation? Even now he might be scribbling away, trying to persuade her that what she's doing to him and their daughter Beth is foolish, disastrous, and finally a tragic thing for the three of them.

No, that's insane. I know Oliver. He's relentless, unforgiving. He could slam a croquet ball into the next block—and has. He isn't going to write any such letter. He gave her an ultimatum, right?—a diktat—and that's that. A week. Four days now. Or is it three? Oliver may be awake, but if he is, he's sitting in a chair in his hotel room with a glass of iced vodka in his hand, his feet on the bed, TV turned on low. He's dressed, except for his shoes. He's not wearing shoes—that's the only concession he makes. That and the fact he's loosened his tie.

Oliver is relentless.

I heat the milk, spoon the membrane from the surface and pour it up. Then I turn off the kitchen light and take the cup into the living-room and sit on the sofa, where I can look across the street at the lighted windows. But I can hardly sit still. I keep fidgeting, crossing one leg and then the other. I feel like I could throw off sparks, or break a window—maybe rearrange all the furniture.

The things that go through your mind when you can't sleep! Earlier, thinking about Molly, for a moment I couldn't even remember what she *looked* like, for Christ's sake, yet we were together for years, more or less continuously, since we were kids. Molly, who said she'd love me forever. The only thing left was the memory of her sitting and weeping at the kitchen table, her shoulders bent forward, and her hands covering her face. *Forever,* she said. But it hadn't worked out that way. Finally, she said, it didn't matter, it was of no real concern to her, if she and I lived together the rest of our lives or not. Our love existed on a 'higher plane'. That's what she said to Vicky over the phone that time, after Vicky and I had set up house-keeping together. Molly called, got hold of Vicky, and said, 'You have your relationship with him, but I'll always have mine. His destiny and mine are linked.'

My first wife, Molly, she talked like that. 'Our destinies are linked'. She didn't talk like that in the beginning. It was only later, after so much had happened, that she started using words like 'cosmic' and 'empowerment' and so forth. But our destinies are *not* linked—not now, anyway, if they ever were. I don't even know where she is now, not for certain.

I think I could put my finger on the exact time, the real turning point, when it came undone for Molly. It was after I started seeing Vicky, and Molly found out. They called me up one day from the high school where Molly taught and said, 'Please. Your wife is doing handsprings in front of the school. You'd better get down here.' It was after I took her home that I began hearing about 'higher power' and 'going with the flow'—stuff of that sort. Our destiny had been 'revised'. And if I'd been hesitating before, well, I left her then as fast as I could—this woman I'd known all my life, the one who'd been my best friend for years, my intimate, my confidante. I bailed out on her. For one thing, I was scared. *Scared.*

This girl I'd started out with in life, this sweet thing, this gentle soul, she wound up going to fortune-tellers, palm readers, *crystal ball gazers,* looking for answers, trying to figure out what she should do with her life. She quit her job, drew out her teacher's retirement

162

money, and thereafter never made a decision without consulting the *I Ching*. She began wearing strange clothes—clothes with permanent wrinkles and a lot of burgundy and orange. She even got involved with a group that sat around, I'm not kidding, trying to levitate.

When Molly and I were growing up together, she was a part of me and, sure, I was a part of her, too. We loved each other. It *was* our destiny. I believed in it then myself. But now I don't know what to believe in. I'm not complaining, simply stating a fact. I'm down to nothing. And I have to go on like this. No destiny. Just the next thing meaning whatever you think it does. Compulsion and error, just like everybody else.

Amanda? I'd like to believe in her, bless her heart. But she was looking for somebody when she met me. That's the way with people when they get restless: they start up something, knowing that's going to change things for good.

I'd like to go out in the front yard and shout something. 'None of this is worth it!' That's what I'd like people to hear.

'Destiny,' Molly said. For all I know she's still talking about it.

All the lights are off over there now, except for that light in the kitchen. I could try calling Amanda on the phone. I could do that and see how far it gets me! What if Vicky heard me dialing or talking on the phone and came downstairs? What if she lifted the receiver upstairs and listened? Besides, there's always the chance Beth might pick up the phone. I don't want to talk to any kids this morning. I don't want to talk to anybody. Actually, I'd talk to Molly, if I could, but I can't any longer—she's somebody else now. She isn't *Molly* any more. But—what can I say?—I'm somebody else, too.

I wish I could be like everybody else in this neighborhood—your basic, normal, unaccomplished person—and go up to my bedroom, and lie down, and sleep. It's going to be a big day today, and I'd like to be ready for it. I wish I could sleep and wake up and find everything in my life different. Not necessarily just the big things, like this thing with Amanda or the past with Molly. But things clearly within my power.

Take the situation with my mother: I used to send money every month. But then I started sending her the same amount in twice-yearly sums. I gave her money on her birthday, and I gave her money at Christmas. I thought: I won't have to worry about forgetting her birthday, and I won't have to worry about sending her a Christmas present. I won't have to worry, period. It went like clockwork for a long time.

Then last year she asked me—it was in between money-times, it was in March, or maybe April—for a radio. A radio, she said, would make a difference to her.

What she wanted was a little clock radio. She could put it in her kitchen and have it out there to listen to while she was fixing something to eat in the evening. And she'd have the clock to look at too, so she'd know when something was supposed to come out of the oven, or how long it was until one of her programs started.

A little clock radio.

She hinted around at first. She said, 'I'd sure like to have a radio. But I can't afford one. I guess I'll have to wait for my birthday. That little radio I had, it fell and broke. I miss a radio.' *I miss a radio.* That's what she said when we talked on the phone, or else she'd bring it up when she'd write.

Finally—what'd I say? I said to her over the phone that I couldn't afford any radios. I said it in a letter too, so she'd be sure and understand. *I can't afford any radios,* is what I wrote. I can't do any more, I said, than I'm doing. Those were my very words.

But it wasn't true! I could have done more. I just said I couldn't. I could have afforded to buy a radio for her. What would it have cost me? Thirty-five dollars? Forty dollars or less, including tax. I could have sent her a radio through the mail. I could have had somebody in the store do it, if I didn't want to go to the trouble myself. Or else I could have sent her a forty-dollar check along with a note saying, *This money is for your radio, mother.*

I could have handled it in any case. Forty dollars—are you kidding? But I didn't. I wouldn't part with it. It seemed there was a *principle* involved. That's what I told myself anyway—there's a principle involved here.

Ha.

Then what happened? She died. She *died.* She was walking home from the grocery store, back to her apartment, carrying her sack of groceries, and she fell into somebody's bushes and died.

I took a flight out there to make the arrangements. She was still at the coroner's, and they had her purse and her groceries behind the desk in the office. I didn't bother to look in the purse they handed me. But what she had from the grocery store was a jar of Metamucil, two grapefruits, a carton of cottage cheese, a quart of buttermilk, some potatoes and onions and a package of ground meat that was beginning to change color.

Boy! I cried when I saw those things. I couldn't stop. I didn't think I'd ever quit crying. The woman who worked at the desk was embarrassed and brought me a glass of water. They gave me a bag for my mother's groceries and another bag for her personal effects—her purse and her dentures. Later, I put the dentures in my coat pocket and drove them down in a rental car and gave them to somebody at the funeral home.

The light in Amanda's kitchen is still on. It's a bright light that spills out on to all those leaves. Maybe she's like I am, and she's scared. Maybe she left that light burning as a night-light. Or maybe she's still awake and is at the kitchen table, under the light, writing me a letter. Amanda is writing me a letter, and somehow she'll get it into my hands later on when the real day starts.

Come to think of it, I've never had a letter from her since we've known each other. All the time we've been involved—six months, eight months—and I've never once seen a scrap of her handwriting. I don't even know if she's *literate* that way.

I think she is. Sure, she is. She talks about books, doesn't she? It doesn't matter of course. Well, a little, I suppose. I love her in any case, right?

But I've never written anything to her, either. We always talked on the phone or else face-to-face.

Molly, she was the letter writer. She used to write me even after we weren't living together. Vicky would bring her letters in from the box and leave them on the kitchen table without a word. Finally the letters dwindled away, became more and more infrequent and bizarre. When she did write, the letters gave me a chill. They were full of talk about 'auras' and 'signs'. Occasionally she reported a voice that was telling her something she ought to do or some place she should go. And once she told me that no matter what happened, we were still 'on the same frequency'. She always knew exactly what I felt, she said. She 'beamed in on me,' she said, from time to time. Reading those letters of hers, the hair on the back of my neck would tingle. She also had a new word for destiny: *Karma.* 'I'm following out my karma,' she wrote. 'Your karma has taken a bad turn.'

I'd like to go to sleep, but what's the point? People will be getting up soon. Vicky's alarm will go off before much longer. I wish I could go upstairs and get back in bed with my wife, tell her I'm sorry, there's been a mistake, let's forget all this—then go to sleep and wake up with her in my arms. But I've forfeited that right. I'm outside all that now, and I can't get back inside! But say I did that. Say I went upstairs and slid into bed with Vicky as I'd like to do. She might wake up and say, *You bastard. Don't you dare touch me, son of a bitch.*

What's she talking about, anyway? I wouldn't touch her. Not in that way, I wouldn't.

After I left Molly, after I'd pulled out on her, about two months after, then Molly really did it. She had her real collapse then, the one that'd been coming on. Her sister saw to it that she got the care she needed. What am I saying? *They put her away.* They had to, they said. They put my wife away. By then I was living with Vicky, and trying not to drink whisky. I couldn't do anything for Molly. I mean, she was there, I was here, and I couldn't have gotten her out of that place if I'd wanted to. But the fact is, I didn't want to. She was in there, they said, because she *needed* to be in there. Nobody said anything about destiny. Things had gone beyond that.

And I didn't even go visit her—not once! At the time, I didn't think I could stand seeing her in there. But, Christ, what was I? A fair-weather friend? We'd been through plenty. But what on earth would I have said to her? *I'm sorry about all this, honey.* I could have said that, I guess. I intended to write, but I didn't. Not a word. Anyway, when you get right down to it, what could I have said in a letter? *How are they treating you, baby? I'm sorry you're where you are, but don't give up. Remember all the good times? Remember when we were happy together? Hey, I'm sorry they've done this to you. I'm sorry it turned out this way. I'm sorry everything is just garbage now.* I'm sorry, Molly.

I didn't write. I think I was trying to forget about her, to pretend she didn't exist. Molly who?

I left my wife and took somebody else's: Vicky. Now I think maybe I've lost Vicky, too. But Vicky won't be going away to any summer camp for the mentally disabled. She's a hard case. She left her former husband, Joe Kraft, and didn't bat an eye; I don't think she ever lost a night's sleep over it.

Vicky Kraft-Hughes. Amanda Porter. This is where my destiny has brought me? To this street in this neighborhood, messing up the lives of these women?

Amanda's kitchen light went off when I wasn't looking. The room that was there is gone now, like the others. Only the porch light is still burning. Amanda must have forgotten it, I guess. Hey, Amanda.

Once, when Molly was away in that place and I wasn't in my right mind—let's face it, I was crazy too—one night I was at my friend Alfredo's house, a bunch of us drinking and listening to records. I didn't care any longer what happened to me. Everything, I thought, that could happen had happened. I felt unbalanced. I felt lost. Anyway there I was at Alfredo's. His paintings of tropical birds and animals hung on every wall in his house, and there were paintings standing around in the rooms, leaning against things—table-legs, say, or his brick-and-board bookcase, as well as being stacked on his back porch. The kitchen served as his studio, and I was sitting at the kitchen table with a drink in front of me. An easel stood off to one side in front of the window that overlooked the alley, and there were crumpled tubes of paint, a palette and some brushes lying at one end of the table. Alfredo was making himself a drink at the counter a few feet away. I loved the shabby economy of that little room. The stereo music that came from the living room was turned up, filling the house with so much sound the kitchen windows rattled in their frames. Suddenly I began to shake. First my hands began to shake, and then my arms and shoulders, too. My teeth started to chatter. I couldn't hold the glass.

'What's going on, man?' Alfredo said, when he turned and saw the state I was in. 'Hey, man, what is it? What's going on with you?'

I couldn't tell him. What could I say? I thought I was having some kind of an attack. I managed to raise my shoulders and let them drop.

Then Alfredo came over, took a chair and sat down beside me at the kitchen table. He put his big painter's hand on my shoulder. I went on shaking. He could feel me shaking.

'What's wrong with you, man? I'm real sorry about everything, man. I know it's real hard right now.' Then he said he was going to fix *menudo* for me. He said it would be good for what ailed me. 'Help your nerves, man,' he said. 'Calm you right down.' He had all the ingredients for *menudo,* he said, and he'd been wanting to make some anyway.

'You listen to me. Listen to what I say, man. I'm your family now, man,' Alfredo said.

It was two in the morning, we were drunk, there were these other drunk people in the house and the stereo was going full blast. But Alfredo went to his fridge and opened it and took some stuff out. He closed the fridge door and looked in his freezer compartment. He found something in a package. Then he looked around in his cupboards. He took a big pan from the cabinet under the sink, and he was ready.

Tripe. He started with tripe and about a gallon of water. Then he chopped onions and added them to the water, which had started to boil. He put *chorizo* sausage in the pot. After that, he dropped peppercorns into the boiling water and sprinkled in some chili powder. Then came the olive oil. He opened a big can of tomato sauce and poured that in. He added cloves of garlic, some slices of white bread, salt and lemon juice. He opened another can—it was hominy—and poured that in the pot, too. He put it all in, and then he turned the heat down and put a lid on the pot.

I watched him. I sat there shaking while Alfredo stood at the stove making *menudo,* talking—I didn't have any idea what he was saying—and, from time to time, he'd shake his head, or else start whistling to himself. Now and then people drifted into the kitchen for beer. But all the while Alfredo went on very seriously looking after his *menudo.* He could have been home, in Morelia, making *menudo* for his family on New Year's day.

People hung around in the kitchen for a while, joking, but Alfredo didn't joke back when they kidded him about cooking *menudo* in the middle of the night. Pretty soon they left us alone. Finally, while the *menudo* was cooking and Alfredo stood at the stove with a spoon in his hand, watching me, I got up slowly from the table. I walked out of the kitchen into the bathroom, and then opened another door off the bathroom to the spare room—where I lay down on the bed and fell asleep. When I woke it was mid-afternoon. The *menudo* was gone. The pot was in the sink, soaking. Those other people must have eaten it! They must have eaten it and grown calm. Everyone was gone, and the house was quiet. The house where the *menudo* had been cooking.

I never saw Alfredo more than once or twice afterwards. After that night, our lives took us in separate directions. And those other people who were there—who knows where they went? I'll probably die without ever tasting *menudo*. But who can say?

Is this what it all comes down to then? A middle-aged man involved with his neighbor's wife, linked to an angry ultimatum? What kind of destiny is that? A week, Oliver said. Three or four days now.

A car passes outside with its lights on. The sky is turning grey, and I hear some birds starting up. I decide I can't wait any longer. I can't just sit here, doing nothing—that's all there is to it. I can't keep waiting. I've waited and waited and where's it gotten me? Vicky's alarm will go off soon, Beth will get up and dress for school, Amanda will wake up, too. The entire neighborhood.

On the back porch I find some old jeans and a sweat-shirt, and I change out of my pajamas. Then I put on my white canvas shoes—'wino' shoes Alfredo would have called them. Alfredo, where are you?

I go outside to the garage, and find the rake and some lawn bags. By the time I get around to the front of the house with the rake, ready to begin, I feel I don't have a choice in the matter any longer. It's light out—light enough at any rate for what I have to do. And then, without thinking about it any more, I start to rake. I rake our yard, every inch of it. It's important it be done right, too. I set the rake right down into the turf and pull hard. It must feel to the grass like it does to us whenever someone gives our hair a hard jerk. Now and then a car passes in the street and slows, but I don't look up from my work. I know what the people in the cars must be thinking, but they're dead wrong—they don't know the half of it. How could they? I'm happy, raking.

I finish our yard and put the bag out next to the curb. Then I begin next door on the Baxters' yard. In a few minutes Mrs Baxter comes out on her porch, wearing her bathrobe. I don't acknowledge her. I'm not embarrassed, and I don't want to appear unfriendly. I just want to keep on with what I'm doing.

She doesn't say anything for a while, and then she says, 'Good morning, Mr Hughes. How are you this morning?'

I stop what I'm doing and run my arm across my forehead. 'I'll be through in a little while,' I say. 'I hope you don't mind.'

'We don't mind,' Mrs Baxter says. 'Go right ahead, I guess.' I see Mr Baxter standing in the doorway behind her. He's already dressed for work in his slacks and sports coat and tie. But he doesn't venture on to the porch. Then Mrs Baxter turns and looks at Mr Baxter, who shrugs.

It's OK, I've finished here anyway. There are other yards, more important yards for that matter. I kneel, and, taking a grip low down on the rake handle, I pull the last of the leaves into my bag and tie off the top. Then, I can't help it, I just stay there, kneeling on the grass with the rake in my hand. When I look up, I see the Baxters come down the porch steps together and move slowly toward me through the wet, sweet-smelling grass. They stop a few feet away and look at me closely.

'There now,' I hear Mrs Baxter say. She's still in her robe and slippers. It's nippy out; she holds her robe at the throat. 'You did a real fine job for us, yes, you did.'

I don't say anything. I don't even say, 'You're welcome.'

They stand in front of me a while longer, and none of us says anything more. It's as if we've come to an agreement on something. In a minute, they turn around and go back to their house. High over my head, in the branches of the old maple—the place where these leaves come from—birds call out to each other. At least I think they're calling to each other.

Suddenly a car door slams. Mr Baxter is in his car in the drive with the window rolled down. Mrs Baxter says something to him from the front porch which causes Mr Baxter to nod slowly and turn his head in my direction. He sees me kneeling there with the rake, and a look crosses his face. He frowns. In his better moments, Mr Baxter is a decent, ordinary guy—a guy you wouldn't mistake for anyone special. But he *is* special. In my book, he is. For one thing he has a full night's sleep behind him, and he's just embraced his wife before leaving for work. But even before he goes, he's already expected home a set number of hours later. True, in the grander scheme of things, his return will be an event of small moment—but an event nonetheless.

Baxter starts his car and races the engine for a minute. Then he backs effortlessly out of the drive, brakes and changes gears. As he passes on the street, he slows and looks briefly in my direction. He lifts his hand off the steering-wheel. It could be a salute or a sign of dismissal. It's a sign, in any case. And then he looks away toward the city. I get up and raise my hand, too—not a wave, exactly, but close to it. Some other cars drive past. One of the drivers must think he knows me because he gives his horn a friendly little tap. I look both ways and then cross the street.

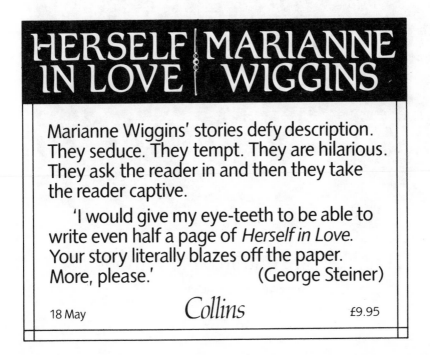

Thursdays are unthinkable without it

From your newsagent. 80p

PATRICK SÜSKIND
A BATTLE

E arly one August evening, when most people had already left the park, two men sat confronting one another across a chess-board. It was in the pavilion on the north-west side of the Jardin du Luxembourg. Although the aperitif hour was drawing near, their game was being followed with such close attention by a good dozen spectators that no one dreamt of leaving the scene until the battle had been decided one way or another.

The interest of the small crowd was concentrated on the challenger. He was a youngish man with black hair, pale in the face and with blasé, dark eyes. He uttered not a word; his expression never changed; only from time to time he rolled an unlit cigarette between his fingers. He was the very personification of nonchalance.

No one knew him; no one had ever seen him play before. And yet from the moment he first seated himself at the chess-board, pale, blasé and silent, and put his pieces in position, there emanated from him so strong an aura that everyone was overcome by the certainty that they were in the presence of a quite extraordinary personality of great and masterly talent. Perhaps it was just his attractive and yet unapproachable appearance, his elegant dress and his handsome physique. Or perhaps it was the calmness and self-assurance of his gestures, or the aura of strangeness and peculiarity that surrounded him—whatever it was, before the first pawn had been moved the onlookers were convinced that this man was a chess-player of the very first order and that he would achieve the miracle secretly desired by them all of beating the local chess star.

This character, a somewhat ugly little fellow of about seventy, was in every respect the exact opposite of his youthful opponent. He wore the blue trousers and woollen jacket flecked with food stains that were the traditional garb of the French pensioner. His shaky hands were speckled with the brown splotches of old age; his hair was sparse, his nose ruby-red, and purple veins marked his face. He possessed no aura whatsoever and he was in need of a shave. He puffed nervously at the butt-end of his cigarette, shifted about restlessly in his folding chair and apprehensively shook his head from side to side non-stop. The bystanders knew him very well. They had all played against him and lost, for, while he was anything but an inspired player, he had the exasperating knack of wearing down his opponents and enraging them by never making a mistake. You could never count on his obliging you with even the smallest lapse of attention. To beat him you actually had to play better than he did. And that, it was presumed, was exactly what was going to happen today. A new master had arrived to knock the star out of the sky. A new master had come to humiliate him, to butcher him move by move, to trample him in the dust and make him taste at last the bitterness of losing. His fate would avenge many an individual defeat.

'Careful, Jean,' they all shouted during the opening moves, 'you're for it this time! You won't beat this one, Jean! You're no match for him! This is your Waterloo, Jean! Look out! You're going to meet your Waterloo today!'

'*Eh bien, eh bien . . .*' responded the old man, shaking his head as with hesitant hand he moved his first white pawn forward.

As soon as the stranger, who had drawn black, began to play, silence reigned in the crowd. No one would have dared speak to him. Shyly attentive, they watched him as he sat silent before the chess-board, never lifting his supercilious gaze from the pieces. They watched as he rolled his unlit cigarette between his fingers and played with quick, assured moves whenever it came to his turn.

The first moves in the game followed the usual pattern. Then there were two exchanges of pawns, the second of which ended with Black keeping a doubled pawn back on a line—a move not usually regarded as advantageous. But the stranger must have accepted the doubled pawn quite deliberately so as to make a way clear for his queen. Obviously he had the same end in view when this led to the sacrifice of a second pawn in a kind of belated gambit which White accepted only with hesitation, indeed almost nervously. The spectators exchanged meaningful glances, nodded apprehensively, and turned expectantly to the stranger.

Momentarily he stops rolling his cigarette, raises his hand, moves it forward and—yes, he moves his queen! He moves her far out, right into his opponent's lines, and by so doing he splits the battlefield in two. A murmur of approval runs through the ranks. What a move! What style! They had suspected that he would move the queen—but to move her so far! Not one of the bystanders—and they were all connoisseurs of the game—not one of them would have dared make such a move. But after all, that's what really makes a true master. A true master plays with originality, daring, determination. To put it simply, a true master plays differently from your average player. And for that reason an average player does not need to understand each individual move made by the master. In fact the spectators did not at this moment quite understand what the queen was meant to be doing in her present position. She was not a threat to anything vital and she was attacking only figures which were well covered. But the purpose and deeper meaning of this move would soon become clear; the master had his own plan—this was certain: you could see it in his impassive expression and his calm and steady hand. After this unconventional move of the queen, it was clear to even the least perceptive spectator that at this chessboard was sitting a genius whose like they would be lucky to see again. For Jean, the old star, they felt only a malicious sympathy. What did he have to offer against such splendid verve? They knew all about him, anyway! He would probably try to extricate himself from the situation with some pettifogging, small-scale moves, by carefully arranged small-scale tactics. And then, after prolonged delay and thought, Jean, instead of making a correspondingly large-scale response to the large-scale move of the queen, pushes on to H4 a little pawn who had been deprived of his cover by the advance of the black queen.

The repeated loss of a pawn means nothing to the young man. He does not reflect for a moment before his queen moves to the right, striking into his opponent's order of battle, and lands on a square from which she at once attacks two pieces—a knight and a rook—and now she pushes forward dangerously near to the king's rank. Admiration widens the eyes of the spectators. What a devil of a fellow Black is! What courage! 'He's a professional,' they whisper, 'a grand master, a veritable Sarasate of chess.' And they all wait impatiently for Jean's counter-move, impatient more than anything to see what Black's next trick will be.

And Jean hesitates. Thinks, torments himself, shifts around in his chair, jerks his head. It is an ordeal to watch him—move, Jean, move, and don't hold up the inevitable progress of events!

And Jean moves. At last. With trembling hand, he places the knight on a square where he is not merely secure from the queen but actually attacks her and covers the rook. Well, well! Not a bad move. But then what else could he have done in this embattled situation? All of us standing here would have done the same. 'But it won't help him,' the whisper goes round, 'Black saw that move coming.'

For already Black's hand is hovering like a hawk above the battlefield. He seizes his queen and moves her—no, he's not moving her back, anxiously, as we would have done, he's moving her just one square to the right! Incredible! People are speechless with admiration. No one really understands the purpose of the move, for the queen is now standing at the edge of the board, threatening nothing, covering nothing. Her position is completely meaningless, and yet she looks so good, maddeningly good, no queen has ever looked so good, solitary and proud in the middle of the opponent's ranks. Jean, too, cannot understand what his sinister opponent is aiming at with this move; he cannot see what trap he is being enticed into; and after much thought and with an uneasy conscience he decides to take another unprotected pawn. He is now, the spectators calculate, three pawns up on Black. But what does that matter? What's the point of numerical superiority when you're faced with an opponent who is obviously thinking strategically, who isn't concerned with numbers but with position, development, super-sudden lightning-fast strokes? Beware, Jean! You'll still be chasing pawns when the next move traps your king.

Now it's Black's turn. The stranger sits there quietly rolling his cigarette between his fingers. This time he thinks for a bit longer than usual, two minutes perhaps. Total silence reigns. Not one of the bystanders dares whisper. Scarcely one of them is still looking at the chess-board. All eyes are fixed on the young man, on his hands and his pale face. Is there not a tiny smile of triumph perceptible in the corners of his mouth? Can one not perceive a very slight flaring of the nostrils such as always precedes great decisions? What will his next move be? What devastating blow is the master about to deal?

The cigarette-rolling stops; the stranger leans forward; a dozen pairs of eyes follow his hand. What will his next move be, what will it be? He takes the pawn from G7—who'd have thought of that? The pawn from G7! The pawn from G7 on to . . . G6!

There follows a moment of complete silence. For a moment even old Jean himself stops trembling and shifting around. Out-and-out rejoicing almost breaks forth in the crowd. They breathe once again; they dig their neighbours in the ribs. Did you see that? What a devil of a fellow he is! *Ça alors!* He lets his queen just be a queen, and simply moves a pawn to G6. Naturally that leaves G7 free for his bishop, that's clear enough, and in the next move but one he'll call check, and then? And then? What then? By then in any case Jean will be finished; that much is quite clear. Just look at him, how strenuously he's thinking.

And yes, Jean is thinking. He thinks for an eternity. Damn the man! Now and again his hand stretches forward and then draws back again. Come on! Move, Jean, for heaven's sake, move! We want to see the master.

Then at last, after five long minutes, as people are beginning to shuffle their feet, Jean dares to make his move. He attacks the queen. With a pawn he attacks the black queen. He tries to escape his fate by means of this delaying tactic. How childish! Black need only withdraw his queen two squares and everything will be back to where it was. It's all over for you, Jean! You've run out of ideas. It's all over . . . Black moves towards—you see, Jean, he doesn't have to spend time thinking. Now it's just a case of blow upon blow. Black moves towards his qu– . . . and for a moment every heart stands still, for Black, contrary to all apparent reason, does not move his queen to save her from that absurd attack by the pawn, no: Black carries out his original plan and puts his bishop on G7.

Baffled, they stare at him. They take half a step backwards, as if awestruck, and look at him uncomprehendingly. He is sacrificing his queen and putting the bishop on G7! And he does it with absolute deliberation and an imperturbable demeanour, sitting there calm and supercilious, pale, blasé and handsome. Their eyes grow a little moist and their hearts warm to him. He's playing as they would love to play and never dare to. They cannot understand why he's playing as he does and they really don't care. Perhaps they even suspect that he is playing suicidally, gambling everything. But all the same, they would love to be able to play like him—splendidly, certain of victory, Napoleonically.

Unlike Jean, whose timid, hesitant game they are able to understand since they play no differently, only less well. Jean's game is sensible. It is orderly, played by the rules, and enervatingly tedious. Black on the other hand creates a miracle with his every move. He offers his own queen as a sacrifice just to put his bishop on G7. When had anyone ever seen anything like it? They are deeply moved by his act. From now on Black can play as he likes, they'll follow him move for move till the very end, whether it be glorious or bitter. For now he is their hero, and they love him.

And even Jean, the opponent, the sober player, preparing with quivering hand to move his pawn into the onslaught on the queen, hesitates as though shy in the face of the glorious hero, and speaks, excusing himself softly as though asking not to be forced into this deed: 'If you give her to me, monsieur . . . I must, yes, I must.' He casts a beseeching look at his opponent. The latter sits there with a face of stone and does not reply. The old man, bruised and shattered, makes his strike.

A moment later the black bishop calls check. Check to the white king! The spectators' emotion turns to enthusiasm. The loss of the queen is already forgotten. To a man they stand behind the young challenger and his bishop. Check to the king! That's how they would have played! Exactly the same, no other way! Check! Cool analysis of the situation would show them straight away that White still has a wealth of possible moves for his own defence, but that thought interests no one. They don't want sober analysis; they only want to see brilliant deeds, attacks of genius and powerful strokes which will knock the opposition out. The game—this particular game—has now only one meaning and interest for them: they want to see the young stranger win and the old star knocked out of the sky.

Jean hesitates and reflects. He knows that no one would put a penny on him any more. But he doesn't know why. He doesn't understand that the others—all of them experienced chess players—do not see the strength and security of his position. He is the stronger by a queen and three pawns. How can they think that he will lose? He cannot lose! Or can he? Is he deceiving himself? Is his concentration failing? Do the others see more than he does? He grows uncertain. Perhaps the fatal trap is already set and at the next move he will tumble into it. Where is the trap? He must avoid it. He must wriggle his way out of it. In any case, he must sell his skin as dearly as he can . . .

And now, clinging to the rules of the game even more cautiously, with ever-increasing care and hesitation, Jean weighs up and considers the situation, and decides to remove a knight and insert him between the queen and the bishop so that the black bishop now stands within the range of the white queen.

Black's response comes without delay. He does not break off the now-impeded attack, but brings up reinforcements: his knight covers the threatened bishop. The audience rejoices. Now the battle proceeds blow upon blow. White calls upon a bishop for help, Black sends a rook to the front, White brings up his second knight, Black his second rook. Both sides mass their forces round the square where the black bishop stands. The square on which the bishop would have had nothing more to do has become the centre of the battle. Why, nobody knows—it is just that Black wants it like this. Every move of Black's, as he escalates the game and brings on a new figure, is greeted with long, open applause. On the other hand White's every move, in his enforced self-defence, is received with undisguised grumbling. Then Black, once again defying all the rules of the game, embarks upon a series of murderous exchanges. The rule-book lays down that such ruthless carnage can scarcely benefit a player at a numerical disadvantage. Black begins it all the same and the audience cheers him on. Never before have they witnessed such a slaughter. Recklessly Black mows down everything within range; he pays no heed to his own losses, pawns fall in rows, knights, rooks and bishops likewise, to the frenetic applause of this expert audience . . . After seven or eight moves and counter-moves the chess-board is laid waste. For Black the result of the battle is grim: he has only three pieces left—the king, one rook and a single pawn. White on the other hand has saved from the Armageddon not just his king and rook but also his queen and four pawns. Any reasonable observer could have no doubt what the end must be and who will win. And in truth there is not doubt in anyone. For now, as before—it is written on the faces still lit up with the dazzle of battle—the spectators hold fast to the conviction that, even if faced with disaster, their man will win. They would still put any money on him and angrily toss aside the merest suggestion of his possible defeat.

The young man too seems completely unmoved by the catastrophic situation. It is his move. He calmly takes his rook and advances him one square further to the right. Silence again reigns in the circle of watchers. Indeed tears come to the eyes of these grown-up men in their devotion to a player's genius. It is like the end of the Battle of Waterloo when the Emperor sends his bodyguard into the conflict long since lost. With his last important piece Black once again goes onto the attack.

White now has his king placed in the last row on G1, with three pawns in the second row in front of him, so that the king is hemmed in and would be in mortal peril were Black to succeed in his apparent plan of moving into the first row with his rook.

This particular way of declaring checkmate on one's opponent is the best known and most commonplace move in the game of chess; one might even say it is the most childish of all moves, since its success depends solely on the opponent failing to recognize the obvious danger and taking no steps to counter it. The most effective of these steps is to open up the line of pawns and so devise an escape route for the king. To try and checkmate an experienced player or even a reasonably advanced beginner with this sleight of hand verges on frivolity. Nevertheless, the delighted audience marvel at their hero's move as though they were witnessing it for the very first time. They shake their heads in boundless admiration. It's true that they know White will have to make a fundamental error to let Black win. But they still believe in Black's victory. They believe wholeheartedly that Jean, the local star, who has beaten all of them, who never permits himself to slip up, will slip up now. And more: they hope he will slip up. They yearn for it to happen. In their hearts they pray fervently that Jean will make this slip . . .

And Jean considers. Nods his head reflectively back and forth, weighs up, as is his wont, the possibilities one against another, hesitates once more—and then his trembling hand, speckled with the brown splotches of old age, clasps the pawn on G2 and sets it down on G3.

The clock on St Sulpice strikes eight. All the other chess players in the Jardin du Luxembourg have long since gone home to their aperitifs. The man who hires out the boards has long since shut up his shop. The group of spectators standing around the two opponents in the centre of the pavilion are the only people left. With wide cow-like stares they contemplate the chess-board, where one small white pawn has settled the fate of the black king. And they still do not want to believe it. They avert their cow-like stares from the depressing terrain of the battlefield and turn them upon the general himself, sitting pale, blasé, handsome and motionless in his folding chair. 'You haven't lost,' their stares are saying, 'you're going to bring about a miracle now. You've foreseen this situation from the very outset, you've brought it about. Now you're going to annihilate your opponent. How you'll do it we don't know—we're just simple players. But you, you miracle-worker, you can do it, you will do it. Don't let us down! We believe in you. Work the miracle, miracle-man, work the miracle and win!'

The young man sat there in silence. Then he rolled his cigarette between thumb and tips of forefinger and middle finger, and put it to his mouth. He lit it, pulled on it, puffed out the smoke over the chess-board, swept his hand through the smoke, let it hover for a moment over the black king and then knocked him over.

To knock a king down as a sign of one's own defeat is a deeply vulgar and ill-tempered gesture. It is as though one is destroying the whole game retrospectively. And it makes a hideous sound when the overturned king hits the board. It strikes into the heart of every chess player.

After the young man had knocked the king over so contemptuously he rose, disdained to glance at either his opponent or his audience, uttered no word of farewell and walked away.

The spectators stood there disconcerted and abashed. They looked at the chess-board in helpless embarrassment. After a moment one or another of them cleared his throat, shuffled his feet and took out a cigarette. What time is it? Quarter past eight already! Heavens, is it as late as that? *Au revoir!* Goodbye, Jean . . . ! And whispering some apologies, they quickly disappeared.

The local star alone remained. He stood the king upright again and began to collect the pieces together into a small box, first the ones which had been taken and then those still standing on the board. As he did this all the individual moves and positions went through his mind, as they always did when a game was over. He had not made a single false move—naturally he hadn't. And yet it seemed to him that he'd never played so badly in all his life. He should have been able to checkmate his opponent in the very opening phase. Anyone capable of that wretched queen's gambit had to be an ignoramus at the game. Usually Jean dismissed such amateurs, mercifully or unmercifully according to his mood, but always swiftly and without misgiving. This time quite clearly his feel for his opponent's true weakness had let him down. Or had he simply grown cowardly? Had he not had sufficient confidence to make short work of this arrogant charlatan in the way he deserved?

No, it was worse than that. He had not wanted to believe that his opponent was so wretchedly bad. And even worse than that: almost to the end of the game he had wanted to believe that he, Jean, was not a match for his opponent. The self-confidence brilliance and youthful aura of the young stranger had made him feel his opponent was invincible. That was why he himself played with such exaggerated caution. And even that was not enough: if he was to be really honest with himself he had to admit that he had admired the stranger, just as the others had done—yes, he had wanted the stranger to win and bring about his, Jean's, downfall in the most impressive and inspired way possible, a downfall he had tired of waiting for over the years, and which would at last have released him from the burden of being the greatest and of always having to beat the others, so that the odious crowd of spectators, envious lot that they were, would finally have been satisfied and he would have had peace at last . . .

But there he was: he had won again. And to him the victory was the most distasteful of all his career, for in his attempt to avoid it he had, throughout the whole game, been forced to disavow and debase himself and lay down his arms before the most miserable, blundering player in the world.

Jean, the local star, was not a man given to great moral perceptions. But this much was clear to him as he shuffled off home with his chess-board under his arm and the box of pieces in his hand:

that he had in truth suffered a defeat today, a defeat which was all the more dreadful and final because there was no way of avenging it and no way of getting even with it through a brilliant victory in the future. And so he decided—he who had never been a man of great decisions either—to call it a day with chess, once and for all.

From now on he would play boules like all the other pensioners: a harmless and sociable game, of more modest moral pretensions.

ISABEL ALLENDE
THE JUDGE'S WIFE

Nicolas Vidal always knew he would lose his head over a woman. So it was foretold on the day of his birth, and later confirmed by the Turkish woman in the corner store the one time he allowed her to read his fortune in the coffee grounds. Little did he imagine though that it would be on account of Casilda, Judge Hidalgo's wife. It was on her wedding day that he first glimpsed her. He was not impressed, preferring his women dark-haired and brazen. This ethereal slip of a girl in her wedding gown, eyes filled with wonder, and fingers obviously unskilled in the art of rousing a man to pleasure, seemed to him almost ugly. Mindful of his destiny, he had always been wary of any emotional contact with women, hardening his heart and restricting himself to the briefest of encounters whenever the demands of manhood needed satisfying. Casilda however appeared so insubstantial, so distant, that he cast aside all precaution and, when the fateful moment arrived, forgot the prediction that usually weighed in all his decisions. From the roof of the bank, where he was crouching with two of his men, Nicolas Vidal peered down at this young lady from the capital. She had a dozen equally pale and dainty relatives with her, who spent the whole of the ceremony fanning themselves with an air of utter bewilderment, then departed straight away, never to return. Along with everyone else in the town, Vidal was convinced the young bride would not withstand the climate, and that within a few months the old women would be dressing her up again, this time for her funeral. Even if she did survive the heat, and the dust that filtered in through every pore to lodge itself in the soul, she would be bound to succumb to the fussy habits of her confirmed bachelor of a husband. Judge Hidalgo was twice her age, and had slept alone for so many years he didn't have the slightest notion of how to go about pleasing a woman. The severity and stubbornness with which he executed the law even at the expense of justice had made him feared throughout the province. He refused to apply any common sense in the exercise of his profession, and was equally harsh in his condemnation of the theft of a chicken and of a premeditated murder. He dressed formally in black, and, despite the all-pervading dust in this god-forsaken town, his boots always shone with beeswax. A man such as he was never meant to be a husband, and yet not only did the gloomy wedding-day prophecies remain unfulfilled, but Casilda emerged happy and smiling from three pregnancies in rapid succession. Every Sunday at noon she would go to mass with her husband, cool and collected beneath her Spanish mantilla, seemingly untouched by our pitiless summer, as wan and frail-looking as on the day of her arrival: a perfect example of delicacy and refinement. Her loudest words were a soft-spoken greeting; her most expressive gesture was a graceful nod of the head. She was such an airy, diaphanous creature that a moment's carelessness might mean she disappeared altogether. So slight an impression did she make that the changes noticeable in the Judge were all the more remarkable. Though outwardly he remained the same—he still dressed as black as a crow and was as stiff-necked and brusque as ever—his judgements in court altered dramatically. To general amazement, he found the youngster who robbed the Turkish shop-keeper innocent, on the grounds that she had been selling him short for years, and the money he had taken could therefore be seen as compensation. He also refused to punish an adulterous wife, arguing that since her husband himself kept a mistress he did not have the moral authority to demand fidelity. Word in the town had it that the Judge was transformed the minute he crossed the threshold at home: that he flung off his gloomy apparel, rollicked with his children, chuckled as he sat Casilda on his lap. Though no one ever succeeded in confirming these rumours, his wife got the credit for his new-found kindness, and her reputation grew accordingly. None of this was of the slightest interest to Nicolas Vidal, who as a wanted man was sure there would be no mercy shown him the day he was brought in chains before the Judge. He paid no heed to the talk about Doña Casilda, and the rare occasions he glimpsed her from afar only confirmed his first impression of her as a lifeless ghost.

Born thirty years earlier in a windowless room in the town's only brothel, Vidal was the son of Juana the Forlorn and an unknown father. The world had no place for him. His mother knew it, and so tried to wrench him from her womb with sprigs of parsley, candle butts, douches of ashes and other violent purgatives, but the child clung to life. Once, years later, Juana was looking at her mysterious son and realized that, while all her infallible methods of aborting may have failed to dislodge him, they had nevertheless tempered his soul to the hardness of iron. As soon as he came into the world, he was lifted in the air by the midwife who examined him by the light of an oil-lamp. She saw he had four nipples.

'Poor creature: he'll lose his head over a woman,' she predicted, drawing on her wealth of experience.

Her words rested on the boy like a deformity. Perhaps a woman's love would have made his existence less wretched. To atone for all her attempts to kill him before his birth, his mother chose him a beautiful first name, and an imposing family name picked at random. But the lofty name of Nicolas Vidal was no protection against the fateful cast of his destiny. His face was scarred from knife fights before he reached his teens, so it came as no surprise to decent folk that he ended up a bandit. By the age of twenty, he had become the leader of a band of desperadoes. The habit of violence toughened his sinews. The solitude he was condemned to for fear of falling prey to a woman lent his face a sad expression. As soon as they saw him, everyone in the town knew from his eyes, clouded by tears he would never allow to fall, that he was the son of Juana the Forlorn. Whenever there was an outcry after a crime had been committed in the region, the police set out with dogs to track him down, but after scouring the hills they invariably returned empty-handed. In all honesty they preferred it that way, because they could never have fought him. His gang gained such a fearsome reputation that the surrounding villages and estates paid to keep them away. This money would have been plenty for his men, but Nicolas Vidal kept them constantly on horseback in a whirlwind of death and destruction so they would not lose their taste for battle. Nobody dared take them on. More than once, Judge Hidalgo had asked the government to send troops to reinforce the police, but after several useless forays the soldiers returned to their barracks and Nicolas Vidal's gang to their exploits. On one occasion only did Vidal come close to falling into the hands of justice, and then he was saved by his hardened heart.

Weary of seeing the laws flouted, Judge Hidalgo resolved to forget his scruples and set a trap for the outlaw. He realized that to defend justice he was committing an injustice, but chose the lesser of two evils. The only bait he could find was Juana the Forlorn, as she was Vidal's sole known relative. He had her dragged from the brothel where by now, since no clients were willing to pay for her exhausted charms, she scrubbed floors and cleaned out the lavatories. He put her in a specially made cage which was set up in the middle of the Plaza de Armas, with only a jug of water to meet her needs.

'As soon as the water's finished, she'll start to squawk. Then her son will come running, and I'll be waiting for him with the soldiers,' Judge Hidalgo said.

News of this torture, unheard of since the days of slavery, reached Nicolas Vidal's ears shortly before his mother drank the last of the water. His men watched as he received the report in silence, without so much as a flicker of emotion on his blank lone wolf's face, or a pause in the sharpening of his dagger blade on a leather strap. Though for many years he had had no contact with Juana, and retained few happy childhood memories, this was a question of honour. No man can accept such an insult, his gang reasoned as they got guns and horses ready to rush into the ambush and, if need be, lay down their lives. Their chief showed no sign of being in a hurry. As the hours went by tension mounted in the camp. The perspiring, impatient men stared at each other, not daring to speak. Fretful, they caressed the butts of their revolvers and their horses' manes, or busied themselves coiling their lassoos. Night fell. Nicolas Vidal was the only one in the camp who slept. At dawn, opinions were divided. Some of the men reckoned he was even more heartless than they had ever imagined, while others maintained their leader was planning a spectacular ruse to free his mother. The one thing that never crossed any of their minds was that his courage might have failed him, for he had always proved he had more than enough to spare. By noon, they could bear the suspense no longer, and went to ask him what he planned to do.

'I'm not going to fall into his trap like an idiot,' he said.

'What about your mother?'

'We'll see who's got more balls, the Judge or me,' Nicolas Vidal coolly replied.

By the third day, Juana the Forlorn's cries for water had ceased. She lay curled on the cage floor, with wildly staring eyes and swollen lips, moaning softly whenever she regained consciousness, and the rest of the time dreaming she was in Hell. Four armed guards stood watch to make sure nobody brought her water. Her groans penetrated the entire town, filtering through closed shutters or being carried by the wind through the cracks in doors. They got stuck in corners, where dogs worried at them, and passed them on in their howls to the newly-born, so that whoever heard them was driven to distraction. The Judge couldn't prevent a steady stream of people filing through the square to show their sympathy for the old woman, and was powerless to stop the prostitutes going on a sympathy strike just as the miners' fortnight holiday was beginning. That Saturday, the streets were thronged with lusty workmen desperate to unload their savings, who now found nothing in town apart from the spectacle of the cage and this universal wailing carried mouth to mouth down from the river to the coast road. The priest headed a group of Catholic ladies to plead with Judge Hidalgo for Christian mercy and to beg him to spare the poor old innocent woman such a frightful death, but the man of the law bolted his door and refused to listen to them. It was then that they decided to turn to Doña Casilda.

The Judge's wife received them in her shady living-room. She listened to their pleas looking, as she always did, bashfully down at the floor. Her husband had not been home for three days, having locked himself in his office to wait for Nicolas Vidal to fall into his trap. Without so much as looking out of the window, she was aware of what was going on, for Juana's long-drawn-out agony had forced its way even into the vast rooms of her residence. Doña Casilda waited until her visitors had left, dressed her children in their Sunday best, tied a black ribbon round their arms as a token of mourning, then strode out with them in the direction of the square. She carried a food hamper and a bottle of fresh water for Juana the Forlorn. When the guards spotted her turning the corner, they realized what she was up to, but they had strict orders, and barred her way with their rifles. When, watched now by a small crowd, she persisted, they grabbed her by the arms. Her children began to cry.

Judge Hidalgo sat in his office overlooking the square. He was the only person in the town who had not stuffed wax in his ears, because his mind was intent on the ambush and he was straining to catch the sound of horses' hoofs, which would be the signal for action. For three long days and nights he put up with Juana's groans and the insults of the townspeople gathered outside the court-room, but when he heard his own children start to wail he knew he had reached the bounds of his endurance. Vanquished, he walked out of the office with his three days' beard, his eyes bloodshot from keeping watch, and the weight of a thousand years on his back. He crossed the street, turned into the square and came face to face with his wife. They gazed at each other sadly. In seven years, this was the first time she had gone against him, and she had chosen to do so in front of the whole town. Easing the hamper and the bottle from Casilda's grasp, Judge Hidalgo himself opened the cage to release the prisoner.

'Didn't I tell you he wouldn't have the balls?' laughed Nicolas Vidal when the news reached him.

His laughter turned sour the next day, when he heard that Juana the Forlorn had hanged herself from the chandelier in the brothel where she had spent her life, overwhelmed by the shame of her only son leaving her to fester in a cage in the middle of the Plaza de Armas.

'That Judge's hour has come,' said Vidal.

He planned to take the judge by surprise, put him to a horrible death, then dump him in the accursed cage for all to see. The Turkish storekeeper sent him word that the Hidalgo family had left that same night for a seaside resort to rid themselves of the bitter taste of defeat.

The Judge learned he was being pursued when he stopped to rest at a wayside inn. There was little protection for him there until an army patrol could arrive, but he had a few hours' start, and his motor car could outrun the gang's horses. He calculated he could make it to the next town and summon help there. He ordered his wife and children into the car, put his foot down on the accelerator and sped off along the road. He ought to have arrived with time to spare, but it had been ordained that Nicolas Vidal was that day to meet the woman who would lead him to his doom.

Overburdened by the sleepless nights, the townspeople's hostility, the blow to his pride and the stress of this race to save his family, Judge Hidalgo's heart gave a massive jolt, then split like a pomegranate. The car ran out of control, turned several somersaults and finally came to a halt in the ditch. It took Doña Casilda some minutes to work out what had happened. Her husband's advancing years had often led her to think about what it would be like to be left a widow, yet she had never imagined he would leave her at the mercy of her enemies. She wasted little time dwelling on her situation, knowing she must act at once to get her children to safety. When she gazed around her, she almost burst into tears. There was no sign of life in the vast plain baked by a scorching sun, only barren cliffs beneath an unbounded sky bleached colourless by the fierce light. A second look revealed the dark shadow of a passage or cave on a distant slope, so she ran towards it with two children in her arms and the third clutching her skirts.

One by one she carried her children up the cliff. The cave was a natural one, typical of many in the region. She peered inside to be certain it wasn't the den of some wild animal, sat her children against its back wall, then, dry-eyed, kissed them goodbye.

'The troops will come to find you a few hours from now. Until then, don't for any reason whatsoever come out of here, even if you hear me screaming—do you understand?'

Their mother gave them one final glance as the terrified children clung to each other, then clambered back down to the road. She reached the car, closed her husband's eyes, smoothed back her hair and settled down to wait. She had no idea how many men were in Nicolas Vidal's gang, but prayed there were a lot of them so it would take them all the more time to have their way with her. She gathered strength pondering on how long it would take her to die if she determined to do it as slowly as possible. She willed herself to be desirable, luscious, to create more work for them and thus gain time for her children.

Casilda did not have long to wait. She soon saw a cloud of dust on the horizon and heard the gallop of horses' hoofs. She clenched her teeth. Then, to her astonishment, she saw there was only one rider, who stopped a few yards from her, gun at the ready. By the scar on his face she recognized Nicolas Vidal, who had set out all alone in pursuit of Judge Hidalgo, as this was a private matter between the two men. The Judge's wife understood she was going to have to endure something far worse than a slow death.

A single glance at her husband was enough to convince Vidal that the Judge was safely out of his reach in the peaceful sleep of death. But there was his wife, a shimmering presence in the plain's glare. He leaped from his horse and strode over to her. She did not flinch or lower her gaze, and to his amazement he realized that for the first time in his life another person was facing him without fear. For several seconds that stretched to eternity, they sized each other up, trying to gauge the other's strength, and their own powers of resistance. It gradually dawned on both of them that they were up against a formidable opponent. He lowered his gun. She smiled.

Casilda won each moment of the ensuing hours. To all the wiles of seduction known since the beginning of time she added new ones born of necessity to bring this man to the heights of rapture. Not only did she work on his body like an artist, stimulating his every fibre to pleasure, but she brought all the delicacy of her spirit into play on her side. Both knew their lives were at stake, and this added a new and terrifying dimension to their meeting. Nicolas Vidal had fled from love since birth, and knew nothing of intimacy, tenderness, secret laughter, the riot of the senses, the joy of shared passion. Each minute brought the detachment of troops and the noose that much nearer, but he gladly accepted this in return for her prodigious gifts. Casilda was a passive, demure, timid woman who had been married to an austere old man in front of whom she had never even dared appear naked. Not once during that unforgettable afternoon did she forget that her aim was to win time for her children, and yet at some point, marvelling at her own possibilities, she gave herself completely, and felt something akin to gratitude towards him. That was why, when she heard the soldiers in the distance, she begged him to flee to the hills. Instead, Nicolas Vidal chose to fold her in a last embrace, thus fulfilling the prophecy that had sealed his fate from the start.

Translated from the Spanish by Nick Caistor

OLIVER SACKS
COLD STORAGE

In 1957, when I was a student of the late Richard Asher, I encountered his patient 'Uncle Toby', and was fascinated by this strange meeting of fact and fable. Dr Asher (who may himself have published something of this story) referred to it sometimes as a 'Rip van Winkle case.' The story often came to my mind, vividly, when my own post-encephalitic patients were 'awakened' in 1969, and it has unconsciously haunted me for years.

Dr Asher had been on a house call to see a sick child. As he was discussing her treatment with the family, he noticed a silent, motionless figure in a corner. 'Who's that?' he asked.

'That's Uncle Toby—'e's hardly moved in seven years.'

Uncle Toby had become an undemanding fixture in the house. His slowing down was so gradual at first that the family didn't notice; but then, when it became more profound, it was—rather extraordinarily—just accepted by the family. He was fed and watered daily, turned, sometimes toileted: he was really no trouble; he was part of the furniture. Most people never noticed him, still, silent in the corner. He was not regarded as ill: he had just come to a stop.

Dr Asher spoke to this waxlike figure. There was no answer, no response. He put out his hand to take the pulse, and encountered a hand cold to the touch, almost as cold as that of a corpse. But there was a faint, slow pulse: Uncle Toby was alive, but suspended, apparently, in some strange icy stupor.

Discussion with the family was odd and disquieting. They showed remarkably little concern for Uncle Toby, and yet, manifestly, they were caring and decent. But, as sometimes happens with an insidious and insensible change, they had accommodated to it as it had happened. But when Dr Asher spoke to them, and suggested that Uncle Toby be brought into hospital, they agreed.

And so Uncle Toby was admitted to hospital, to a specially equipped metabolic care unit. His temperature could not be measured by an ordinary clinical thermometer; so a special one, reserved for hypothermics, was fetched: it registered sixty-eight degrees Fahrenheit. Uncle Toby's temperature was thirty degrees below normal. A suspicion was formed, immediately tested and confirmed: Uncle Toby had virtually no thyroid function, and his metabolic rate was reduced almost to zero. With scarcely any thyroid function, any metabolic stimulator or 'fire', he had sunk into the depths of a hypothyroid (or myxoedema) coma: alive, but not alive; in abeyance, in cold storage.

It was clear what to do—it was a simple medical problem: we had only to give him a thyroid hormone, thyroxine, and he would come to. But this warming up, this refiring of metabolism, would have to be done very cautiously and slowly; his functions, his organs had accommodated to his hypometabolism. If his metabolism were stimulated too quickly, he might have cardiac or other complications. So slowly, very slowly, we started him on thyroxine, and very slowly he started to warm up . . .

A week passed. There was nothing to see, though Uncle Toby's temperature was now seventy-two degrees. It was only in the third week, with the body temperature now well over eighty degrees, that he began to move . . . and talk. His voice was exceedingly low, slow, and hoarse—like a phonograph record croaking round at a single revolution per minute (some of this croakiness was due to myxoedema of the vocal cords). His limbs, too, had been stiff and swollen with oedema, but grew lither and more limber now with physiotherapy and use. After a month, though still cool, and slow in speech and motion, Uncle Toby had clearly 'awakened', and evinced animation, awareness and concern.

'What's happening?' he asked. 'Why am I in hospital? Am I ill?' We countered by asking him what *he* had been feeling. 'Sort of cool, sort of lazy, slowed-down, you know.'

'But Mr Oakins,'—we only called him 'Uncle Toby' among ourselves—'what came in between feeling cool, feeling slow, and finding yourself here?'

'Nothing much,' he answered. 'Nothing I know of. I suppose I must have been really ill, passed out, and the family brought me here.'

'And how long had you passed out for?' we asked, in a neutral tone.

'How long? A day or two—couldn't be any longer—my family would be sure to bring me in.'

He scanned our faces curiously, intently.

'There's nothing more to this, nothing unusual?'

'Nothing,' we reassured him, and made a quick exit.

Mr Oakins, it seemed, unless we misunderstood him, had no sense that any time had elapsed, certainly not any great length of time. He had felt queer; now he was better—simple, nothing to it. Could this be what he actually believed?

We were given vivid confirmation of this later that same day, when the staff nurse came to us in some agitation. 'He's quite lively now,' she reported. 'He has a real need to talk—he's talking about his mates, his work. About Attlee, the King's illness, the 'new' Health Service, and so on. He's no idea what's going on *now*. He seems to think it's 1950.'

Uncle Toby, as a person, a conscious entity, had slowed down and stopped as he had gone into coma. He had been 'away', 'absent', for an unconscionable time. Not in a sleep, not in a trance, but in a deep and mindless coma. And now he had emerged, the years of coma were a blank. It was not amnesia, not 'disorientation'; his higher cerebral functions, his mind, had been 'out' for seven years.

How would he react to the knowledge that he had 'lost' seven years—that much of what was exciting, important, dear to him, had passed irretrievably away? That he himself was no longer 'contemporary', but a piece of the past, an anachronism, a fossil strangely preserved?

Rightly or wrongly, we decided on a policy of evasion (and not only evasion, but frank deceit). This was planned, of course, as a temporary measure, until he had the physical or mental strength to come to terms with things, to withstand a profound shock.

The medical staff made no efforts, therefore, to disabuse him of his belief that it was 1950. We watched ourselves closely, lest we give anything away; we forbade any careless talk; we also forbade visitors; and we inundated him with newspapers and periodicals from 1950. He read these avidly, though expressed surprise, on occasion, at *our* ignorance of the 'news', and the disgraceful, yellowed, dilapidated condition of the papers.

And now—six weeks had passed—his temperature was almost normal: he looked fit and well, and considerably younger than his years.

At this point came the final irony. He started to cough, to spit blood; he had a massive haemoptysis. Chest x-rays showed a mass in his chest; and bronchoscopy a highly malignant, rapidly proliferating 'oat-cell' carcinoma.

We managed to find chest films, routine x-rays, from 1950, and there we saw, small and overlooked at the time, the cancer he now had. Such highly malignant, fulminating carcinomas are apt to grow rapidly, and be fatal in months. Yet he had had this in 1950. It seemed evident that this cancer, like the rest of him, had been arrested, in cold storage.

Now he was warmed up, the cancer raged furiously, and Mr Oakins expired, in a fit of coughing, a matter of days later.

His family let him sink into a coldness which saved his life; we warmed him up, and, in consequence, he died.*

POSTSCRIPT (1987). Last month I was contacted by Mrs D., a woman in her fifties, who had been labelled as having 'apathetic depression', and treated with antidepressants (tricyclics, MAO inhibitors, etc.) for *twenty-nine years* to no effect. It was then realized—after almost three decades of misdiagnosis— that she was, and had been all along, markedly hypothyroid (though not nearly so profoundly as Uncle Toby).

Hypothyroidism, though it may produce obvious changes (facial puffiness, oedema of limbs, slowly-returning reflexes, hoarseness of voice, coldness, lethargy and apathy), can be

---

* The question of the wisdom of giving medication, in particular naturally-occurring hormones, without considering their total effect on the organism and person, was frequently stressed by Dr Asher. He would note how a diagnosis of 'hypothyroidism' in an elderly person might immediately prompt the administration of thyroid hormone, and how this, in turn, might tip the patient into coronary insufficiency or heart failure. Such patients (he would stress) might be 'better off' left alone—and he wondered whether their diminution of thyroid function might not be a physiological or adaptive measure, designed to reduce the load on an ailing heart (indeed, anti-thyroid drugs were given at one time for treatment of angina or heart failure, precisely in order to do this).

Oliver Sacks

strangely overlooked by family, close friends and even the physicians of the affected person, because the changes are so gradual that it is easy to adjust to them. Another person, a new pair of eyes, may spot the trouble in a moment. Sometimes, however, the physical signs are not marked, and there is only a change in mental and emotional status—this was first described by Richard Asher, in his famous paper 'Myxoedematous Madness'.*

Mrs D. was started on thyroxine, and in six months restored to metabolic health. She feels very well now, but has a certain sense of anachronism and outrage: 'I've lost twenty-nine years,' she says. 'I feel cheated of life. I found I was out-of-date, out of sync. Everything and everyone had moved on, while I had stood still.' She has now (like some of my *Awakenings* patients) 'caught up' in a sense, made a grateful and graceful accommodation, though some sense of loss, of grief, and of anger, still persists.

---

* In the *British Medical Journal*, 10 September 1949 and reprinted in *Talking Sense* (Pitman Medical Books, 1972), pp. 77–95.

JONATHAN SCHELL
PARADISE

One day in the autumn of 1968, in the tiny Siberian village of Korenskaya, some 300 miles from the Arctic Circle, the Russian poet Joseph Brodsky, who was twenty-four years old and had been sent to Korenskaya to serve a five-year term of internal exile for the crime of 'parasitism', picked up an anthology of English poetry and, intending to turn to the poems of T. S. Eliot, found himself reading instead W. H. Auden's poem 'In Memory of W. B. Yeats', which includes the lines:

> Time that is intolerant
> Of the brave and innocent
> And indifferent in a week
> To a beautiful physique,
>
> Worships language and forgives
> Everyone by whom it lives;
> Pardons cowardice, conceit,
> Lays its honours at their feet.

Brodsky was thunderstruck. Another reader coming upon these lines might conclude that Auden was merely affirming, in diffident, lightly mocking diction, the ancient faith of the poet that in his poems he, as well as those about whom he writes, can live beyond death and survive the general ruin of time. Brodsky, however, detected in the word 'worships' a new note, a new thought. And that new thought set in motion in his mind a stream of further thoughts about time, language and other matters which has continued to flow down to this day. They lie at the core of his collection of critical and autobiographical essays, *Less Than One*. Brodsky was so astonished when he read Auden's lines that at first, as he looked out of the small window of his shack at the familiar 'muddy dirt road with a few stray chickens on it,' he doubted that he had correctly understood what he had read. 'But for once the dictionary didn't deceive me,' he writes, in an essay on Auden. 'Auden had indeed said that time (not the time) worships language.' He goes on:

> For 'worship' is an attitude of the lesser towards the greater. If time worships language, it means that language is greater, or older, than time, which is, in turn,

older and greater than space. That was how I was taught, and I indeed felt that way. So if time—which is synonymous with, nay, even absorbs deity—worships language, where then does language come from? For the gift is always smaller than the giver. And then isn't language a repository of time? And isn't this why time worships it? And isn't song, or a poem, or indeed speech itself, with its caesuras, pauses, spondees, and so forth, a game language plays to restructure time? And aren't those by whom language 'lives', those by whom time does, too? And if time 'forgives' them, does it do so out of generosity or out of necessity? And isn't generosity a necessity anyhow?

Thus does Brodsky build the rudiments of a kind of metaphysics out of the overtones of a single expression. It is characteristic of Brodsky that he attributes the substance of his thinking to another writer's lines (as if everything that he subsequently worked out was nothing more than a protracted elucidation of what Auden had packed into the one word 'worships'), presenting his thinking as merely the continuation of a broader train of thought that, implicitly, neither began with him nor will end with him; but it's also characteristic that he persists in his elucidation until he has arrived at novel, and sometimes extreme, conclusions. For example, if language is 'greater' than time, and time 'absorbs deity', then language must in some sense be greater than God. Linguistics here seems to have swallowed up theology.

As is evident in the quaint scholasticism of such notions as that the gift is 'smaller' than the giver, and that language is 'greater', hence 'older', than time, Brodsky is not proceeding according to the rules either of strict logic or of historical or scientific analysis. Yet there is rigour in the thinking. In this passage, Brodsky seems to have proceeded by making use of Auden's expression that time 'worships' language to summon up an entire theological tradition, in which man, time, language and God are arranged in a hierarchy; then, making use for his own purposes of the simple organizing principle of hierarchy—that some things are 'higher' and therefore 'greater' (not to mention 'older') than others—he rearranges the elements. In other passages, he proceeds by means of a kind of relentless application of a metaphor or idea, extending it farther and farther afield, until something new gets said. For example, in the title essay, we find the surprising assertion that grass 'is propaganda'. Moving back a sentence, we read, 'Because of its plenitude, the future is propaganda.' Continuing back up the page to the previous paragraph, we discover the author as a schoolboy sitting in a Soviet class-room, finding in himself rebellious feelings against the ever-present portrait of Lenin, usually wearing 'that meaningless expression on his face which could be mistaken for anything, preferably a sense of purpose.' The rebellion was Brodsky's first lesson in 'estrangement' and led him to the belief that 'whatever there was in plenitude' was 'some sort of propaganda'. Even grass.

But whether he is delving into the meaning of the use of a single word, or appropriating antiquated logic to his needs, or pressing an idea to its limits, Brodsky is at pains to reason his way forward. There is courtesy and respect for the reader implicit in this procedure. Some writers use reasoning to back up dogmatic claims: strict logic, like mathematics, is supposed to compel the mind's assent. Other writers, though, use reasoning actually to disclaim dogmatic authority, for argumentation can serve to open up the process of thought to the reader's inspection, inviting him into the very workshop in which thoughts are forged. Brodsky's writing has this open quality. It is perhaps especially invaluable when, as is also the case in his essays, feeling is deep. Deep feeling always has the potential to be used to browbeat or bully the reader, but Brodsky routes feeling through the civilizing channels of argument, where writer and reader meet on assumed common ground. He does not so much hold emotion in check as pay it out in the currency of thought—in argued howls, reasoned elation, deduced sobs. T. S. Eliot wrote of G. K. Chesterton that although his brain 'swarms with ideas, I see no evidence that it thinks.' Just the opposite is the case with the brain of Joseph Brodsky. It is incessantly thinking, but we find in it little evidence of 'ideas'.

It has been said that it is a characteristic of scientific genius to be able to dwell unwaveringly over a long period on a scientific problem until it yields its answer. Brodsky has mental stamina of this sort. He meditates, he broods, and his thinking has the elongated quality of these mental activities. (In his poem 'St. Pietro' he dwells, without repetition, on the fog-enshrouded landscape of the town for more than a hundred lines, before arriving at a few more or less explicit thoughts regarding the sea, life, memory and time: he brews metaphysics out of mist.) It's an elongation, however, that has nothing to do with long-windedness; his prose, as befits a poet, is highly compressed. The result is abundance. From within the covers of this book, a small mountain range of new thinking about the role of literature in history and in life in general shoulders its way up into the intellectual landscape. It includes what is perhaps the most original thinking in a generation—since W. H. Auden and Hannah Arendt turned their minds to these questions— on the responsibilities of artists and writers in times of great and pervasive evil. It is one of the many pleasures of his collected essays that Brodsky devotes himself to generous-spirited, line-by-line appreciation of individual poets of the twentieth century (they are Constantine Cavafy, Anna Akhmatova, Osip Mandelstam, Marina Tsvetaeva, Eugenio Montale, Derek Walcott and Auden), but along the way he says enough of a general nature to constitute a full-fledged poetics of and for our time.

In the period between the two world wars, when fascism was on the rise, many writers in the Western democracies, including Auden, lent their pens to the anti-fascist and other political causes. The results, some of these writers, again including Auden, later came to believe, were neither great literature nor effective politics—and in some instances, certainly, were political mischief. Part of the reason may be suggested by the old saying that truth is the first casualty of war. It's a casualty that, within limits, armies and political parties are ready and able to sustain, but that literature, for which the pursuit of truth is of the essence, is likely to find fatal. Gone to war, literature, it seems, kills itself off before it can get in the first blow against the enemy—a poor result for both art and causes. The epitaph for this particular movement may have been Auden's lines, which also happen to appear in his poem on the death of Yeats:

> For poetry makes nothing happen; it survives
> In the valley of its saying, where executives
> Would never want to tamper.

The poem was published in 1939, the year in which the Soviets and the Nazis signed their short-lived non-aggression pact, and the Second World War began. In those circumstances, Auden's announcement of withdrawal—as poet-combatant, anyway—from the fight gave the measure of the depth of his new conviction. In any case, whatever poets and other writers thought they could or couldn't accomplish politically, the armies by then had massed, and were about to take matters into their own hands.

In the East, meanwhile, where Stalin had risen to power, the situation was of course quite different: there the question was not how much writers might like to interfere in politics but the other way around, with slow death from cold and starvation in a camp being a strong possibility for the writers. While it might be that 'executives' did not wish to tamper with poetry, commissars decidedly did; in fact, they set out not just to tamper with literature but to run it from the ground up. Curiously, however, even as the state sought to assume the role of the writer, it abandoned the role—more or less traditional to it—of fundamental record-keeper of the nation's political and other common experience. Like an army that leaves its home territory unprotected when it invades another country, the state left a vacuum, and this vacuum came to be filled, eventually, by none other than the persecuted writers. And remembrance was a role that literature could play just by being itself. In the Soviet Union, writers did not have to rush to the barricades; the barricades rushed to them, causing great hardship, but also giving to their work a political importance that it would not have had if they had been left alone. The difference was that whereas in ordinary times the oblivion against which a piece of writing pits itself is the normal and inevitable one of death and the forgetfulness that comes with the passage of time, under totalitarianism that oblivion is organized, speeded up and turned to a political purpose. In deploying its commemorative power against this state-sponsored amnesia, 'poetry' is still making nothing happen, yet it is saving much from being destroyed; and while its role is still not 'political', in the sense of enlisting itself in causes, its political importance nevertheless becomes great.

This literature, concerned as it must be with conveying basic information that is otherwise unavailable, calls for a documentary, journalistic style—in short, for the techniques of realism. In a time when the state would like everyone to forget how many people it has killed and who they were, the most important mission may be to supply particular facts—to provide individual headstones for individual victims. Stylistic innovation, understandably, tends to be passed up. Brodsky points out that 'Narrating a tale of mass extermination, one's not terribly keen to unleash the stream of consciousness . . .' In the case of Aleksander Solzhenitsyn—certainly the greatest of the practitioners of the literature of remembrance—stylistic conservatism goes hand in hand with political and cultural conservatism. He looks back with fondness on the days when an authoritarian Russian state was allied with the Orthodox Church, and regards modern times, from the Middle Ages down to the present, with the deepest suspicion. At the same time, he looks on European influences on Russia as mostly baneful. Russia's salvation, he believes, will come from its past, and in particular from its own spiritual traditions represented by the Orthodox faith.

By now, the experiments both with the politicization of literature in the West and with the more fruitful discovery of the commemorative power of literature in the East are well known. Brodsky, however, though keenly aware of both, strikes out on a new and unexpected path. Certainly, the last thing he would recommend would be the enlistment of literature in the service of political causes; in fact, as he sees it, the best path for literature to follow is deliberate flight from anything bearing the slightest resemblance to political propaganda. That was the lesson of Lenin's picture on the class-room wall, and it applied to writing much more directly than to grass. It is the very essence of literature, he believes, to pursue what is individual, what is new, what is seen anew. But to see things anew requires stylistic innovation, and stylistic innovation tends to be lost in the face of tragedy. To save the memory of the mistress's eyes from oblivion, the words themselves must be memorable; but, to save the victims of the state from the same fate, a plain recitation of the facts alone may seem most appropriate. Brodsky is adamant in his insistence on originality. Life itself, he finds, is defective because it tends to lack this quality. It is too repetitive, too much like grass. To gain distinction and meaning, life needs language. Hence, it is not enough that art should imitate life—the programme of literary realism; art should add a whole other dimension to life. Speaking of Dostoyevski, who is one of Brodsky's literary heroes, he writes, 'His art was anything but mimetic; it wasn't imitating reality; it was creating, or, better still, reaching for one . . . He simply felt that art is not about life, if only because life is not about life. For Dostoyevski, art, like life, is about what man exists for.' Twentieth-century Russian prose, however, has, to Brodsky's regret, taken the realistic path—or, rather, remained stuck in it. He attributes this choice of style also to another cause, and it is a surprising one—Tolstoy. His 'mimetic avalanche', Brodsky says, diverted several generations of Russian writers from the more promising path indicated by Dostoyevski, whom Brodsky somewhat surprisingly regards as a master of linguistic invention. The Tolstoyan highway, we are told, led steadily downhill—'via Chekhov, Korolenko, Kuprin, Bunin, Gorky, Leonid Andreev, Gladkov'—to 'the pits of socialist realism'.

Encountering this view, in which Tolstoy, Chekhov and Solzhenitsyn are somehow brought into association with Stalinist hacks and all are rejected in favour of a superior, but largely abstract 'road not taken', the reader may feel like voicing any of a number of protests. The legions of Tolstoy admirers are certain to be offended. What is more serious, the reader may find it out of order that, in the face of so much tragedy, questions of literary style are given such importance. For Brodsky, however, the matter of style is inseparable from the matter of language, and since language is the medium through which life finds its very meaning, and the meaning of life is what life is *for,* it follows that the question of style is intrinsic to the main goal of life. Literature, and, more generally, the search for meaning through language, is for him the path taken by the spirit trying to find its way morally as well as aesthetically in the world. As he puts it baldly, 'By itself, reality isn't worth a damn; it's perception that promotes reality to meaning.' Something like this was the faith, he tells us, of his generation, for which 'books became the first and only reality whereas reality itself was regarded as either nonsense or a nuisance.' This extreme, unabashed, bookish Platonism, in which the mundane world is brushed aside in favour of a superior one to be found in literature, has a long history in Russia. Pushkin informs us of 'young provincial ladies . . . brought up in the open air, beneath the shade of the apple trees' who have gained 'all their knowledge of life and of the world from books.' Pushkin's picture is idyllic and Brodsky's desperate, but the feeling that in books there is a life as good as, or better than, the one outside them is the same. In Brodsky, this faith reaches a new pitch as well as gaining a new historical context and new metaphysical underpinnings, all of which lead him to the apotheosis of poetry and language expressed in his reflections on Auden's lines on language and time.

Just how far Brodsky is prepared to go in this direction, and with what justification, is revealed in a pair of essays on the twentieth-century Russian poetess Marina Tsvetaeva. The first is about prose pieces of hers, and the second is an analysis, seventy pages in length, of her poem 'New Year's Greetings', which was addressed to her friend Rainer Maria Rilke shortly after his death in 1926. The two essays emerge as a full-scale defence of artistic creativity as being essential to, rather than a distraction from, ethical responsibility. Artistic creativity has often been regarded as ethically suspect, if only because of its unpredictability, which threatens to undermine settled ethical precepts. But for Brodsky it is just this capacity for bringing forth the new that makes it indispensable to ethics. His position is not one of art for art's sake. He still places the meaning of the work first, but he regards that meaning as reachable only through the most fanatical and unswerving obedience to the demands of aesthetics, which is to say, above all, to the phonetic and rhythmic and stylistic demands of language. Language, as he sees it, *is* a means to an end—the end being meaning—but that end will never be reached unless the writer surrenders himself to the means: to language itself. Some of Brodsky's most eloquent writing in these essays describes, in passages that illustrate the points they are making, the process of writing. For example:

> Poetic language possesses—as does any language in general—its own particular dynamics, which impart to

psychic movement an acceleration that takes the poet much farther than he imagined when he began the poem. Yet this is, in fact, the principal mechanism (temptation, if you will) of creative work; once having come into contact with it (or having succumbed to it), a person once and for all rejects other modes of thought, expression—conveyance. Language propels the poet into spheres he would not otherwise be able to approach, irrespective of the degree of psychic or mental concentration of which he might be capable beyond the writing of verse. And this propulsion takes place with unusual swiftness: with the speed of sound—greater than what is afforded by imagination and experience. As a rule, a poet is considerably older when he finishes a poem than he was at the outset.

Or:

The true mover of speech, let us repeat, is the language itself, that is, the liberated verse-mass milling the theme and almost literally splashing up when it hits a rhyme or an image.

In these passages, it seems to me, Brodsky assigns to language the role that, since Freud, we are used to assigning to the unconscious mind. Freud found in the unconscious mind the source of the amazing abundance poured forth in creative work that so greatly exceeds what we feel is the capacity of the conscious mind. Brodsky finds the additional source in language—everyone's common possession. The Freudian writer reaches 'down' into himself, into the dark, hidden depths of feeling, impulse and memory. The Brodskian writer reaches 'sideways', where the riches of language—the rhymes, the cadences, the associations, the connections—await discovery. The Freudian writer digs; the Brodskian writer is 'propelled'—indeed, he is 'accelerated'—along the pathways of language. In this process, a rhyme scheme is not a limitation on meaning but an incitement to it; a poetic form is not a restriction on feeling but a vehicle carrying it to expression. Hence, 'a poet's biography is in his vowels and sibilants, in his meters, rhymes, and metaphors.' In discovering the sources of creativity in the commonly held possession of language rather than in the privacy of the self's depths, Brodsky brings creativity closer to ethics. For care in the use of language—the medium shared by artists and politicians—has, as everyone knows by now, important political consequences. Brodsky's view of creativity as a linguistic journey also helps to explain his dislike of the politicization of art—of what in the United States is sometimes called 'consciousness-raising'. That project—otherwise known as propagandizing—assumes that the writer already knows what is right, and that his job is to raise the reader's mind to this predetermined elevation. For Brodsky, however, the goal is not to arrive again at what is already known or believed, or to push someone else there, but to travel oneself to some new place.

The idea of racing off at the speed of sound towards unknown destinations has a devil-may-care sound to it, but Brodsky insists that in fact this path is the most rigorous and responsible of all. 'Rational enterprise, choice, selection' are not thereby given up, he assures us; they are 'entrusted to hearing'—'focused into hearing'— as if in a 'miniaturization' or 'computerization' of analytical processes. Hearing can be trusted to choose wisely because of the double, 'phonetic' and 'semiotic', nature of language. But it is not only phonetics and semiotics that are inseparably paired, it is also 'aesthetics and ethics'. Sometimes Brodsky seems to mean by this that devotion to language is the first responsibility of the poet to his art, and, as such, an 'ethics' for the profession; at other times, though, he seems to mean much more—that this devotion is the means by which the conscience of society is best attuned for its task of discriminating between good and evil. It can perform this task in part because the individual mind, off in pursuit of new, hitherto undreamed-of shades of meaning, is immunized against the cliché-ridden, mass-produced speech in whose name evil is so often done; in part because the artist, subordinating himself to the 'dynamic, logic and laws of his artifice,' is led to a new sensibility that offers both him and his audience what is 'perhaps the only route of departure from the known, captive self,' and, for that matter, from the captivity of his time and place; but mostly because artistic pursuit is a process of spiritual elevation through which people first detach themselves—'estrange' themselves—from their immediate world and then rise above it to gain a glimpse of what life is for.

Foreseeing that charges of 'élitism' and unfairness may be levelled against his championship of rigorous aesthetic standards, he answers—rightly, it seems to me—that in artistic and intellectual work there is a necessary hierarchy based on talent and excellence, the abandonment of which leads to 'equating wisdom with idiocy.' But while it is essential to acknowledge that artistic ability is granted to a minority on the basis of talent, it is troubling to suppose that ethical or spiritual ability has been granted on a similar basis. An artistic élite is one thing; a spiritual élite another. The spiritual path, one would like to think, lies open to all. But it may not be necessary to assign too narrow a meaning to Brodsky's use of the words 'poetic' and 'artistic'.

I am reminded of what Hannah Arendt says about moral discrimination in her book *The Life of the Mind.* She notes that in the make-up of Adolf Eichmann, an evil-doer on a big scale, there seemed to be no positive or active cause—such as fanatic intensity, monumental ambition, consuming greed—for the evil; rather there was 'an absence'—an absence of thought: 'thoughtlessness'. The absence manifested itself in the employment of 'clichés, stock phrases, adherence to conventional, standardized codes of expression and conduct.' That led Arendt to wonder whether the 'activity of thinking'—by which she meant not philosophical inquiry or any other specialized professional activity but simply 'the habit of examining and looking at whatever occurs'—might not be the best antidote to evil. The evil she had upper-most in her mind was not the sort that occurs when an individual commits one of the seven deadly sins but the mass evil that breaks out when whole societies lose their bearings and plunge collectively into criminality. It is at these moments that the Eichmanns of the world, who otherwise would probably spend their lives relatively harmlessly, can commit horrifying crimes out of pure thoughtlessness. They only have to go along with what the whole of organized society now sanctions and rewards. In these moments, the moral challenge for the individual is not, as sometimes may be the case in happier times, to find the strength to adhere to an ethical code professed by society, but to find an individual path to sanity when society has gone mad—to remain upright morally when the world around him has turned upside down. And it is in these moments, too, that the radical independence of the world advocated, in their different ways, by

Brodsky and Arendt, proves its full worth. Both insist that the individual's resistance to the prevailing dogma should not be some new dogma. Since thoughtless acceptance of dogma is the root of the evil, it is hard to recommend adherence to some other dogma as an acceptable solution. Then one would be at best only a step away from supporting similar evils backed up by a different ideological content. And that seems to be why both Brodsky and Arendt offer, as the best path of resistance, not a better set of precepts for people to cling to but a mental process—be it 'thought' or 'poetry'; not the mind holding fast to received knowledge but the mind in motion: the mind awake, stirred, responding, discriminating, open, alive.

The adoption of the aesthetic sense as the guide to meaning generally (of which ethical meaning forms only a part) raises other questions. For Brodsky, in literature the aesthetic sense is above all a linguistic sense, which he sees as the motor force of poetry, carrying the poet along verbal pathways to the marriage of sound and significance. At the same time, he regards translation as the 'main vehicle' by which civilization develops. Yet poetry, they say, is what is lost in translation—for in the new language the old meaning must be married to new sounds. But if language is at the heart of civilization, and poetry is at the heart of language, yet poetry is what is lost in translation, it doesn't sound as if civilization is going to be very successful. A closely related question is raised by another conflict between sound and meaning: that between 'synthesis'—the process by which the poet, using his 'three hundred-and-sixty-degree bat-radar', assembles his material from all points of the compass and compresses it into the poetic line—and 'analysis', the orderly, linear, sequential process by which the prose-bound literary critic must operate when he analyses a poem. Brodsky is categorical in his ranking of poetry and prose. Poetry is on top, prose at the bottom, on the grounds that poetry makes far greater use of the phonetics and rhythm of language than prose does. To seek to 'approach analytically a phenomenon whose nature is synthetic is doomed,' he warns, as have many other poets before him. It's advice, though, that he proves unable to heed, for after giving it he immediately plunges into his seventy pages of line-by-line exegesis of the Tsvetaeva poem—a tour de force of analysis.

An interesting light is shed on these riddles by a thought

mentioned in passing in another essay—that poetry itself can be seen as an act of 'translation': translation of the poet's 'meaning', much of which escapes even the most inspired writing. In the Tsvetaeva essay, he notes that Tsvetaeva claims that the language 'most native' to her is neither Rilke's German nor her own Russian but 'the Angelic'. Angelic—which we can take to be the language of meaning itself, from which the poem is an imperfect translation—is a language that everyone, poets and non-poets alike, has in common, although no one can speak it. It is the foundation for a common humanity that is expressed, always imperfectly, always provisionally, in various translations, starting with the original poem. (This view of meaning and language corresponds to the view of truth and language held by Lessing, who, in a remark quoted by Arendt in an essay on his work, said, 'Let each man say what he deem the truth, and let the truth itself be commended to God.') Seen in the light of this view of the relationship between poetry and meaning, the Tsvetaeva essay becomes a drama on many levels of civilization in the form of translation. At least four languages are involved: Angelic, German, Russian and English. If prose and poetry (analysis and synthesis) are counted as 'languages', that makes six. First there are Rilke's translations from the Angelic—his poems. Then there is Tsvetaeva's rendering of Rilke's life of poetry—her poem 'New Year's Greetings'. Then there is Brodsky's translation of this poem into the 'language' of prose (prose which, incidentally, was originally written in Russian and then translated into English.) The poem itself, it seems significant to mention, is not given in full in translation in the essay; only the lines directly analysed by Brodsky are offered. To the extent that part of the poem is missing, the reader is given a commentary without a text. And that seems appropriate, for the English reader, to whom the poem in its original Russian is unavailable, feels that Brodsky's analysis gives us the poem more fully than the most brilliant complete translation ever could. In this essay, analysis becomes translation—suggesting that analysis may not be doomed after all, if only because it is so useful in translating the works of one culture for another, with both analysis and translation being possible because poetry is already a 'translation', and therefore no stranger to the process. All of which may say something about prose. No one has ever said that prose is what gets lost in translation. Prose gets through. Presumably, it is what is left over after the poetry has been lost. If translation is the main vehicle of civilization, then prose must be, too—a noble role, notwithstanding Brodsky's low ranking of it. In making this case for prose, I would offer Brodsky's essay on Tsvetaeva—a literary marvel in its own right—as Exhibit A. In this analytic act of translation—of civilization—even the poetry, one feels, gets through.

Venturing farther along the path of the soul's aesthetic-spiritual progress, Brodsky discovers a 'poetic paradise' that he clearly finds superior in many respects to the paradise of religion. He takes as his text some lines from the Tsvetaeva poem on Rilke, in which, trying to picture his life in the afterlife, she asks him:

> How is writing going in the sweet life
> Without a desk for your elbow, or brow for your hand?

In this half-corporeal, half-etherealized picture of Rilke, in which, through a sort of other-worldly decomposition (sparing some parts of the body while claiming others), he is found still in possession of his elbow but with no desk to lean it on, and still in possession of a hand (fully equipped with a palm) but with no forehead to rest upon it (a depiction that, séance-like, reduces him to the writing part of the body), Brodsky finds the clues to his ideal of 'the poetic version of "eternal life".' As suits a theological, or quasi-theological, 'proof' (and as is characteristic of Brodsky's prose in any case), the reasoning is careful. The missing desk and head, he points out, create 'negative tangibility', giving to absent things a vividness that not only is a lot more than 'non-being' but, in his opinion, actually 'surpasses being in its tangibility.' Brodsky is telling us again—and on no point is he more insistent—that art is not a more or less faded reflection or imitation of life but an 'independent reality', which does nothing less than disclose life's meaning. Naturally, the more significant the missing thing, the more significant is its new life in the poem, and when the missing thing is a whole poet, and when, in addition, the poet was himself engaged in reflecting on 'the entire phenomenal and speculative world,' then what is made tangible negatively is that whole phenomenal and speculative world. The 'next world'—the world of the poem, the world after death, the world in which what is absent is made present—is thereby set in motion and becomes inexhaustible. Here Brodsky presents us with the striking idea of an absence capable of evolution—an absence with a rich life of its own. Since death is the supreme form of absence, death emerges as 'nothing but a continuation of language.' And the next world, poetically speaking, is 'materialized into a part of speech, into a grammatical tense.' Thus is born the idea of the poetic paradise.

Thinking over this poetic paradise, in which art outshines life, eternity has taken up residence in grammar, and death has been transmuted into a stream of words, one would naturally like to know just where in, or beyond, the world it is situated. Is one's 'afterlife' going to take place in the heads of poets and their readers? Is heaven being located in the world, in the precinct of art? Or is art being elevated above the world into a transcendent realm? Is the new realm available to all, through their common possession of language? Is 'poetry' to be taken literally as verse, or is the word meant in some broader sense? Are there social consequences? (In his essay on Derek Walcott, Brodsky says that the poetic calling is 'the most sound programme of social change there is.') Political ones? Is a pantheon of poets now to replace, or be added to, the pantheon of saints? (Brodsky does suggest that we should 'worship' Auden on the basis of his poetry.) Brodsky, who arrives at his vision on a fairly high plane of abstraction, does not address these questions, but there can be no doubt that he is speaking, at least in part, of the enterprise of civilization as a whole. That is, the new afterlife evidently does depend on the living, who can be aware of the dead and their doings in life only because there is such a thing as civilization. The characteristics of paradise that he finds in civilization are spiritual purity (or, at any rate, the striving for it), an afterlife and a potential endlessness or eternity. The idea of eternity is especially important. Associated with religious paradise, eternity signifies perfection, the end of change, absoluteness, finality. As an aspect of civilization, it signifies just the opposite: imperfection, ceaselessness of change, the provisionality of all present forms of culture. As usual, Brodsky makes the point in the form of a statement about language. For time, he says, 'is literally an afterword to everything in the world, and the poet, who constantly deals with the self-generating nature of language, is the first to know this.' In other words, here on earth there is nothing that can be said, no matter how revelatory it may be, that cannot be added to, revised or superseded—that does not call for, and summon up, a sequel. The poet's obedience to the call of language rather than to any particular truth that has already been put into words—in effect, giving his highest allegiance to the *next* thing that is going to be said—turns out to have large implications. It means that, if he understands his own calling, and is faithful to it, he will grasp that no word spoken can ever be the last word, that no truth is the final truth. That is why language, via time, 'absorbs deity'. Indeed, it absorbs one deity after another, and discovers new ones as well. In her poem to Rilke, Tsvetaeva continues to interrogate him about paradise, and Brodsky quotes the lines

> Am I right, Rainer, God is a *growing*
> Baobab? Not a Golden Louis.
> There's not just one God, right? Above him there
>   must be yet another
> God?

For 'Art is something more ancient and universal than any faith with which it enters into matrimony, begets children—but with which it does not die.' In the last analysis, this may be what 'time . . . worships language' means: that civilization is never completed, nor should we ever expect it to be.

One feature of the ecclesiastical paradise that the poetic one must do without is bliss. It must do without even the consolation in the face of evil offered by religious faith, for, rejecting the all-inclusive claims of every dogma, it requires us to face without explanation what Brodsky, interpreting Tsvetaeva's poetic vision, calls simply 'the unacceptability of the world.' For Brodsky, this unacceptability is metaphysical and spiritual bedrock. What makes the world unacceptable decidedly includes the deaths at the hands of the Soviet state of millions of blameless people, but those events, and the revolution that precipitated them, are singular only in that they were an 'absolute baring—to the bone'—of 'the core of existence' as a whole. To 'accept' such events—to relinquish one's anger, to permit oneself to be consoled in any way, by religion or anything else—is for him a form of spiritual collapse. Teachings of acceptance, he believes, may even play into the hands of the state, which would like nothing better than for everyone to accept what it has done.

The temptation to beat a horrified retreat from the suffering and disorder of our time to the comfort of the 'traditional values' of one dogmatic faith or another are always present, as events in the Middle East, the United States and elsewhere make clear. To the dogmatist, once The Word has been spoken, all that remains is repetition and exegesis; thereafter, all work is basically missionary work. Implicit in every dogma is a dream of stasis—of a world ordered according to a revelation that has already been handed down. In such a world, any 'afterword' can at best be tolerated, at worst suppressed. This is the germ of violence and repression which is latent in all dogma, no matter how benign its substance. In opposition to these static faiths, Brodsky offers his vision, based on his understanding of art and artistic creativity, of a world civilization that is unfinished and in principle unfinishable. In this vision, the place for endlessness is not in heaven but on earth, and the spiritual abundance that is bound to be brought forth by new generations is not to be feared or merely tolerated. It is welcomed and affirmed.

The prisoner is permitted to exchange letters with members of his family and receive visits from them to the extent stipulated by the corrective-educational grade under which he is serving his sentence. If it is in the interests of his re-education, he may be permitted to exchange letters with other people as well, and/or to receive visits from them. To ensure that the educatonal impact of the prison term is achieved, the prisoner's letters are censored.

(Law Fifty-nine of the Czechoslovak Penal Code, dealing with the serving of prison sentences.)

In the last week of May 1982, six days before my release from prison, Václav Benda and I were moved from the bookbinding workshop to Bloc One, where Václav Havel was being kept.* Both Havel and I were on the morning shift, the weather was fine and the courtyard fairly open, so I was able to spend my remaining

---

* Václav Havel, Jiří Dienstbier and Václav Benda were among six signatories of Charter 77 convicted of subversion in Prague in October 1979, as a result of their work for VONS, the Committee for the Defence of the Unjustly Persecuted. Havel was sentenced to four and a half years in prison, Benda four years and Dienstbier three.

In January 1980 Havel was sent to prison in Heřmanice, in North Moravia, and in March that year met up with Dienstbier and Benda there. In July 1981 he was transferred to Plzeň-Bory prison, where he was kept until January 1983, when he became seriously ill with pneumonia. He was moved to prison hospital in Prague, and subsequently released to 'home care'. No decision has so far been made as to whether he must serve the remainder of his sentence.

Altogether Havel wrote 144 letters to his wife, Olga. In 'Under Eastern Eyes' (*Granta* 20), Timothy Garton Ash writes about a recent meeting with Havel.

afternoons strolling with him in the most remote of the prison areas, the wryly-named Bory 'Versailles' (here, in spite of the prison workshops and rubbish heaps, a few traces of an ancient garden remained). Over the long months we had exchanged no more than a few words: words snatched at odd moments—at meal-times or the occasional sports event, at the gatherings to celebrate the Victorious February or the October Revolution, at a rare concert of recordings of works by Bach, or at the prison entrance, when the members of the laundry staff (which included Havel) returned to their cells.

For me, at least, things were coming full circle—indeed, with my imminent release there was something of the euphoria we had felt in Heřmanice, in January 1980, when after seven months of isolation in the interrogation cells we were suddenly allowed to speak to each other, to prepare our snacks together and sit next to each other while watching the evening news. Strangely, of the two of us, Havel was in the better mood. As long as the others remained behind, my own freedom meant little to me and my departure seemed incomplete. Havel, however, viewed my release as the first of many and as a cause for optimism. A tireless systematizer (his effects were folded in his cubby-hole with the precision you would expect of a newly graduated military officer), he kept giving me instructions, asking me to repeat everything over and over, point by point, and laughing with me as we plotted my return to the outside world.

His letters, especially, were important to him. Aware as he was of the campaign being waged abroad in connection with our trial and imprisonment, he was afraid that he might enter the public consciousness as a 'professional revolutionary' or 'dissident'—not, as he wished, as a writer, a seeker after truth, but as a kind of cultural cruise missile, deployed by one superpower against another. He was against bullshit, regardless of where it might come from. If he was primarily against home-grown bullshit, it was simply because he lived in Czechoslovakia and it was his duty to start at home. 'If I lived elsewhere,' he said, 'I would doubtless be trying to prevent the construction of a new runway at Frankfurt Airport, collecting signatures against the installation of Pershing and cruise missiles and voting for the Green Party.'

On 7 January 1980, those of us sentenced in the VONS trial were led out in hand-cuffs from our interrogation cells into the Pankrác courtyard, put on a bus and placed well apart among the other prisoners—bound, in strict isolation, for our North Moravian prison.

On arriving in Olomouc, Havel, Benda and I were told to board the Heřmanice bus. We were given no other instructions, but nervously tried to sit down next to each other. Even here we were not allowed to smoke, eat or speak. Cautiously, I fished out a photograph of the group, smuggled in during a Christmas visit, and gave it to Havel, who managed to hide it without the guards noticing. In Heřmanice we were taken down into the cellar—are all prison changing-rooms located in the cellar?—and from there to a registration and arrivals department. The next day we started working—cutting wire out of PVC insulation. It was freezing cold, but at least we were together. And it seemed at first that we would stay together: not only had we been sent to the same prison, but we were billeted in the same section, worked in the same factory and were even able to talk to one another.

A few days later the prison governor called us in and explained this surprising state of affairs: although our crimes may have been political, we would serve our sentence in an ordinary prison camp. Instead of the ideal conditions (as he put it) in which our colleague Jiři Lederer was detained, we would be lining up in the open courtyard, exposed to the rain and snow, queuing for our meals in the company of common criminals.

It sounded terrifying. However, it wasn't long before these 'common criminals' were giving us paté, lard and bacon, searching out clean shirts with buttons on them, not to mention discrediting or beating up any informer planted on us. Others in our situation would have been scrubbing the latrines, but the only job they assigned us was sweeping out the 'culture room' (the room with the TV set). (We later showed our gratitude and scrubbed the latrines anyway.) Of course, some of the prisoners spied on us; some, to improve their conditions, informed on us. Men in prison are a reflection of society in general—but distorted, heightened: the mask of convention is torn aside and they behave as their nature dictates. While any weakness is mercilessly and cruelly punished and abused—and violence openly displayed—any strong character trait is respected, and the qualities of every newcomer are fully acknowledged.

Our journey into this world had been intimated (doubtless unintentionally) by the commentaries of *Rudé právo* and TV reportage. As a result, we were soon being asked to help in almost every situation: to write applications for the reopening of prisoners' cases, to complain about illegal treatment, to advise on broken marriages and psychological crises—suicide, poker and the love-lives of Prague actresses. More than that, in an environment where every man regarded every other man as an informer, we were accepted, thanks in no small part to the activities for which we had been sentenced. And thanks to the prisoners getting to know us, we were treated as exceptions—men to whom it was possible to entrust anything without fear of repercussions. This fact was quickly grasped by the governor when he informed us—loudly—that we would not be setting up a branch of VONS in his prison, and duly sent Havel and Benda to the punishment cells for having written some letters on behalf of an illiterate gypsy.

The first activity he forbade us was writing—any writing. This included a ban on making notes. In order, he said, that we wouldn't be millionaires after our release, he would subject us, if we attempted to pursue this particular line, to thirty days' solitary confinement.

All that remained were the letters home. According to the regulations, we were allowed to write four pages once a week. Prisoners were permitted to write about personal and family matters only—nothing else: nothing about conditions or the serving of their sentences. What exactly consituted a personal matter? It seemed to escape the authorities that the serving of one's sentence was the most personal matter of all. And how do you explain to such people that, to a writer, writing about literature was a personal matter?

Letter-writing was the only way to communicate with the outside world, the only regular contact with one's family, apart from a one-hour visit once every three months. It was also the only creative outlet for those accustomed to writing as a way of life. At the same time, it was a struggle. The first problem was finding a time and a place. At the beginning we managed, occasionally, to write our letters together in the common-room. Then the governor banned us from congregating there, denouncing us as class enemies—adding, by the by, the interesting fact that all *coups d'état* were hatched in prison. Our letters were written usually on Saturdays and Sundays, between queuing for breakfast, the compulsory film screening, lunch, the head-count, or the evening news on TV; in the middle of tidying up or the various irksome activities which constitute the fiction of re-education; or in a room where people snored, quarrelled, used dope, or fought. Here we each tried to snatch a few valuable minutes—learning how to piece together four cogent pages, how to say as much as possible about the situation, how to detail one's state of mind and yet not provoke the displeasure of the censors.

More often than not the letter failed to get through. It didn't concentrate on personal matters. It touched on forbidden matters. It ridiculed permitted matters. It was mischievous. It was illegible. The handwriting was too small. The lines were too closely spaced. The margins had not been observed. It was in code. It was an essay.

Incidentally, the predicament of letters from home was the same. On one occasion the governor wanted to put me in a cell for something my brother wrote. He confiscated a letter from Václav Benda's wife, in which she informed him that 'the stove was smoking'—what did she mean by that? Havel was denied a letter because his brother had the temerity to use an English expression. It was as if our relatives were also under prison rules.

To begin with we did our best to understand the rules—even to conform to them. We read our letters to one another and discussed the chances of their being let through. We were constantly surprised. One letter, which we judged quite innocent, would be confiscated, while another, in which we tried to go to the limit of the rules (as we understood them), got through. We were frustrated, inevitably—eventually to be liberated by the realization that a thinking man's desire for order and logic was just as futile in prison as it was outside. There were no rules: whether the letters would be released depended solely on the mood or caprice of the governor and the other censors. The confiscation of a letter was often an unspoken punishment. Informers might repeat some unfavourable news about us, a foreign radio station perhaps mention our presence in Heřmanice. However maddening this may have been, there was nothing we could do about it.

Occasionally, then, we exchanged letters in the changing-room, merely in order to discuss them. The themes of the letters often continued conversations begun over our semolina pudding or during the line-up for work (indeed, at any opportunity which presented itself). We wrote with our colleagues in mind, with the satisfaction that if the letter did not get through, at least the other two would see it. If we wanted to communicate something important to those at home, we wrote in such a way that at least one of our three letters would stand a chance of getting through. Sometimes all three were confiscated. When this happened regularly, we let it be known (in front of informers) that we would not bother writing at all. Our next letters got through. A lengthier disruption of our correspondence would have brought undesirable publicity.

Havel was a frequent target for persecution, mainly because of his success abroad as a playwright: the source of irritation being the belief that he had earned large sums of money. If his alleged earnings were enough to make many admire Havel, they were likewise enough to make others envy him. Havel's polite and courteous behaviour—in contrast with the brutal arrogance of the prison authorities—may have given the governor and some of the warders the impression that he was weak and that it would be easy to break him. They were greatly provoked, and consequently irritated, by him—for the most part because his evident embarrass-ment when he was being bullied was followed not by his submission, but by a quiet, unyielding perseverence incomprehensible to them. They confiscated one of his letters, saying that it was essayistic. 'You keep going on about the order of the spirit, the order of being,' the governor shouted. 'The only orders that need concern you are ours.' When the governor forbade Havel to write essays, ordering him to write only about himself, he started a series on his fifteen different moods. After the eighth, the governor forbade him to humber them. The remaining seven are unnumbered: they, like the two letters we publish here, exist nevertheless.

Jiří Dienstbier

Translated from the Czech by Pavel Stránský and Alan Mason

6 September 1981

Dear Olga,

I'm sure you remember the end of Ionesco's *The Chairs*, when the Orator comes on to give the assembled public an extremely important message: it amounts to the sum total of all that the Old Man and Old Woman have learned during their lifetime— knowledge they must pass on to the world before they leave it; knowledge that will reveal some fundamental truth and explain 'how it all is.' The Orator, it is implied, is going to acquaint his audience with the true meaning of life. But the long-awaited speech consists merely of utter gibberish.

Many have interpreted this as expressing the author's conviction that communication is impossible, that two people can never come to an understanding about anything, much less the 'meaning of life', because life has no meaning: all is vanity and man is hopelessly submerged in total meaninglessness. Hardly unexpected, therefore, that Ionesco is for many the dramatist of absolute scepticism and nihilism.

What Ionesco meant is his own business. I mention the play now not because I want to impose my own explanation on it, but because the motif of the Orator seems to me a useful starting point.

Notice: the Old Man and Old Woman—aware of how significant their message is, and the importance of giving it to the world in a comprehensible form—do not deliver the message themselves, but hire a professional communicator.

If the Orator's purpose was really to inform the public of the meaning of life, then he failed. Why? Because the meaning of life is not a snippet of unfamiliar information conveyed by someone who knows it to someone who doesn't—as an astronomer might tell us the number of planets in the solar system, or a statistician how many alcoholics there are. The mystery of being and the meaning of life are not 'data', and people cannot be separated into those who know the data and those who don't. None of us becomes 'better' than anyone else simply by learning something others have not learned, or rather by encountering some fundamental 'truth' that others have missed. Safarik correctly distinguishes between truth and information: information is portable and transmissible; truth is less simple. (In any case, history has adequately demonstrated that the more people who succumb to the delusion that truth is a commodity which can readily be passed on, the greater the horrors that follow—because this delusion inevitably leads to the conviction that the world can be improved simply by spreading the truth as quickly as possible. And what quicker way to spread it than by violence?)

As I understand it, 'the meaning of life' is not 'objectively' knowable or graspable as a concept at all.

For me, the notion of some complete and finite knowledge, that explains everything and raises no further questions, relates clearly to the idea of an end—an end to the spirit, to life, to time and to being. However, anything meaningful ever said on the matter (including every religious gospel) is remarkable for its dramatic openness, its incompleteness. It is not a conclusive statement so much as a challenge or an appeal—to something that is, in the highest sense, living; to something that overwhelms us or speaks to us, obliges or excites us; to something that accords with our innermost experience and may even change our entire life, but which never, of course, attempts to settle unequivocally the unanswerable question of meaning. Instead, it tends to suggest how to live with the question.

Is that too little? I don't think so. Living with the question means constantly 'responding' to it, or rather, having some form of living contact with that meaning, always hearing a faint echo of it. It means not an end to the problem, but an ever-closer co-existence with it. Though we cannot 'answer' it in the traditional sense of the word, we, by longing for it and seeking after it, confront it indirectly over and over again. We are a little like the blind man touching the woman he loves, whom he has never seen and never will. The question of the meaning of life is not a full stop at the end of life, but the beginning of a deeper experience of it. It is like a light whose source we cannot see, but in whose illumination we nevertheless live—whether we delight in its incomprehensible abundance or suffer from its incomprehensible paucity.

Ultimately, being in constant touch with this mystery is what makes us genuinely human. Man is the only creature who is both a part of being (and thus a bearer of its mystery) and aware of that mystery as a mystery. He is both the question and the questioner, and cannot help being so. It might even be said that, through man, being can inquire after itself.

The first serious confrontation with the question of meaning does not occur only when one feels that life has lost its meaning; it also happens at the moment when, as a result of one's own reflections, one is seriously touched by meaning itself. This moment also constitutes the beginning of man's history as a human being, of the history of culture, of the history of what we might call 'the order of the spirit.'

This is a history not of 'answering', but of 'questioning'; it does not begin with a life whose meaning is already known, but with a life knowing itself ignorant of its own meaning and prepared to come to terms with this hard fact constantly.

This 'coming to terms with meaning' is the most complex, the most obscure and at the same time the most important metaphysical experience one can go through in life.

I don't know any other way of tackling the question of 'the meaning of life' than undergoing the experience personally and trying to report on it. In one way or another, this is what I've been trying to do from the outset in my letters, and I intend to carry on, in the hope that whatever I manage to squeeze out in these difficult circumstances will be taken neither literally nor too seriously, but as a stream of improvised attempts to articulate my unarticulated 'inner life'. Above all, let me not sound like Ionesco's Orator.

I can't wait for the visit!

Kisses,
Vasek

---

13 March 1982

Dear Olga,

I am thinking of the contradiction that many have seen between, on the one hand, those actions of mine which supposedly betray me as an incorrigible 'idealist', always willing to have another go at smashing the wall down with his head in the naïve belief that he can change the world—and, on the other hand, my writing, which, they say, betrays me as a pessimist and a sceptic, if not an outright nihilist, incapable of believing that anything can ever turn out for the best.

Well, I'd like to put the matter straight.

First, if a person doesn't remain completely silent, if he says what he thinks now and again, and simply behaves as his sense of responsibility dictates, this doesn't mean that he is an 'idealist' or a 'dreamer', or that he harbours illusions of changing the world. (On the contrary: such people are all the more likely to display a good-humoured self-deprecation.) It means merely that he is trying to behave 'normally'—that is, freely and with dignity, in harmony with himself.

Secondly, when a reviewer of *The Mountain Hotel* remarked that the play came out of the very depths of my despair, I had to laugh. I do often write in a state of agitation, depression, unhappiness and despair, because I find writing so difficult, and because I am so seldom satisfied with what I write. But when—in happy moments—my work goes well and proceeds as I had imagined or even better, I rejoice and am as happy as a child. My feelings when I write relate almost exclusively to how the work is going, and hardly at all to what the writing is about.

I find it inconceivable that the source of my writing or my desire to write might be despair, and in any case I don't know why I, of all people, should feel hopeless. I simply observe with deep absorption the world around me; I select from it those motifs that speak to me personally and have a certain special inner charge. From this an important message may radiate, if properly understood and developed—a message associated with what I take to be the 'central themes'. From such motifs, with happy absorption, I ultimately build the tiny artificial constructions which are my plays. The better my work goes, the more I am drawn along by 'being manifesting itself', and the greater my joy. If people call my plays absurd, depressing, upsetting, shocking or even—as they say—'dead-end', this is certainly not because I have surrendered to such moods while writing them. Rather it is just because it seems right, because I was pulled that way by the thing itself; because it seemed the most authentic way of touching on the central themes and opening them up in a suggestive way; because I suppose that way corresponds to my general experience of the world—quite simply, because I like it that way, it entertains me that way, and I consider it to be just right. And when I do manage to get something right, I try to forget I have written it and imagine going to the theatre to see it as an ordinary member of the audience. My sense then is that, however absurd, tragic, depressing or cruel it might be, and despite its upsetting qualities—indeed through them—I would certainly find it delightful, liberating and elevating, perhaps to the point of tears. I would be delighted to hear things called by their proper names once more, delighted that being was revealed in all its fullness, and therefore that all was not yet lost. Such an experience can't possibly depress me—in fact, it greatly strengthens my conviction that somehow everything makes sense: our life, our toiling and moiling, our god-forsaken world; in short, that there is some genuine hope left. What really depresses me is to see on the stage something completely different: a slimy, insinuating, clever, seductive, devilishly ethical lie.

Thirdly, it should be more or less obvious why there is no real contradiction between what is (mistakenly) taken for my 'naïve idealism' and my 'pessimism': they are merely two intrinsic and (in my personal feelings) inseparable aspects of the same existential tendency. Because I believe in the meaning of being and need to touch it continually by trying to make sense of my own existence in the world, I struggle constantly against nonsense, and write about it all the time with as much joyful radicalism as I can muster. Only by ceaselessly squaring accounts with nonsense and holding up the mirror to its constant victories, can I strengthen in myself the experience of meaningfulness and give substance to my faith. And if, at the outset of this 'futile' commitment and my writing about 'futility', there is faith, a feeling of meaningfulness and joy, then at the end of it the faith is deepened, the meaningfulness strengthened and the joy supreme: for this is the joy of those who have tasted the 'life in truth'.

I kiss you,
Vasek

Translated from the Czech by Paul Wilson

Olga Havloná

If Samuel Beckett had been born in Czechoslovakia we'd still be waiting for Godot.

Samuel Beckett's "Waiting for Godot" is banned in Czechoslovakia.

In fact, any writing that differs from the opinions of the Czech government is banned in Czechoslovakia.

Luckily, Beckett does not live in Czechoslovakia, but what of those writers who do?

Fortunately, some of their work can be read in Index on Censorship, a magazine which fights censorship by publishing the work of censored poets, authors, playwrights, journalists and publishers.

We publish work from all over the world regardless of politics, religion or race.

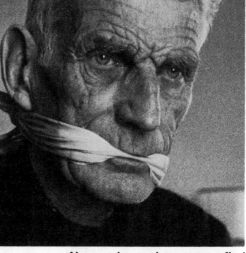

Our contributions come from wherever work is censored.

We also publish commentaries, first-hand testimonials, factual reports and a country by country chronicle.

You'll always find publishers, writers and journalists at the front of the struggle for free speech.

Now you know where you can find their work.

Please write to us for a free copy of our magazine at: 39c Highbury Place, London N5 1QP or you can telephone us on: 01-359 0161.

Index on Censorship for crying out loud.

IAN JACK
FINISHED WITH
ENGINES

My father wrote a kind of autobiography in the years before he died. I have it now beside me in a big brown paper envelope, 150 pages of lined foolscap covered with the careful handwriting—light on the up-stroke and heavy on the down—which he learned on a slate in a Scottish schoolroom eighty years ago. He called these pages 'a mixture of platitudes and personal nostalgia.'

My father's life spanned eight decades of the twentieth century, but he met nobody who mattered very much and lived far removed from the centre of great events. He was born in the year the Boer War ended, in a mill town in the Scottish lowlands. A Co-operative Society hearse took him to a crematorium in the same town six months before Britain fought what was probably the last of its imperial wars, in the Falklands. He was too young for the Somme and too old to be called up for El Alamein. He never saw the inside of Auschwitz and knew nobody who did. He neglects to tell us his role (if any) in the General Strike. He worked for most of his life as a steam mechanic (though he always used the word 'fitter'); a good one, so I have been told by the people who worked beside him.

He started work as a fourteen-year-old apprentice in a linen mill on five shillings a week and progressed through other textile factories in Scotland and Lancashire, into the engine-room of a cargo steamer, down a coal pit, through a lead works and a hosepipe factory. He loved applying for jobs—would study the advertisements, remove the cap from his fountain pen, rest the lined foolscap on a chess-board he had made for himself, and write steadily in an armchair near the fire—and only fate in the shape of unwelcoming managements prevented his moving to work in jute mills on the Hoogli or among a colony of French progressive thinkers in the South Pacific.

He did not prosper. Instead he ended his working life a few miles from where he began it, and in much the same way: in overalls and over a lathe and waiting for the dispensation of the evening hooter, when he would stick his leg over his bike and cycle home. He never owned a house and he never drove a car, and today there is very little public evidence that he ever lived.

Few of his workplaces survive. The cargo steamer went to the scrapyard long ago, of course, but even the shipping line it belonged

235

to has vanished. The coal pit is a field. Urban grasslands and car parks have buried the foundations of the mills. The house he grew up in has been demolished and replaced with a traffic island. The school where he learned his careful handwriting has made way for a supermarket. As a result, I am one of the sons of the manufacturing classes whom de-industrialization has disinherited; in many respects it is a benign disinheritance, because many of the places my father worked were hell-holes, but it is also one so sudden and complete that it bewilders me.

S till, there is this 'mixture of platitudes and personal nostalgia.' But I'm exaggerating the paucity of what he left behind. There was actually *much* more than the contents of the brown envelope. There were books, suits from Burtons, long underpants, cuff-links, shirt armbands, pipes which continued to smell of Walnut Plug, the polished black boots he always preferred to shoes, half-empty bottles of Bay Rum, tools in tool-boxes, shaving brushes, cigarette cards, photograph albums, photographs loose in suitcases, tram tickets, picture postcards sent from seaside resorts and inland spas—Rothesay and Llandudno, Matlock and Peebles. *Here for the week. Weather mixed. Lizzie and Jim.* What a man for collecting! Even here, interleaved among the foolscap, I find a card from the Cyclists' Touring Club for the Christmas of 1927, a bill from the Spring Lodge Hotel (family and commercial) for sixteen shillings and fourpence and a menu from the mess of the cargo steamer *Nuddea* dated 12 October, 1928 (that day's lunch, somewhere in the tropics, comprised pea soup, fried fish, roast sirloin of beef). And in a smaller envelope inside a larger one is a pamphlet on humanist funeral ceremonies, for 'when it is desired that no reference should be made to theological beliefs but, rather, to the ethical and natural aspects of human life.'

He left no explicit instructions, but the hint is clear enough. We only half-obliged. We did not stand at the lectern and read aloud, from the scraps of card which tumble from this smaller envelope:

> I want no heaven for which I must give up my reason and no immortality that demands the surrender of my individuality.

Or:

> Forgive me Lord, my little joke on thee
> and,
> I'll forgive your one big joke on me.

The truth is that a strident proclamation of my father's doubt would have sat strangely out of kilter with the last quarter of the twentieth century in Britain. Who, in this country of the don't-knows, now doubts doubt? It would have been like listening, that day in the crematorium, to the proposition that the earth moved round the sun.

I was born in 1945 and grew up in the Scotland of the 1950s. But in our house we lived in the 1910s and 20s as well, concurrently. The past sustained us. It came home from work every evening with flat cap and dirty hands and drew its weekly wages from industries which even then were sleep-walking their way towards extinction.

Our village lay at the northern end of the Forth Bridge, three large cantilevers which had been built with great technical ingenuity, and at some cost to human life, to carry the railway one and a half miles over the Firth of Forth. It was opened by the Prince of Wales in 1890. The village was unimaginable without the bridge. Its size reduced everything around it to the scale of models: trains, ships, the village houses—all of them looked as though they could be picked up and thrown into a toy cupboard. The three towers rose even higher than our flat, which stood in a council estate 250 feet above the sea. On still summer mornings, when a fog lay banked across the water and the foghorns moaned below, we could see the tops of the cantilevers poking up from the shrouds: three perfect metal alps which, when freshly painted, glistened in the sun. Postcards sold in the village post office described the bridge as the world's eighth wonder, and went on in long captions to describe how it had been built. More than 5,000 men had 'laboured day and night for seven years' with materials which included 54,160 tons of steel, 740,000 cubic feet of granite, 64,300 cubic yards of concrete and 21,000 tons of cement. They had driven in 6,500,000 rivets. Sixty workers had been killed during those years, some blown by gales into the sea and drowned, others flattened by falling sheets of steel.

For several decades the bridge dazzled Scotland as the pinnacle of native enterprise, and then slowly declined to the status of an old ornament, like the tartan which surrounded its picture on tea towels and shortbread tins. People of my father's generation had been captivated by its splendour and novelty. Pushing his bike as we walked together up the hill, he would sometimes say ruefully: 'I became an engineer because I wanted to build Forth Bridges.'

From quite an early age I sensed that something had gone wrong with my father's life, and hence our lives, and that I had been born too late to share a golden age, when the steam engine drove us forward and a watchful God was at the helm. Scotland, land of the inventive engineer! Glasgow, the workshop of the world! I hoped the future would be like the past, for all our sakes.

My father began his apprenticeship in 1916 in one of Dunfermline's many linen mills. The town was famous for the quality of its tablecloths and sheets—'napery' used to be the generic word—and ran along a ridge with a skyline spiked by church steeples and factory chimneys. The gates of my father's first factory were only a few hundred yards from his home. He writes:

> We oiled and greased and greased and oiled . . . pirn winding frames, bobbin winding frames, cop winding frames, overpick and underpick looms, dobbie machines, beetles, calenders and shafting. There was never an end to shafting! A main shaft approximately 250 feet in length driving thirty-two wing shafts of an average length of seventy-five feet. This was all underfloor . . . and eight of these wing shafts had to be oiled every day when the engine stopped for the mill dinner hour.

Later he moved to the blacksmith's shop, where he made 'hoop iron box-corners' for the packing department and learned how to handle a hammer and chisel. 'Chap, man, chap!' said the blacksmith. 'Ye couldnae chap shite aff an auld wife's erse.' Eventually, towards the end of his apprenticeship, he was transferred to the engine house:

Sometimes I would be allowed to attend the mill engine for a week or a fortnight . . . taking diagrams from each cylinder with an old Richards Indicator, and studying the cards, I felt just as a doctor must feel when sounding his patient's lungs with a stethoscope. If the cards were all right and the beat of eighty-five revs per minute had become automatic listening, then I could relax, and, as smoking was just tolerated in the engine house, have a Woodbine. It is said that the ratio of the unpleasant to the pleasant experiences in life is as three to one. The engine 'tenting' [tending] was one of those pleasant intermissions.

Reading this, I try to construct a picture of my father thirty years before I knew him. There he sits next to the cascading, burnished cranks of the mill engine. I know from snapshots that he has curly black hair and a grave kind of smile. Perhaps he's reading something—H.G. Wells, a pamphlet from the Scottish Labour Party, the Rubáiyáe of Omar Khayyam. The engine pushes on at eighty-five revolutions per minute. Shafting revolves in its tunnels. Cogs and belts drive looms. Shuttles flash from side to side weaving tablecloths patterned with the insignia of the Peninsular and Oriental Steamship Company and the Canadian Pacific Railway. Stokers crash coal into the furnaces—more heat, more steam, more tablecloths—and black clouds tumble from the fluted stone top of the factory chimney, to fly before the south-west wind and then to rise and join the smoke-stream from a thousand other work-places in lowland Scotland: jute, cotton and thread mills, linoleum factories, shipyards, iron-smelters, locomotive works. Human and mechanical activity is eventually expressed as a great national movement of carbon particles, which float high across the North Sea and drop as blighting rain on the underdeveloped peasant nations to the east.

In 1952, after twenty-two years working in Lancashire, my father returned to Scotland, to his old factory. It was his tenth move, and a complete accident: the result of yet another letter to an anonymous box number underneath the words 'Maintenance Engineer Wanted'.

My mother, surrounded by people who called her husband Jock (his name was Harry) and talked of grand weeks in Blackpool, had fretted to be home among her 'own folk', but my father hadn't minded Lancashire. He liked to imitate the dialect of the cotton weavers and spinners; it appealed to his sense of theatre, just as the modest beer-drinking and the potato-pie suppers of the Workers' Educational Association sustained his hope that the world might be improved, temperately. The terraced streets shut my mother in, but my father, making the best of it, found them full of 'character': men in clogs with Biblical names—Abraham, Ezekiel—and shops that sold tripe and herbal drinks, sarsaparilla, dandelion and burdock. He bought the *Manchester Guardian* and talked of Lancashire people as more 'go-ahead' than the wry, cautious Scotsmen of his childhood. Lancastrians were sunnier people in a damper climate. They had an obvious folksiness, a completely realized industrial culture evolved in the dense streets and tall factories of large towns and cities. Lancashire meant Cottonopolis, the Hallé Orchestra playing Beethoven in the Free Trade Hall, knockers-up, comedians, thronged seaside resorts with ornamental piers. In Fife, pit waste encroached on fishing villages and mills grew up in old market towns, but industry had never completely conquered an older way of life based on the sea and the land.

Later he would talk of Bolton as though he had been to New York, as a place of opportunity, with witty citizens who called a spade a spade. A Lancashire accent, overhead on a Scottish street, would have him hurrying towards the speaker. Often he was disappointed:

'Do you mind me asking where you're from?'

'Rochdale.'

'Och, I'm sorry, I thought it might be Bolton.'

We moved back to Fife. The furniture went by van while we came north by train, behind a locomotive with a brass name-plate: *Prince Rupert*. I was seven. I held a jam-jar with two goldfish, whose bowl had been trusted to the removers, as Prince Rupert hauled us over the summits of Shap and Beattock. The peaks and troughs of telegraph wires jerked past like sagging skipping ropes. Red-brick terraces with advertisements for brown bread and pale ale on their windowless ends gave way to austere villas made of stone. The wistfulness of homecoming overcame my parents as we crossed the border; Lancashire and Fife then seemed a subcontinental distance apart and not a few hours' drive and a cup of coffee on the motorway. Our carriage was shunted at Carstairs Junction and we changed stations as well as trains in Edinburgh. Here English history no longer provided locomotive names. We had moved to new railway territory, with older and quainter steam engines named after glens, lochs and characters from the novels of Sir Walter Scott. At dusk we sped across the Forth Bridge behind an Edwardian machine called *Jingling Geordie*, sailing past our new home and on towards the small shipbuilding town where my mother's father had settled.

When I awoke the next morning rivetters were already drilling like noisy dentists in the local shipyard, and express trains drifted, whistling, along the embankment next to the sea. The smells of damp steam and salt, sweet and sharp, blew round the corner and met the scent of morning rolls from the bakery. Urban Lancashire could not compare with this and, like my mother, I never missed it. But what was linear progress for a seven-year-old may have been the staleness of a rounded circle for a man of fifty: this little industrial utopia of my childish eye had foundations which were already rotting.

Two days later we moved a few miles down the coast and into our home beside the Forth Bridge, and my father went to work in his new-old factory. It was a shock:

> The scrap merchants were at work; they had removed most of the looms and machinery from the old weaving shed, which made it a most cheerless place. The blackbirds were nesting in the old Jacquard machines. All the beam engines had gone and the surface condenser on top of the engine house in the mill road was now standing dry and idle. The latest engine (installed in 1912) was a marine-type compound; it was also standing idle with the twelve ropes still on the flywheel. The engine packing and all the tools were still in the cupboard, the indicator, all cleaned, lay ready to take diagrams; there was even a tin of Brasso and cloths

for polishing the handrails. It seemed as if everything
was lying in readiness for an unearthly visitor to open the
main steam valve. But there was no steam, everything
was cold and silent . . .

The views from our new house were astounding. On the day we
moved in, in October 1952, I stood at the top of the outside stair and
watched a procession of trains crossing the bridge and a tall-
funnelled cargo steamer passing below, unladen and high out of the
water, its propeller playfully flapping the river. Pressing my nose
against the front-room window and squinting to the left I could see
Edinburgh Castle. In Lancashire all we could see from our windows
were back gardens and washing and more houses like our own, with
all the doors painted in council green. My parents' phrase, 'moving
up home to Scotland', took on a literal meaning. It was as though we
had been catapulted from a pit bottom into daylight.

In 1956, the summer before Suez, my father took us to
Aberdeen. It was my first proper holiday and the first evidence,
perhaps, of a slightly increased disposable income: all previous
excursions had been to the homes of aunts and grandparents. That
spring we studied the brochures which declared Aberdeen 'the
Silver City with the Golden Sand', and the word 'boarding house'
became part of the evening vocabulary. My father chose a name and
address and corresponded with the landlady. My mother didn't like
the sound of it: she noticed that the address did not carry the
distinguishing asterisk which marked the approval of Aberdeen's
town hall. But my father tutted and persisted: it would be fine; the
landlady sounded a nice wee woman. We went by train (an express;
high tea in the dining car) and then by bus to a grey suburb in the lee
of a headland where the North Sea sucked and boiled. It quickly
became obvious that the house was 'off the beaten track', a phrase
and a situation which always recommended themselves to my
father. It lay a change of buses away from the beach but very close
to a fish meal factory. The smell of rotting fish hung over the street
and crept into the house, to slide off the polished Rexine of the sofa
and chairs but impregnate permanently the dead collie dog which
the landlady had converted into a rug. The whiff of more marine
life, cooking in pots, came from the kitchen. We ate boiled and fried

haddock for a week and were reminded constantly that Aberdeen was then the premier fishing port of Europe. This was twenty years before the oil came in.

At night I shared a room with a young man who had an institutional haircut and dug for a living in a market garden. Other young men, equally shorn, emerged for the breakfast kippers. Mrs MacPhail, the widowed landlady, had claimed them after they had reached the age limit of the 'special schools' that contained them during adolescence. On the first morning we walked to the lighthouse and stared forlornly across the harbour mouth towards the inaccessible beach. My father said we would just have to make the best of it; the other lodgers were 'decent enough laddies . . . a wee bit simple but hardly proper dafties . . . there's no harm in them.' And there wasn't. On wet evenings the hardly-dafties took me to the cinema, and on the night before we left they gave us a concert in the room with the dog rug. My room-mate, Johnny, sang 'If I Were a Blackbird I'd Whistle and Sing.' Another hummed 'A Gordon For Me' through a comb and paper. A third placed a favourite new record on the radiogram and again and again we heard: 'Zambezi! Zambezi, Zambezi! Zam!' The next morning my father—who had a terrible fear of missing trains—rose at an extraordinarily early hour to pay the bill and surprised the landlady, naked and trying to cover herself with the remains of her pet collie.

More than twenty years later, he would mention the experience whenever the word Aberdeen looked likely to occur in a conversation, even if the rest of us had been talking about the oil rigs now moored in the firth outside the house, or what would happen to the country when the oil ran out.

My father went on cycling back from his lathe until well into the 1960s. The new decade was good to us both. I left home at eighteen and gladly entered pubs, football grounds and dance halls. Films and television plays began to represent British life as we thought we knew it. When *Saturday Night and Sunday Morning,* the film of Alan Sillitoe's novel, came to the local Regal, I was thrilled to see scenes of conscientious men working at milling machines and lathes. 'Poor bastards,' says Albert Finney in the role of the new British hero, the young worker who sticks up two fingers at respectability and grabs what he can get.

The film kindled a suspicion within me that this was the definitive verdict on my father, apparently a dupe who had worked for buttons for nearly fifty years. It was an ignorant, adolescent judgement: my father was not a 'poor bastard' and surprising things began to happen to him. I came home late one Saturday night and found him roaring with laughter at a satire show on television. He joined the Campaign for Nuclear Disarmament and worked for it long after I, an earlier but more faint-hearted member, had left. He won a couple of thousand pounds on the football pools (a total ignorance of football led to the correct forecast; virtue, for once, had its reward) and took my mother on sea voyages to Egypt and the Soviet Union, two countries which had fascinated him since Howard Carter found Tutankhamun's tomb and the Bolsheviks stormed the Winter Palace. He grew jollier and, rather than offering bitter homilies against masonic foremen and the unfairness of piece-work, settled into a new role as a teller of quaint stories.

In 1967 he retired with a present of twenty pounds in an envelope and a determination to enjoy himself. He read books on Egyptology, went to evening classes in Russian, cultivated his garden and watched quiz shows and documentaries on television. This is the passage of my father's life I know least about. Somehow we missed our connection. I neglected him, no longer went out with him on the bike, barely listened to the stories I thought he would always be there to tell.

As the old died the village filled up with new people: wives who wore jeans and loaded small cars at the nearest supermarket, husbands who drove what twenty years before would have seemed an impossible distance to work. Couples gutted old cottages and painted knock-through rooms in white, hung garlic from their kitchen shelves. In these houses 'lunch' and 'supper' supplanted 'dinner' and 'tea', but their owners, searching for a past to embellish their modern lives, went burrowing into history to uncover village traditions which had been invisible for forty years. The only village celebration of my childhood had been the one to mark the Coronation, when New Testaments and children's belts in red, white and blue had been distributed. Now an annual gala day was revived, with a bagpiper at the head of the procession, and a 'heritage trail' signposted in clean European sans-serif as though it were an exit on an autobahn. Meanwhile most of the village shops closed and vans stopped calling with the groceries. Steam locomotives no longer thundered up the gradient. The Davidsons went quiet and then dispersed. My father gave up reading newspaper stories which told of 'fights to save jobs'. Once he threw down the local weekly in disgust: 'There's nothing in here but sponsored walks and supermarket bargains.' He cycled still, taking circuitous routes to avoid the new motorways and coming home to despair at the abundance of cars. Usually on these trips he would revisit his past. The Highlands, fifty miles away, were now beyond him, but even in his seventies he could still manage to reach the Fife hills and the desolate stretch of country which had once been the Fife coalfield. He brought back news to my mother. 'Do you mind the Lindsay Colliery? It's all away, there's nothing there but fields.' Factories had gone, churches were demolished, railway cuttings filled up with plastic bottles and rusty prams.

Once around this time we visited an exhibition of old photographs in Dunfermline, his birthplace. One picture showed a street littered with horse dung and small boys standing in a cobbled gutter: the High Street, circa 1909. My father went up close. 'That's me on the left there. I remember the day the photographer came.' We looked at a boy with bare feet and a fringe cropped straight across the forehead. The photograph and the man beside it were difficult to reconcile. Quite suddenly I realized how old my father was. Afterwards he talked about writing his 'life story' and we encouraged him; for months of evenings and afternoons he sat in the easy chair with the chessboard and the foolscap on his knee, writing with his fountain pen and smiling.

He became, I suppose, like the people he had always cherished: a character. Like the photograph, he was now of historic interest, and sometimes when I came up from London I expected to find him surrounded by tape recorders and students from the nearest university department of oral history. That did not happen. One day he collapsed into the potato patch he'd been digging. Cancer was diagnosed, eventually, but he never asked for the diagnosis and was never told. For many weeks my mother nursed him as he slipped in and out of pain and consciousness. The pills did

·not seem to work; he whimpered and cried aloud like an abandoned baby, an awful sound. The doctor decided to change the medication to an old-fashioned liquid cocktail of alcohol, morphine and cocaine. After the first dose he rose bright-eyed from the pillows and saw me, up from London.

'What's yon big lazy bugger doing here?'

Those were his last words to me, and my mother worried that I'd been hurt. 'He's never spoken about you like that before. I don't know what came over him.'

We decided that it was bravado induced by alcohol, but I wondered. I remembered all the times I'd failed to help him in the garden; my uselessness with a chisel and saw; and my job, where I never got my hands dirty, or at least not literally. Or perhaps he was simply bored and had decided to liven people up.

The crematorium was a new building, concrete and glass, which had been built (as my father would have been the first to tell his mourners) near the site of one of the first railways in the world. The moorland to the east held mysterious water-filled hollows and old earthworks, traces of an eighteenth-century wagonway which had carried coal from Fife's first primitive collieries down to sailing barques moored at harbours in the firth. Here my father had played in the summers before 1914, uncovering large square stones with bolt-holes which had once secured the wagonway's wooden rails. Here also we had gone for walks on Sundays in the 1950s, smashing down thistleheads and imagining the scene as it must have been when horses were pulling wooden tubs filled with coal. The world's first industrial revolution sprang from places such as this; it had converted our ancestors from ploughmen into iron moulders, pitmen, bleachers, factory girls, steam mechanics, colonial soldiers and Christian missionaries. Now North Britain's bold participation in the shaping of the world was over. My father had penetrated the revolution's secrets when he went to night school and learned the principles of thermo-dynamics, but as the revolution's power had failed so had he. His life was bound up with its decline; they almost shared last gasps.

What I would like to experience most of all would be to find myself freed, even if only for a moment, from the weight of my body. I wouldn't want to overdo it—just to hang suspended for a reasonable period—and yet I feel intensely envious of those weightless astronauts whom we are permitted to see all too rarely on our TV screens. They seem as much at ease as fish in water: they move elegantly around their cockpit—these days quite spacious—propelling themselves forward by pushing gently off invisible walls, and sailing smoothly through the air to berth securely at their work place. At other times we have seen them conversing, as if it were the most natural thing— one of them 'the right way up', the other 'upside down' (but of course in orbit there is neither up nor down). Or we have seen them take turns to play childish games: one flicks a toffee with his thumbnail, and it flies slowly and in a perfectly straight line into the open mouth of his colleague. We have seen an astronaut squirt water from a plastic container into the air: the water does not fall or disperse but settles in a roundish mass which then, subject only to the weak forces of surface tension, lazily assumes the form of a sphere. What do they do with it then? It can't be easy to dispose of without damaging the delicate structures upholding its surface.

I wonder what it would take to make a documentary that would link together these visions, transmitted by some miracle from the satellites that flash past above our heads and above our atmosphere. A film like that, drawn from American and Soviet sources, and with an intelligent commentary, would teach everybody so much. It would certainly be more successful than the nonsense that is put out today, more successful too than porno movies.

I have also often wondered about the experiments, or more particularly the simulation courses which aspiring astronauts have to undergo and which journalists write about as if they were nothing out of the ordinary. What sense is there in them? And how is weightlessness simulated? The only technique imaginable would be to close the candidates in a vehicle in free-fall: a plane or an elevator such as Einstein postulated for the experiment designed to illustrate the concept of special relativity. But a plane, even in a vertical fall, is braked by the resistance of the air, and a lift (or rather, a fall) has additional frictional forces acting on the cable. In both cases, weightlessness (or *abaria* to the die-hard classicists) would not be complete. And even in the best case—the quite terrifying scenario of a plane dropping like a stone from a height of five or ten or twenty miles, perhaps with an additional thrust from the engines in the final stages—the whole thing would last no more than a few tens of seconds: not enough time for any training or for measuring physiological data. And then there would be the question of stopping . . .

And yet almost all of us have experienced a 'simulation' of this decidedly non-terrestrial sensation. We have felt it in a childhood dream. In the most typical version, the dreamer becomes aware with joyous amazement that flying is as easy as walking or swimming. How could you have been so stupid as not to have thought of it before? You just scull with the palms of your hands and—hey presto—you take off from the floor, moving effortlessly; you turn around, avoiding the obstacles; you pass skilfully through doors and windows, and escape into the open air: not with the frenetic whirring of a sparrow's wings, not with the voracious, stridulant haste of a swallow, but with the silent majesty of the eagles and the clouds. Where does this presentiment of what is now a concrete reality come from? Perhaps it is a memory common to the species, inherited from our proto-bird-like aquatic reptiles. Or maybe this dream is a prelude to a future, as yet unclear, in which the umbilical cord which calls us back to mother earth will be superfluous and transparent: the advent of a new mode of locomotion, more noble even than our own complicated, unsteady, two-legged style with its internal inefficiencies and its need of external friction between the feet and the ground.

From this persistent dream of weightlessness, my mind returns to a well-known rendition of the Geryon episode in the seventeenth canto of the *Inferno*. The 'wild beast', reconstructed by Dante from classical sources and also from word-of-mouth accounts of the medieval bestiaries, is imaginary and at the same time splendidly real. It eludes the burden of weight. Waiting for its two strange passengers, only one of whom is subject to the laws of gravity, the wild beast rests on the bank with its forelegs, but its deadly tail floats 'in the void' like the stern-end of a Zeppelin moored to its pylon. At first, Dante was frightened by the creature, but then that magical descent to Malebolge captured the attention of the poet-scientist, paradoxically absorbed in the naturalistic study of his fictional beast whose monstrous and symbolic form he describes with precision. The brief description of the journey on the back of the beast is singularly accurate, down to the details as confirmed by the pilots of modern hang-gliders: the silent, gliding flight, where the passenger's perception of speed is not informed by the rhythm or the noise of the wings but only by the sensation of the air which is 'on their face and from below'. Perhaps Dante, too, was reproducing here unconsciously the universal dream of weightless flight, to which psychoanalysts attribute problematical and immodest significance.

The ease with which man adapts to weightlessness is a fascinating mystery. Considering that for many people travel by sea or even by car can cause bouts of nausea, one can't help feeling perplexed. During month-long spells in space the astronauts complained only of passing discomforts, and doctors who examined them afterwards discovered a light decalcification of the bones and a transitory atrophy of the heart muscles: the same effects, in other words, produced by a period of confinement to bed. Yet nothing in our long history of evolution could have prepared us for a condition as unnatural as non-gravity.

Thus we have vast and unforeseen margins of safety: the visionary idea of humanity migrating from star to star on vessels with huge sails driven by stellar light might have limits, but not that of weightlessness: our poor body, so vulnerable to swords, to guns and to viruses, is space-proof.

Translated from the Italian by Piers Spence

Primo Levi died on 11 April, after a fall at his home in Turin. His death was reported by Italian newspapers as 'apparent suicide'.

LETTERS

The New Right and Bradford

To the Editor

In his article, 'Bradford' (*Granta* 20), Hanif Kureishi gives the impression that Ray Honeyford was dismissed from his school in Bradford as a result of spontaneous protests among parents; that these protests were provoked by articles in the *Salisbury Review*—a journal which expounds a nationalist, and perhaps even racist, ideology; and that the *Salisbury Review* is part of a sinister new phenomenon called the 'New Right', a movement whose members include not only myself, but also a large number of well known and influential people.

The Honeyford case is open to many interpretations, and I am no more likely than Mr Kureishi to have obtained the distance necessary for an objective assessment. Nevertheless, here are the facts as I perceive them.

Mr Honeyford published an article, expressing his indignation at policies which were being imposed on Bradford schools in the name of 'multi-cultural' education. He argued that these policies were incompatible with the purpose (as he saw it) of the British education system, which is to prepare children, whatever their ethnic origins, for life in British society. In the course of his argument, Mr Honeyford made some severe criticisms of Pakistan (criticisms which I, and many supporters of Miss Bhutto, endorse); he also failed to mince his words. Mincing, however, is obligatory, when discussing the question of race, and Mr Honeyford soon discovered his mistake.

His article fell into the hands of a left-wing member of Bradford council, and was noticed by activists in the local university (which has prominent departments of sociology, social policy and peace studies, where the *Lumpenintelligentsia* has found a congenial power base). The article was brought to the attention of other activists, and within no time had excited the interest of the local mosques, which are run by Islamic fundamentalists. The elders of the mosques greatly resented Mr Honeyford's charge that children were often taken away from school illegally during term time. Moreover, Mr Honeyford was already in disfavour with them, having criticized the mosques for the violent punishments which they administer to the children in their care. According to Mr Honeyford, children often came to school after their Koranic classes severely beaten. It is unfortunate, of course, that Mr Honeyford's tolerance towards the reactionary version of Islam is so slender—almost as slender, indeed, as Mr Kureishi's tolerance towards the reactionary version of conservative politics. But at least Mr Honeyford tried to fulfil his duty as a headmaster, in defending children who would otherwise have found no protector.

The net result, however, was that the mullahs and the hard left combined to organize a boycott of Mr Honeyford's school. Threats and intimidation were used to gain compliance. One greengrocer came to apologize to Mr Honeyford, saying that he could not send his child to school—although he wished to do so. If he did, he had been told, his shop windows would be smashed. Mr Ansari, the school bus driver, was actually beaten up when he continued to fulfil what he saw to be his duty. Organized agitators appeared on the 'picket lines' outside Drummond Middle School, and of course the university and its student union played an important role in mobilizing their cohorts to attend. Eventually the intimidation became intolerable, and Mr Honeyford, perceiving the damage that was being done to the children, decided that he had no choice but to resign.

To Mr Kureishi the affair has quite another aspect. He too sees a conspiracy—but one coming from the 'Right', in which Mr Honeyford is not the innocent victim but the culpable *agent provocateur*. He feels certain that this is so, since he has read various comments about myself and the *Salisbury Review,* which entitle him to say that 'the essential tenet of the New Right is expressed in the editorial of the first issue of the *Salisbury Review*', and to identify that tenet in the following words: 'the consciousness of nationhood is the highest form of political consciousness.'

As a matter of fact, the editorial in question says no such thing. In the course of discussing the universal possibility of conservatism, the editorial argues as follows:

. . . a version of conservatism flourishes wherever [local] attachments flourish. Even if it is true that the consciousness of nationhood is the highest form of political consciousness, that is itself a general truth about the human condition, as capable of elucidation in the language and preconceptions of foreign peoples as in the symbols of English Tory politics.

A contentious utterance, certainly, but surely not one capable of bearing the sinister interpretation that Mr Kureishi wishes to impose on his unfairly extracted 'central tenet'.

Mr Kureishi completes his intellectual sketch with another quotation, this time alleged to be from an article of mine:

Those who are concerned about racism in Britain, that call British society 'racist', have no genuine attachment to British customs and institutions, or any genuine allegiance to the Crown.

In so far as I have ever written anything resembling that clumsy sentence, it is in an article in *The Times,* warning of the dangers of anti-semitism. The article begins as follows:

The campaign to portray British society in general, and the Conservative Party in particular, as 'racist' is gathering momentum. If I were convinced that those most active in prosecuting it had any genuine attachment to British customs and institutions, or any genuine allegiance to the Crown, I should feel more sympathy. But when the very same people urge us, from the platforms placed at their disposal by such bodies as the GLC, to destroy the traditional school curriculum, and to censor textbooks, in the interest of 'multi-cultural' education, then I doubt their motives. For what is the purpose of such a change, if not to perpetuate the conditions which have traditionally led to racial conflict? What is 'multi-cultural education', if not a means to ensure that our minorities continue to identify themselves as such, and so remain detached from the political condition which surrounds them, enduring victims of an enduring disadvantage?

The opening two sentences might honestly be held to imply the sentence quoted by Mr Kureishi. On the other hand, they do not really imply it, as the context shows. You may not agree with the paragraph, but surely it contains a *possible* view, and one which you could hold without being a racist? The fact that it is the very same view as the one defended, in different words, by Mr Honeyford, is not sufficient to establish the existence of a 'New Right' conspiracy.

Similar misrepresentation occurs elsewhere in Mr Kureishi's article— for example, in his discussion of John Casey's now notorious contribution to the *Salisbury Review*, on the 'politics of race'. Such misrepresentation and obloquy are, however, most unfortunate. It is important for Mr Kureishi, and for the minorities whose interests he so ably defends, that open discussion of questions of race, culture and immigration should be permitted. It is in no one's interest that people should be hounded from their employment, like Mr Honeyford, or arbitrarily persecuted on hearsay evidence, like Miss McGoldrick of Brent, merely for having expressed a view or made a remark which others judge to be 'racist'. And it is in everyone's interest that people should entertain, in a spirit of free inquiry, opinions which others regard as outrageous, in order that the truth should at last be known. As Mr Kureishi shows, in his description of the unfortunate Asian taxi-drivers, savagely beaten by a gang of white thugs, the problems are real, and the social order of Britain depends upon our solving them.

Roger Scruton
Editor, *The Salisbury Review*
London

Notes on Contributors

Michael Ignatieff's new book, *The Russian Album,* published in May, is an exploration of his Russian ancestry. He also presents the Channel Four discussion programme, *Voices.* **Bruce Chatwin** is the author of four books. The latest of these, *The Songlines,* in which 'Dreamtime' is included, is published by Jonathan Cape on 25 June. **Ryszard Kapuściński**'s most recent book is *Another Day of Life.* The interview with him in this issue was conducted at his home in Warsaw. The second volume of **John Berger**'s 'Pig Earth' trilogy, *Once in Europa,* has just been published in the United States. **Patrick Süskind**'s first novel, *Perfume,* appeared last year. His play *The Double Bass,* which has been broadcast on Radio Three, will be published in September. He lives in Munich. **Isabel Allende** is the author of two novels, *The House of the Spirits* and *Love and Shadows.* She left Chile following the military takeover, and now lives in Colombia. **Ed Graza** has been visiting the North-west Frontier Province since 1980, shortly after the Soviet invasion of Afghanistan. **Richard Ford**'s novel *A Piece of My Heart* will be published in June. His first collection of short stories, *Rock Springs,* follows in the spring. **Oliver Sacks** has published four books, the most recent of which is *The Man Who Mistook His Wife For A Hat.* **Primo Levi**'s 'Weightless' was first published in *La Stampa.* His latest book, *The Wrench,* has just been published in Britain. He died on 11 April this year. **Jonathan Schell** is the author of *The Fate of the Earth* and *The Abolition.* Early this year he left the *New Yorker,* where he had been a staff writer, and he now teaches at the Institute of Politics at the Kennedy School of Government in Cambridge, Massachusetts. **Ian Jack** writes for the *Observer* and for *Vanity Fair.* 'Finished with Engines' is taken from the Prologue to a collection of his journalism, *Before The Oil Ran Out,* published by Secker & Warburg. **Raymond Carver**'s selected poems, *In a Marine Light,* will be published by Collins Harvill in June. **Václav Havel**'s play *Temptation* has just received its British première in a Royal Shakespeare Company production at the Other Place in Stratford.

BACK ISSUES

6: A LITERATURE FOR POLITICS: 'Interviews with Argentine Soldiers from the Falklands'; Jeremy Seabrook and Trevor Blackwell, 'Mrs Thatcher's Religious Pilgrimage'; Boaz Evron, 'An Indictment of Israel'; Milan Kundera, 'The Story of a Variation'; Ariel Dorfman, 'How to Read the Comics'; Nadine Gordimer, 'A City of the Dead, A City of the Living'; Peter Weiss, 'The Aesthetics of Resistance'; and others. 336 pages. Limited stocks; please list alternative choice.

7: BEST OF YOUNG BRITISH NOVELISTS: Martin Amis, 'Money'; William Boyd, 'Extracts from the Journal of Flying Officer J.'; Maggie Gee, 'Rose on the broken'; Kazuo Ishiguro, 'Summer after the War'; Adam Mars-Jones, 'Trout Day by Pumpkin Light'; Salman Rushdie, 'The Golden Bough'; Graham Swift, 'About the Eel'; and thirteen others. 320 pages.

8: DIRTY REALISM—NEW WRITING FROM AMERICA*: Jayne Anne Phillips, 'Rayme—a Memoir of the Seventies'; Elizabeth Tallent, 'Why I Love Country Music'; Richard Ford, 'Rock Springs'; Raymond Carver, 'The Compartment'; Tobias Wolff, 'The Barracks Thief'. Plus Michael Herr, 'The State of the State of Things'; Angela Carter, 'Sugar Daddy'; Carolyn Forché, 'El Salvador: an Aide-Mémoire'. 256 pages.

9: John Berger, BORIS: Gabriel García Márquez, 'The Solitude of Latin America'; Mario Vargas Llosa, 'The Story of a Massacre'; Don McCullin, 'El Salvador'; Patrick Marnham, 'The Border'; Graham Swift, 'A Short History of Coronation Ale'; Russell Hoban, 'Pan Lives'; T. C. Boyle, 'Greasy Lake'; and others. 256 pages.

11: MILAN KUNDERA: Ian McEwan, 'An Interview with Milan Kundera'; Milan Kundera, 'Soul and Body', 'A Kidnapped West or Culture Bows Out'. Plus Salman Rushdie, 'Outside the Whale'; Martha Gellhorn, 'Testimonial'; Redmond O'Hanlon, 'Deeper into the Heart of Borneo'; Gabriel García Márquez, 'Mystery without End'; Mario Vargas Llosa, 'Cheap Intellectuals'; and others. 256 pages.

14: AUTOBIOGRAPHY: Norman Lewis, 'Jackdaw Cake'; Beryl Bainbridge, 'Funny Noises with our Mouths'; Breyten Breytenbach, 'Punishable Innocence'; William Boyd, 'Alpes Maritimes'; Josef Škvorecký, 'Failed Saxophonist'; Don McCullin, 'A Life in Photographs'; Jaroslav Seifert, 'Skating with Lenin'; Adam Mars-Jones, 'Weaning'; Bernard Crick, 'On the Orwell Trail'; and others. 256 pages.

15: James Fenton, THE FALL OF SAIGON: Nadine Gordimer, 'The Essential Gesture: Writers and Responsibility'; George Steiner, 'A Conversation Piece'; Salman Rushdie, 'On Günter Grass'; Günter Grass, 'The Tin Drum in Retrospect'; John Berger, 'Go Ask the Time'; Ryszard Kapuściński, 'Warsaw Diary'; Marilynne Robinson, 'The Waste Land'; Richard Ford, 'On Harley-Davidson'; and others. 288 pages.

16: SCIENCE: Oliver Sacks, 'Excesses'; Italo Calvino, 'The Loves of the Tortoises'; Primo Levi, 'Chromium'; Stephen Jay Gould, 'Adam's Navel'; Lewis Thomas, 'Co-operation for the Birds'; Plus Germaine Greer, 'Women and Power in Cuba'; David Hare, 'Nicaragua: An Appeal'; Tim O'Brien, 'Quantum Jumps'; David Mamet, 'The Bridge'; Mary Gordon, 'The Imagination of Disaster'; and others. 256 pages.

Granta 1–5, 12–13 are now out of print.

All prices include postage and packing in UK, overseas add £1 per order.

17: Graham Greene, WHILE WAITING FOR A WAR: Milan Kundera, 'Prague: A Disappearing Poem': Patrick Marnham, 'In Search of Amin'; Heinrich Böll, 'A Letter to My Sons'; Joseph Lelyveld, 'Forced Busing in South Africa'; Kazuo Ishiguro, 'October, 1948'; Alice Munro, 'A Queer Streak'; Doris Lessing, 'My Mother's Life'; John Updike, 'Italo Calvino'; Amos Oz, 'Notes from Israel'; Hanif Kureishi, 'Erotic Politicians and Mullahs'; and others. 256 pages.

18: THE SNAP REVOLUTION, James Fenton in the Philippines: Mark Malloch Brown, 'Aquino, Marcos and the White House'; John Berger, 'The Accordion Player'; Alice Munro, 'A Queer Streak (Part Two): Possession'; Seamus Deane, 'Haunted'; Adam Nicolson, 'Wetness'; David Hare, 'Joint Stock: A Memoir'; George Steiner, 'Desert Island Discs'; Gianni Celati, 'Thoughts of a Storyteller on a Happy Ending'; Primo Levi, 'Tadpoles'. 256 pages.

19: MORE DIRT: New Writing from America: Richard Ford, 'Empire'; Jayne Anne Phillips, 'Fast Lanes'; Richard Russo, 'Fishing with Wussy'; Ellen Gilchrist, 'Memphis'; Joy Williams, 'Escapes'; Louise Erdrich, 'Knives'; John Updike, 'Getting the Words Out'; Adam Mars-Jones, 'Slim'; Mary Benson, 'A True Afrikaner'; Primo Levi, 'From Lab to Writing Desk'. 256 pages

20: IN TROUBLE AGAIN – A Special Issue of Travel Writing: Redmond O'Hanlon, 'Amazon Adventure'; Salman Rushdie, 'Eating the Eggs of Love'; Martha Gellhorn, 'Cuba Revisited'; Norman Lewis, 'The Shaman of Chichicastenango'; Ryszard Kapuściński, 'A Tour of Angola'; Hanif Kureishi, 'Bradford'; Timothy Garton Ash, 'Under Eastern Eyes'; and others. 256 pages.